Introduction
to
Political
Inquiry

RICHARD L. COLE

GEORGE WASHINGTON UNIVERSITY

Introduction
to
Political
Inquiry

Macmillan Publishing Co., Inc.
New York
Collier Macmillan Publishers
London

Macmillan Publishing Co., Inc.,
866 Third Avenue, New York, New York 10022

Collier Macmillan Canada, Ltd.

Library of Congress Cataloging in Publication Data
Cole, Richard L
 Introduction to political inquiry.

 Includes bibliographies and index.
 1.   Political science research.   I. Title.
JA86.C5   320'.07'2   79-13140
ISBN 0-02-323350-8

Printing:1 2 3 4 5 6 7 8   Year:0 1 2 3 4 5 6

TO PAM

One
Whose
Imagination
Knows
No
Bounds

Preface

This book is intended to serve as an introduction to the conduct of systematic political research. It is not a text in statistics; it does not cover in exhaustive detail every technique which scholars may find useful in pursuing political research. It does discuss some of the basic concepts and techniques of empirical political research and does offer suggestions and advice to assist the beginning researcher in the various stages of political research. In so doing, two major themes are pursued: first, political research is an enjoyable, rewarding experience; and second, for maximum satisfaction such research should be conducted in an orderly, systematic fashion. To help convey the first of these themes, examples from the political science literature are used throughout to illustrate the various techniques and concepts discussed. These examples should demonstrate the excitement of political and policy research; but, still, there is no substitute for actually participating in a research effort. It is hoped that the student may on several occasions have the opportunity to participate in such research activities and that in so doing the methods and suggestions discussed here will be found useful.

A major feature of this text is that it attempts to carry the reader through the entire process of systematic research — topic selection, literature review, hypothesis formation, data collection, data handling, data analysis, and report writing. Each of these, of course, is a very specialized topic, and each has its own areas of controversy and distinct body of literature. It is obvious that no single text can exhaustively explore the many complexities of each of these topics. The great risk in preparing a text such as this is that the coverage given each topic may be too shallow or diluted to be of much use. Yet it is my belief that a useful purpose is served by a text which attempts to introduce to the novice researcher these issues in an integrated and illustrated fashion. What may be lost in depth of coverage is at least partially compensated by a greater appreciation of the entire research process including a clearer understanding of the relationship of each phase to all others. In selecting the topics to be covered and in deciding the emphasis to be given, I attempted to answer two questions: (1) which topics would the student find most useful in understanding and evaluating contemporary political and policy research?; (2) which methods and techniques would be found by beginning researchers to be most helpful in conceiving of and carrying out their own individual or group research projects? Thus, no attempt is made here to cover all possible methods and techniques. Of these topics which are included, greater attention is given to some (such as survey research design, observational data collection techniques, and statistical measures of association) and correspondingly less to others (such as experimental research design, archival and documentary means of data collection, and statistical tests of inference). Admittedly, these represent personal preferences, but I believe that the student completing this text will be able to intelligently and critically deal with the bulk of contemporary political science research and will be in a position to carry out at least moderately challenging and sophisticated political research. I am confident that the energetic student may pursue, through the references and citations provided, any topic for which he or she desires more specialized information. Above all, I hope the text conveys the message that good political research is systematic, not haphazard, and that — in spite of major recent advances in computer technology, data availability, and packaged statistical programs — quality research is still heavily dependent on skilled and imaginative human judgment. It is this perspective which, it seems to me, often is missing in the more specialized and focused methods texts.

This text assumes no previous statistical knowledge and is intended primarily as an introductory guide to those having little or no training in empirical research. It is not a text overly concerned with mathematical derivations or statistical computation. Rather, in those sections where statistics are discussed, the stress is on the conditions under which such techniques should be applied and the proper interpretation of results. The exercises concluding each chapter are designed to further illustrate the points raised and to assist in student understanding and mastery of the concepts and techniques discussed. To illustrate various topics and techniques, I have relied often on data supplied by the Inter-University Consortium for Political and Social Research and especially its 1976 American National Election Study. The data for the 1976 study were originally collected by the Institute for Social Research, the University of Michigan, under a grant from the National Science Foundation. Neither the original collectors of the data nor the Consortium bear any responsibility for the analyses or interpretations presented here.

In preparing this text, I owe many debts of gratitude and many expressions of appreciation. My former teacher, William Shaffer of Purdue University, read and commented on the entire manuscript. His suggestions, as always, were outstanding; as always, he rescued me from many errors. I was fortunate to have had the excellent comments and criticisms of Helenan Lewis of Western Michigan University and of my colleagues and friends at the George Washington University, Susan Carroll, John Dirkse, Eva Liebhold, Cynthia

McClintock, and Stephen Wayne. Each of these gave unselfishly of their time and considerable talents and each offered needed support and encouragement at various stages of the effort. Clark Baxter of Macmillan is to be commended for his cheerful and professional guidance of this project from its earliest stages to the final product. Mr. Stuart Goldstein assisted in checking the accuracy of the statistics and data presented, Ms. Callie Gass helped with the permission requests, and Ms. Maureen Kacznski typed portions of the original manuscript. I am indebted to all of these for their services as well. I am grateful to the Literary Executor of the late Sir Ronald A. Fisher, F.R.S., and to Dr. Frank Yates, F.R.S. and to Longman Group, Ltd., London, for permission to reprint Tables B, C, and D from their book *Statistical Tables for Biological, Agricultural and Medical Research* (6th edition, 1974). I am fortunate to be able to conclude this text with examples of student research papers authored by Robin B. Steiner and Steven M. Schneider. No other has contributed more to this effort than my wife, Pam, whose patience and understanding provided inspiration throughout. To all of these, and more, go my sincerest thanks.

Richard L. Cole
The George Washington University

Contents

1

CONDUCTING SYSTEMATIC POLITICAL RESEARCH

The Trauma

It's early September. You have just taken your seat in your first political science course of the new academic year. As you are renewing acquaintances with last year's friends, the instructor enters and hands out a syllabus for the course. Listed among the course requirements is an independent research paper. The paper is to be a major effort, carefully researched and footnoted; original sources are to be cited; hypotheses are to be formulated and tested; empirical analysis is encouraged; standard manuscript style is to be followed. The paper is due 3 weeks prior to the last class session. You have never prepared a major research paper before; you know nothing about the subject matter of this course. You begin to ask yourself if you should drop the course; you wonder if you should abandon political science as a major. How will you ever select an appropriate topic, carry out the research, and write the report— all in about 3 months?

Actually, most students discover, as soon as initial anxiety levels have lowered, that conducting independent research can be the most rewarding of academic experiences. Finally, one is freed from the rigors of lectures, note taking, memorization, and class examinations and allowed to pursue one's own intellectual interests. The product of the research represents one's own work, reflective of one's own talents, imagination, and creativity. Independent research is, in a word, "fun." But for maximum satisfaction, research should be carried out in a systematic and orderly fashion. Otherwise, the results can be meaningless and the effort frustrating, indeed.

The Focus of This Book

To say that political research must be orderly is not to suggest that systematic research will always result in startling revelations or that seemingly haphazard research is bound to be unproductive. It certainly is not to deny the critical role of the human imagination — the true wellspring of creative, innovative research. In his celebrated study of street-corner urban men, Elliot Liebow quotes his mentor, Hylan Lewis, as being fond of exclaiming, "The scientific method is doing one's darndest with his brains, no holds barred."[1]

The scientific process unquestionably involves the application of the human intellect to the solving of problems deemed important by the scientific community and society at large. In solving such problems, the intellect must not be harnessed; curiosity must not be bridled. To do so would stagnate scientific research.

However, to say that research should proceed systematically *is* to imply that there exist procedures and guidelines which, if followed, serve to maximize the rewards and satisfactions of the research endeavor and to increase the probability that such research will have important payoffs. Learning these procedures is similar to learning to play a musical instrument. For the beginning researcher, the process may at first seem awkward, cumbersome, and "mechanical." For the established researcher, these procedures become second nature; they are followed almost unconsciously. Like the skilled musician, the task of the researcher is to meld these techniques with a "no holds barred" imagination to accomplish a harmonious and well-blended product.

Comparing Systematic and Unsystematic Research

When we refer in this book to systematic and unsystematic research, we are not distinguishing between honest and dishonest work. It is assumed at the outset that all students recognize the difference between honest and dishonest research and that work which is plagiarized, faked, misrepresented, or otherwise purposefully distorted cannot be tolerated.

Unsystematic research can be conducted by the most diligent and conscientious of students. Many elements of unsystematic research, in fact, may be quite legitimate and may appear very "scientific." The unsystematic researcher may even be unaware of the flaws in his or her methodology.

---

[1] Quoted in Elliot Liebow, *Tally's Corner: A Study of Negro Streetcorner Men* (Boston: Little, Brown and Company, 1967), p. 235. This study is examined more closely in Chapter 3. This quote also is attributable to the noted physicist, P. W. Bridgman. See: Morris Kline, *Mathematics: A Cultural Approach* (Reading, Mass.: Addison-Wesley, 1962), p. 50.

Systematic research skills, in short, are not automatically acquired; they must be learned.

Perhaps an appreciation of the topics to be covered in this book can best be gained by first considering some examples of unsystematic research. While unsystematic research can take many forms, there are a few typical cases. Everyone is familiar with the "Scrambler." This is the student who (usually the weekend before the paper is due) in one hurried trip to the library checks out a few books and makes photocopies of what appear to be some important journal articles on a particular topic, carries all this back to his or her room, spreads the materials in front of the television set, fixes a sandwich or two, and then scrambles through all this material while watching an afternoon football game. It is assumed that sometime during the third or fourth quarter a fully developed research product will emerge. What typically emerges is an unimaginative paper, poorly researched, poorly cited, and smeared with mustard. The student, and instructor, will be disappointed with the effort.

Also typical of unsystematic research is the method used by the "Data Masher." This is the student who at least collects some data on a particular topic, ambles to the computer center with the data set, mashes the data through the computer (correlating every variable with every other), then frantically searches through the printouts for significant correlations (the data masher usually assumes that unless astonishingly high correlations are found, all is lost). Having found some strong correlations, the student then prepares, ex post facto, some hypotheses that can be supported by these findings and shapes the report accordingly.

Frequently encountered also is the "Names and Terminology Shuffler." This student will find all the major works on a particular topic and, in "cut-and-paste" fashion, shuffle, more or less randomly, the findings of previous research into a single paper. The result may have no uniform theme or may make no original contribution, but the student believes that the instructor will at least be impressed with citations from the major scholars and apparent familiarity with the terminology in a particular field.[2]

In each of these examples, the students, in fact, are adopting *portions* of the systematic approach to research. It is certainly important to spend some time at the library, to become familiar with the major works and terminology in a field, to develop hypotheses, to find empirical evidence pertaining to the hypotheses, and perhaps to actually utilize the computer to perform some analysis. In isolation, however, none of these measures represents systematic research. It is not enough to selectively apply segments of the research process to your effort — these phases must be integrated in an orderly and systematic fashion. Otherwise, the process is likely to be tedious, the experience frustrating, and the results unrewarding.

[2]In formulating these research strategy typologies, I owe a debt to Irvin L. White, whose insightful paper, "Planning and Organizing for Research: A Guide for Beginners" (unpublished), makes similar arguments.

3

Compare the Scrambler, the Masher, and the Shuffler with the "Systematic Researcher." This student first carefully develops several possible research topics, evaluates each, selects the one with the greatest potential, thoroughly reviews the literature in the selected area, clearly and precisely develops hypotheses that can be examined and tested within the time frame and with the resources available, collects the appropriate data for the testing of hypotheses, applies the appropriate analytic techniques, and prepares a report relating the findings to some body of theory or important policy issue. Such research not only will be well received but, even more important, the results will be personally rewarding and satisfying. The researcher is assured that his or her efforts add, even if only incrementally, to that which is known about a particular issue. The results represent real contributions to knowledge.

The Element of Timing

The systematic approach to political research is the approach to be promoted in this text. The following chapters are organized according to the major stages in the research effort. The student will find in those chapters many specific, and hopefully helpful, research suggestions. Additionally, one overall factor that must always be considered in conducting a research effort is time. Perhaps no other single element is so crucial to research success as this one. Alternatives can often be found for the other research ingredients, but time is the one element for which there is no substitute. Social science research is especially time-consuming, and the researcher must be aware of the time available and plan accordingly.

Of course, the amount of time required for each stage of the research process will vary widely. Researchers who must collect their own data will have to devote more time to this phase than persons relying on available information. Those applying more sophisticated and complex analytic techniques will need more time for this stage than those satisfied with more basic, and less time-consuming, routines.

Still, it is possible to suggest a *very* rough guide to the amount of time that should be allotted to each stage. Table 1.1 assumes a time frame of 13 weeks (or about the time most students will have in one semester). Obviously, those having more or less time will have to adjust these intervals accordingly.

The time suggested for the initial stages of topic selection, literature review, and hypothesis formation (5 weeks) may seem excessive. Indeed, more senior researchers may require much less time for these activities. On the other hand, the initial stages are the most important phases of the research process. Beginning researchers, in particular, will have to invest a great deal of time in becoming familiar with the indexes, abstracts, and other sources required for the completion of these phases and in simply thinking through the feasibility

TABLE 1.1
Suggested Time Allotments and Chapter Keys for Each Stage
of the Systematic Research Process

Stages in the Research Process	Suggested Time Allotment	Chapter Keys
Topic selection	2 weeks	2
Literature review	2 weeks	2
Hypothesis formation	1 week	2
Data collection	3 weeks	3
Coding and punching data	1 week	4
Data analysis	2 weeks	5–9
Report writing and rewriting	2 weeks	10
Total	13 weeks	

of pursuing a particular project. It is assumed, as well, that beginning researchers will consider and discard several topics before finally settling on the one that is to be pursued. Thus about one-third of the total time available may productively be devoted to the early stages, but after this the student should be ready to proceed without delay to the remaining tasks.

Concluding Comments

This text, then, pursues two themes: (1) political research should be thought of as an enjoyable opportunity, not a traumatic exercise; and (2) for maximum satisfaction, research must be carried out in a systematic, orderly fashion. The techniques of research can be taught; many suggestions will be introduced in the following chapters. But the greatest teacher is personal experience. It is hoped that this guide will be used by the student in conjunction with his or her own research effort. Only then will the rewards and satisfaction of political research be fully appreciated.

Exercises

1. a. Discuss the differences between *unsystematic* research and *dishonest* research.
   b. How can one distinguish between these?
   c. What are some likely consequences of each?
2. a. Discuss the differences between *systematic* and *unsystemayic* research.
   b. What stages of research characterize systematic research?
   c. What are the advantages of systematic over unsystematic research?
3. a. It is suggested that the adequate time is an especially important ingredient to successful social science research. Discuss some reasons why you would expect social science research to be especially time-consuming.
   b. Are some strategies of social science research likely to be even more time-consuming than others?

5

   c. Why is the answer to part (b) likely to be "yes"?

4. a. Select three empirical studies in political science (books or articles) that you find interesting and report the approximate amount of time the authors appear to have allocated to each stage of the research process as discussed in this chapter.

  b. Could the time allocated by these authors to the various stages of research have been shortened without significantly sacrificing the quality of the research?

  c. How might this have been accomplished?

2

THE EARLY STAGES OF THE RESEARCH PROCESS: SELECTING THE TOPIC, REVIEWING THE LITERATURE; FORMULATING HYPOTHESES

The inital stages of research are the most critical. The topic selected and the hypotheses developed set the tone for the entire effort and establish the framework within which the other major issues of the research process — such as data collection, research design, and methods of analysis — will have to be addressed.

Of these early phases, the actual selection of a topic is the most difficult for which to provide a specific set of guidelines. Topic selection is highly personal; an idea that may seem fascinating to one person may appear dull and unimaginative to another. Further, the ability to conceive and define a useful research topic that can be successfully carried out within the parameters of available time and resources requires considerable experience and skill. For most scholars, these skills must be developed and honed over a period of time; we learn through trial and error. The beginning student will not have had these experiences, but some general guides can be suggested. A research idea is generated and criteria are applied to evaluate the potential of the idea. How this is done is the subject of the following sections.

Selecting a Potential Topic

The initial idea for a possible topic may come from several sources. Of course, some instructors may assign one topic to the entire class, particular topics to particular students, or may provide a list of topics from which the student is to make a selection. In these instances the initial decisions have already been made or at least substantially narrowed. More typically, however, students must make these decisions themselves.

The idea for a topic may originate solely with the student. You may have decided to take the course in Urban Politics, Western European Governments, International Relations, or Voting Behavior because you already have an interest in the subject matter. You may already know that your interest lies in the area of nineteenth-century urban machine politics, the French party system, the United Nations, or American voting patterns. This is a beginning. From here you proceed to define a manageable and interesting topic.

Or, you may have taken the course precisely because you know very little about the particular subject matter, and consequently ideas for research topics are not immediately forthcoming. In such situations one should begin simply with a review of the content of the text(s) assigned for the course. By examining chapter titles and subheadings, one begins to appreciate the broad areas of concern in that subject area.

For more ideas, the student might consult the *International Encyclopedia of the Social Sciences*, a publication consisting of articles by leading social scientists. Each article describes some of the major issues and questions in a particular subject area, summarizes important findings, and provides additional references to major works. The *Encyclopedia* is thus an invaluable source of research ideas and testable hypotheses.

Let us assume that the student has decided to pursue a research topic in the general area of American voting behavior. Turning to the section "Voting" in the most recent (1968) version of the *Encyclopedia*,[1] the student will find an article by Donald Stokes, a leading scholar in this field. In that article Stokes discusses the methods of voting analysis, the range of voting studies, and the major problem areas (such as participation, partisanship and political socialization, and class and group influences). Also, a bibliography of approximately 60 major sources is provided. The student should come away from this essay with many ideas for researchable topics, together with suggestions for ways to pursue these topics.

Additionally, the student should examine, even if very cursorily, the leading journals and periodicals. In the past few years a number of specialized journals have appeared in many areas of political interest (such as urban affairs, criminology, and comparative politics). A simple review of the titles of articles appearing in these journals will give the student a very good idea of contemporary research interests in that field. Having followed these steps, the student should have several ideas of potential researchable topics.

---

[1] A supplement to the *Encyclopedia*, soon to be published, is to contain biographies of over 200 eminent social scientists.

After formulating several general ideas for potential research, it is time to consult with the instructor and to begin the process of narrowing the list to one or a few topics that are capable of completion with the resources available and the time allotted. The instructor will have additional ideas concerning topic feasibility, data sources, and resource materials. At this stage, several criteria are to be applied by the researcher in narrowing the list to the single topic that will be pursued.

Criteria for Evaluation

Student Interest

A question often asked of instructors by students is: "What project do you want me to pursue?" The more appropriate question to ask, when options are provided, is: "What project would be of most interest to *me*?" In the case of a semester's project, several weeks will be devoted to the research effort. In the case of a Master's thesis or doctoral dissertation, several months (perhaps even years) will be required. It is mandatory that the researcher select a topic that will be appealing for at least this period of time. Nothing can be so onerous as a dull research project, and nothing so detracts from the ultimate quality of the final product than lack of researcher enthusiasm. If you find after initial explorations that the topic does not appeal to you, get another topic.

Discipline Significance

It is not enough that the topic be of interest to the researcher; it should also be of interest to the broader community of scholars in that field. One major purpose of research is to add to existing knowledge. Even brief semester projects should be placed clearly into the context of existing theory or related to questions of obvious policy relevance. The student of voting behavior, for example, probably would not find a consuming interest by scholars in exploring the relationships between the public's choice of political candidates and brands of deodorant preferred.

More substantial topics, such as a case study of referendum voting in a particular city, become even more relevant when placed in the broader theoretical context of factors associated with voting behavior in all American cities. Or, a study of attitudes of local decision makers becomes more important when related to the process of policy making in that locality.

Graduate students and senior undergraduates will generally be familiar with the significant issues in a particular area, so the application of this criterion will be almost automatic. For those unfamiliar with a discipline's major issues, a quick examination of social science indexes and abstracts (to be discussed below) will indicate other work that is being conducted in the chosen area. If the student finds no reference in the literature relating to the topic he or she is considering, the topic is probably of no interest to the broader discipline or is too difficult to be pursued. In either case, the student should look for another topic.

Manageability

Additionally, the researcher must be concerned with the selection of a manageable topic. It is usually not too difficult to conceive of interesting and significant ideas. The problem often is selecting a topic that can be completed within the time allotted and with the resources available. Social science research can be very time-consuming and expensive. In conducting a project involving surveys, for example, consider the effort involved in drafting the questions, printing the surveys, coding and punching the results, analyzing the data, and writing the report. Even if surveying a very small sample (say, 100 individuals or less), such a project requires a large expenditure of time and resources. A project involving surveys might be appropriate for an entire class in which different students are assigned different tasks, but it would be very difficult for one student to manage in one semester's time. In pursuing an empirically oriented study, then, it is suggested that students consider using data *already* collected and, if possible, already available for computer use (Chapter 3 discusses some of these important sources of data).

The researcher must also be *realistic* in selecting a topic. Although it would be interesting and perhaps significant to conduct an interview study of a state's legislative body, politicians are very busy people and it is doubtful that the student could be afforded enough time with a large-enough sample to make the study worthwhile. On the other hand, an interview study of legislative aides, or of legislators themselves when the legislature is out of session, might be possible.

All of this is simply to say that in selecting a topic, the researcher must, at the outset, apply a good deal of foresight and common sense. Know your own time and resource limitations; and select a topic that is realistic and manageable.

Ethical Considerations

All people involved in research dealing with human subjects are becoming increasingly sensitized to the moral and ethical issues involved. In adopting the scientific method to behavioral research, social scientists cannot adopt the laboratory scientist's lack of concern with the subject matter.[2] Although the chemist need have little regard for the "welfare" of the elements in the test tube, the behavioral scientist must be totally concerned with the welfare of his or her human subjects. Human experimentation must be *voluntary*, and those participating in the study must be fully apprised of whatever risks may be

---

[2]This, of course, is not to imply that laboratory scientists do not have to worry about the consequences of their research or the use to which that research might be put; only that behavioral scientists, in addition to this, have to be especially concerned with the welfare of their human subjects.

involved. Maximum care must be taken to ensure that human subjects are not embarrassed, insulted, or otherwise psychologically or physically harmed by the research.

Illustrative of the growing awareness of these issues, the *American Political Science Association* issued in 1968 a statement entitled "Ethical Problems of Academic Political Scientists,"[3] outlining some areas of particular concern. Included in that report are special references to student–teacher relationships, political activity of academic political scientists, government-sponsored political research, and integrity of scholarship. Further, the Department of Health, Education, and Welfare has issued guidelines and regulations on the protection of human subjects in medical and nonmedical research. All students of politics should be thoroughly familiar with these two documents and with their own obligations as political researchers.

Although everyone would agree that participants in social science research should not be harmed by their participation, it is sometimes difficult to know just when research oversteps legitimate boundaries. When calling on the phone, mailing out a questionnaire, or knocking on a door, survey researchers are intruding into someone's life. No matter how innocent or innocuous the questions, the researcher has disturbed and altered someone's routine, even if only briefly.[4] When granted an interview with a public official, the researcher removes that individual, even if just for a short period of time, from public responsibilities. Although political researchers take these risks in the hope that the information gained will extend our understanding of human behavior and ultimately enrich the human condition, it is mandatory that intrusions be kept to a minimum. Surveys and interviews are to be conducted at the *interviewee's* convenience; the questions asked are to be kept to the minimum necessary.

When evaluating a research topic dealing with human subjects, one important criterion to be applied is that of ethics. In a word, human subjects must be treated with *dignity*. If there is the slightest doubt that this will not be the case, the topic should be abandoned.[5]

Problem Familiarity

Having followed these steps, the student should have settled on a general research area and should be at least reasonably certain of the feasibility and

[3] This report is reprinted in *P.S., Newsletter of the American Political Science Association,* 1 (Summer 1968).

[4] A similar point is made by Earl R. Babbie, *Survey Research Methods* (Belmont, Calif.: Wadsworth Publishing Company, Inc., 1973), pp. 348–349.

[5] For more in-depth discussions of the important topic of ethics in political research, see Stuart W. Cook, "Ethical Issues in the Conduct of Research in Social Relations," in Claire Selltiz, Lawrence S. Wrightsman, and Stuart W. Cook, *Research Methods in Social Relations,* 3rd ed. (New York: Holt, Rinehart and Winston, Inc., 1976), pp. 199–250; Neil M. Agnew and Sandra W. Pyke, *The Science Game,* 2nd ed. (Englewood Cliffs, N.J.: Prentice-Hall, Inc., 1978), pp. 181–194; and Babbie, *Survey Research Methods,* pp. 347–358.

desirability of proceeding. It is always tempting at this stage to leap to the data-collection and analysis phases of the research process. Admittedly, these are important and exciting phases of research. First, however, attention must be paid to other, also important, stages of the research process. One of these is *problem familiarity*. The researcher must become thoroughly familiar with the available literature in the area.

The review of the literature further assists in narrowing the topic and in placing the research in the proper theoretical or policy context. Through immersion in the literature, the researcher becomes familiar with the approaches and techniques used by others, with the sources of data available, and with the important questions that remain to be answered. In short, the literature-review process tells us what has been previously attempted in the area, which approaches have been successful and which have not been so successful, and what issues remain to be answered. These are indispensable clues to the research effort.

It is at this stage that the researcher turns to the library. For the reasons cited above, the library and its personnel are essential to the conduct of systematic research. Yet, the library experience can be very frustrating, especially for the novice researcher. Tens of thousands of books and articles are published each year, so it is impossible even for experts to keep up to date with every piece of published research in their fields. For the library experience to be truly productive, this phase of the research process must be carried out deliberately and expeditiously. Assisting in the maximum use of the library's resources are a number of guides which quickly alert the researcher to the materials that are most directly and immediately related to the topic being pursued. It is essential that the researcher become thoroughly familiar with these tools.

Continuing with our example of the student interested in the area of American voting behavior, let us follow this student as he or she might proceed with the problem-familiarity stage. The results of these efforts will be the further narrowing of this broad field to a research topic of manageable proportions and the development of appropriate hypotheses to be tested.

The Card Catalog

One place to start would be the card catalog. Beginning researchers are generally at least basically familiar with the card catalog, which typically lists holdings by author, title, and subject. The student might look up the topic of interest under the appropriate subject heading in the card catalog and locate and review all books therein listed.

Although the card catalog is obviously useful, it has several limitations. As one student of information sources in political science has found, "The Library of Congress (one widely used library classification scheme) subject terms employed do not always reflect the currently accepted terminology of political science and are frequently too broad or too general. In a disturbing number of instances the subject entry used is either false or fails to locate the desired material."[6] Additional limitations of the card catalog are that it will typically list only books and reports (to the neglect of professional articles, magazines, newspapers, and the like), the subject headings of the card catalog typically are rather broad, and a time lag of some months usually exists from the publishing of a book to its acquisition and cataloging by the library. While the card catalog is *one* helpful source, more efficient means for proceeding with problem familiarity are available. In this regard, the student will find most useful various reference indexes and abstracts.

Indexes

Social Science Index. The *Social Science Index* (H. W. Wilson Company, New York; formerly the *Social Sciences and Humanities Index*) is an extremely important reference source to recent articles appearing in the social science journals. Published quarterly (with cumulative annual editions), the *Social Science Index* provides an author and subject index of over 270 periodicals in the fields of anthropology, area studies, economics, environmental sciences, political science, psychology, public administration, sociology, and related subjects. The researcher interested in American voting behavior would find in the June, 1978 volume, under the subject heading "Voting," the following articles relating to the United States:

Cross-over voting in a 1976 open presidential primary. R. D. Hedlund. Pub Opinion Q 41:498–514 Wint'77–78

Elections and the mobilization of popular support. B. Ginsberg and R. Weissberg. bibl Am J Pol Sci 22:31–55 F'78

Extrapolating laboratory exposure research to actual political elections. J. E. Grush and others. bibl J Pers Soc Psychol 36:257–70 Mr'78

From confusion to confusion: issues and the American voter (1956–1972). M. Margolis. Am Pol Sci R 71:31–43 Mr'77; Reply with rejoinder. G. M. Pomper. 71:1596–7 D'77

Partisan identification and electoral choice: the hostility hypothesis. M. A. Maggiotto and J. E. Piereson. bibl Am J Pol Sci 21:745–67 N'77

Political involvement and partisan change in presidential elections. J. T. Pedersen. bibl Am J Pol Sci 22:18–30 F'78

The first entry tells us that an article on the subject of U.S. voting behavior entitled "Cross-over Voting in a 1976 Open Presidential Primary" by R. D. Hedlund will be found in Volume 41 of *Public Opinion Quarterly*, pages 498–514, the winter 1977–1978 issue. From their titles, the student makes an initial judgment as to which articles seem most related to the specific voting behavior issues in which he or she is most interested. Entries listed in the

[6]Frederick Holler, *The Information Sources of Political Science* (Santa Barbara, Calif.: American Bibliographical Center, 1971), p. 7.

Social Science Index with "bibl" (such as the second listing above) include extensive bibliographic references. These articles are often particularly useful for researchers. Since the *Social Science Index* is published annually, the user will want to examine the listings for a few previous years as well.

Public Affairs Information Service Bulletin. A second useful index for the political scientist is the *Public Affairs Information Service Bulletin* (PAIS, Inc., New York). Published since 1915, PAIS provides an index of publications on subjects that bear on contemporary public issues and the evaluation of public policy, with emphasis on factual and statistical information. PAIS includes in its index professional periodicals, books, government documents, and reports of public and private organizations. Under the topic "Voting" in the 1977 volume are listed over 30 entries, including selections from *Congressional Quarterly*, *U.S. News and World Report*, *The Wall Street Journal*, and various social science journals and law reviews.

Reader's Guide to Periodical Literature. Another index that may be of use is the *Reader's Guide to Periodical Literature* (H. W. Wilson Company, New York). Published annually since 1900, the *Reader's Guide* indexes by subject and author over 150 periodicals. Less professional in orientation than the *Social Science Index* or *PAIS*, the *Reader's Guide* includes in its coverage a wide variety of periodicals, ranging from the *Yale Review* and the *Bulletin of the Atomic Scientists*, to *Time*, *Newsweek*, *Reader's Digest*, and *Popular Mechanics*. Listed under the topic "Voting" in the March 1977–February 1978 edition of the *Reader's Guide* are the following entries:

Apathetic voter. A. McCarthy. Commonweal 104:105+ F 18 '77
Helping patients to vote. W. G. Lee. il MH 61:14–16 Summ'77
Meet Mrs America: B. Lowrey as average American voter. J. Miller. por
    New Repub 176:19–21 Ap 9 '77
On non-voters. E. M. von Kuehnelt-Leddihn. Nat R 29:153 F 4 '77
Yes for permitting weekend voting. il Nations Bus 65:6 Mr '77

Comparing these listings with those under the topic "Voting" in the *Social Science Index*, one can see that the *Reader's Guide* is much more general and less scholarly in orientation. However, a lag of some years usually exists between an area of current popular interest and the publication of scholarly research on that issue. For very contemporary issues, the *Reader's Guide* can sometimes be the most useful index.

Newspaper Indexes. Useful also for reference to very current topics are the indexes of some major newspapers. Among those newspapers currently indexed and available on microfilm in most libraries are *The New York Times*, *The Washington Post*, *The Wall Street Journal*, and the *Christian*

Science Monitor. Looking up the topic of "voting" in the *New York Times Index* of July 1 to July 15, 1978, the reader is referred to the topic "Elections," where reference is found to articles dealing with the changing politics of the South, political wives, campaign financing, entertainers as fund raisers, and former President Ford's role in the 1978 Congressional elections.[7]

Abstracts

Also useful are social science abstracts. Abstracts differ from indexes in that they attempt in a short paragraph (usually fewer than 500 words) to summarize the important points of the cited material. Because they provide more information, and therefore take longer to compile, abstracts may be less complete and somewhat less current than indexes. Still, they provide an extremely useful tool and the researcher will want to consult these as well.

The Universal Reference System: Political Science, Government, and Public Policy Series. Perhaps the most useful of the abstract sources is *The Universal Reference System: Political Science Series* (IFI/Plenum Data Company, New York, under the general editorship since 1974 of George W. Johnson). First published as a 10-volume set in 1967 and updated annually since then, the *Universal Reference System* each year abstracts books, pamphlets, articles, and chapters on subjects of interest to political scientists. Under the heading "Voting" in the 1977 *Annual Supplement* are listed over 140 entries. One of these was the following:

ERIKSON R., "THE INFLUENCE OF NEWSPAPER ENDORSEMENTS IN PRESIDENTIAL ELECTIONS: THE CASE OF 1964" CHOOSE VOTING POL/BEHAV. PAGE 143 X2403

This listing indicates the author of this entry, the title of the article, some additional key terms (Choose, Voting, Pol/Behav), and the location of the abstract (page 143 X2403). Turning to page 143, listing 2403 of the *Universal Reference System*, the following abstract of this article is found:

---

[7] A new index that political scientists may find helpful is *The Federal Index* (Cleveland, Ohio: Predicasts, Inc.). Beginning in 1976, *The Federal Index* focuses on the federal government (the executive, the Congress, the independent agencies, and the courts) and various domestic issue areas (such as the economy; environment and energy; health, education, and welfare; and so forth). Published monthly, *The Federal Index* limits its coverage to five sources: the *Congressional Record*, the *Federal Register*, *The Weekly Compilation of Presidential Documents*, the *Commerce Business Daily*, and *The Washington Post*. Although obviously not as broad in its coverage as the other publications, the special focus of this index may be quite useful for political and policy analysts.

2403 ERIKSON R.
"THE INFLUENCE OF NEWSPAPER ENDORSEMENTS IN PRESIDENTIAL ELECTIONS: THE CASE OF 1964"
AMERICAN JOURNAL OF POLITICAL SCIENCE, 20 (2) (May 76), 207–231.
This paper estimates the influence of newspaper endorsements on voting behavior in U.S. presidential elections. The analysis focuses on the impact of newspaper endorsements in the 1964 presidential election – the one recent presidential election in which a considerable number of newspapers endorsed the democratic candidate. It is argued that newspaper endorsements exert an important influence.

The abstract, it can be seen, again lists the author and the title, and presents a paragraph summary of the contents of the article. At this point, the researcher may decide whether this article is really important to his or her topic. If so, the abstract indicates the location of the article (*American Journal of Political Science*, May, 1976, pages 207–231).

International Political Science Abstracts. A second abstract of considerable utility is the *International Political Science Abstracts.* Published bimonthly since 1950 by the *International Political Science Association* (Paris), this volume provides an index and abstract of articles appearing in political science journals listed by major headings: Political Science: Methods and Theory; Political Thinkers and Ideas; Governmental and Administrative Institutions; Political Process: Public Opinion, Attitudes, Parties, Forces, Groups and Elections; International Relations; National and Area Studies. Listed under the topic "Voting" in the 3–4 issue of the 1977 volume are several articles, one of which is the following:

ABERBACH, J. D. — Alienation and voting behavior today. Society 13(5), July– Aug. 76: 19–26.

The primary theoretical concern of this article is to refine our ideas about the effects of political alienation on voting behavior. The major substantive theme is the impact of two forms of alienation — political trust and political efficacy — on candidate choice in American presidential elections. Data analyzed are from the 1968 and 1972 elections studies of the University of Michigan's Center for Political Studies. Extensive comparisons to a previous study of the 1964 presidential contest are used to increase perspective and to modify existing hypotheses. Subjects covered include the zero-order effects of alienation on voting behavior, the interaction between political trust and political efficacy in determining voter choice, and the impact of party identification and attitudes on political issues on the relationship between political trust and the vote. The conclusion stresses the implications of the findings for the future course of American electoral politics, especially the likelihood of a major party realignment.

Dissertation Abstracts. A final source, one especially useful when the researcher is interested in locating the most recent works in a particular area, is *Dissertation Abstracts International* (University Microfilms International, Ann Arbor, Michigan). *Dissertation Abstracts International* (DAI) is a monthly compilation of abstracts of doctoral dissertations submitted to University Microfilms International by more than 375 colleges and universities in the United States and Canada. The DAI is divided into two broad categories: (1) sciences, and (2) humanities, where political science listings are found. The abstract itself is indexed by author and key word. Looking up the key words "Vote," "Voter," and "Voting," in the January, 1978 abstract volume, several dissertations are found, including those dealing with voting behavior in an urban school district, voter equality, money and votes, and referendum voting. An abstract about one-half page in length accompanies each listing. Most dissertations listed in DAI are available on microfilm from University Microfilms.

Properly used, the indexes and abstracts alert the researcher to the available works in a particular area of interest. By examining titles and summary abstracts, the student further narrows the potential field of research topics. Within the broad area of American voting behavior, for example, the student will soon find that some topics appear more feasible and personally interesting than others.

Of course, abstracts and indexes are only signaling devices; they do not substitute for actually reviewing the material itself. But they do assist the researcher in discarding extraneous information and in focusing on that which is truly relevant for his or her particular interest. Those materials will then be sought in the library's holdings for more thorough review, and the process of topic narrowing is continued.

Finally, the result of these efforts should be the selection of a research topic of manageable proportions and sufficient student interest. From the library's vast holdings the researcher may have found a few dozen books and articles, even fewer perhaps, which are most directly related to the specific topic chosen. But these few sources will sharply define the topic, place it in its proper theoretical or policy context, indicate sources of data, and reveal important questions that should be pursued. The researcher is now equipped to proceed to the hypothesis-formation stage.

Hypothesis Formation

Having completed the literature-review stage, the researcher should be thoroughly familiar with existing theory and research in the area of particular interest. From this body of knowledge, hypotheses are developed. Hypotheses are testable statements relating two or more concepts or variables. Theories are usually too broad and imprecise to be directly testable; hypotheses are explicit statements of expected relationships. As

McGaw and Watson have put it, "Hypotheses link abstract theories to the empirical world."[8]

Hypothesis formation is a critical stage in the process of systematic research and cannot be lightly dismissed. Two extremely important functions are performed by the explicit formation of hypotheses. First, hypotheses provide a means of theory evaluation. As a result of hypothesis testing, the researcher is able to offer some evidence relating to the utility of the theory itself. If testing indicates the hypotheses as formulated to be true, this provides some empirical verification of the theory. Failure to substantiate the hypotheses raises questions concerning the validity of the theory.[9] Of course, neither positive confirmation of the hypotheses nor failure to substantiate the hypotheses provide absolute proof of the theory's validity. Any number of factors may affect empirical testing, including the failure to develop adequate hypotheses, poor sampling, and unaccounted for variables. Still, the testing of hypotheses provides some empirical linkage between theory and the real world. It is also true that, even following the best of procedures, the results of hypothesis testing rarely will provide complete verification or falsification of a theory. More likely, the testing will indicate those *circumstances* under which the theory seems to apply and those under which it may be less applicable. In any case, the formation and empirical examination of hypotheses is vital to theory evaluation.

The second important role of hypotheses in the conduct of systematic political research is in providing guidance and direction in the data-collection stage. The hypotheses developed will dictate the nature of data that must be collected. Suppose that the student interested in voting behavior establishes the following as one hypothesis to be examined: "Alienated citizens are more likely than nonalienated citizens to support extremist political candidates." In the data-collection phase it becomes imperative that this student gather information on individuals which will provide some measure of their alienation *and* their candidate preferences. A thousand other pieces of information may be collected, but unless some measures of these two specific variables (alienation and candidate preference) are gathered, the researcher cannot succeed in testing the original hypothesis.

Perhaps the beginning student will feel more comfortable in developing his or her own testable hypotheses after reviewing the work of more experienced researchers. Examining any issue of the leading political science journals, numerous examples of hypothesis articulation will be found. The student interested in voting behavior, for example, would run across a recently

---

[8] Dickinson McGaw and George Watson, *Political and Social Inquiry* (New York: John Wiley & Sons, Inc., 1976), p. 153.

[9] It should be noted that hypotheses may be developed from empirical observation as well as deduced from theory. Also, empirical testing can never absolutely prove a hypothesis to be true; but such testing can at least lend support to a hypothesis, and this, in turn, lends supports to the theory from which the hypothesis is derived.

published article on the subject of voter turnout by Steven Rosenstone and Raymond Wolfinger.[10] Following their review of the literature, Rosenstone and Wolfinger state:

> Two general [hypotheses] about the effect of registration are suggested by the literature… (1) The more time and energy required to vote, the lower the probability that an individual will vote. (2) [Since] the costs of voting affect some people more than others; registration laws have their greatest impact on people with less education.[11]

These hypotheses state with precision the issues to be pursued and the variables to be examined. The beginning researcher would profit from a personal examination of other hypotheses developed in the political science literature.

Admittedly, the state of social science theory is such that it is not always possible to extract from the literature hypotheses as elegant and precise as those developed by Rosenstone and Wolfinger. One may find theories that conflict in their predictions, or one may be interested in an area where little formal theory is available or where the theory that is available is too underdeveloped to be of much use. In such cases, it might be possible to "borrow" hypotheses from a more established area. The student of domestic intergovernmental relations, for example, might productively adopt hypotheses generated from the rather large body of theory dealing with international relations. Or, the researcher might state his or her hypotheses as low-level propositions or even as questions. In any case, it is critical at this stage of the research process to give considerable thought to the questions that the research must answer. Even seasoned researchers sometimes forget to devote appropriate consideration at the outset to the nature of the data that will have to be collected to address the issues of concern. This almost automatically ensures project failure. The attempt, at least, to precisely set out hypotheses to be tested, *before* beginning the data-collection stage, will substantially reduce the probability of making this fatal research error.

Concepts: The Building Blocks

Hypotheses, it has been stated, relate two or more concepts. Concepts can be defined as abstract terms used to represent sets of characteristics. Concepts, Kenneth Bailey says, "are simply mental images or perceptions [which] may be impossible to observe directly, such as love or justice, or [which] may have referents that are readily observable, such as a tree or a table."[12]

---

[10]Steven J. Rosenstone and Raymond E. Wolfinger, "The Effect of Registration Laws on Voter Turnout," *American Political Science Review*, 72 (March, 1978), pp. 22–45.

[11]*Ibid.*, p. 28. Rosenstone and Wolfinger actually use the word "propositions" rather than "hypotheses." In this instance, however, I believe the two words are essentially interchangeable.

[12]Kenneth D. Bailey, *Methods of Social Research* (New York: The Free Press, 1978), p. 33.

Examples of concepts often used in political research are: social status, power, influence, group cohesion, alienation, leadership, political efficacy, socialization, and political culture. To be useful for empirical analysis concepts must be operational. As is used here, operational means measurable; the concepts being used must be susceptible to measurement. The researcher must be able to translate the concepts being examined into observable and definable events. Satisfactory indicators of the concept must be found or developed.[13] This is the very important process of *concept operationalization*.

Here, too, the beginning student would profit from an examination of attempts by more senior researchers to operationalize their concepts. Consider again the Rosenstone and Wolfinger study of voter turnout. For their data source, Rosenstone and Wolfinger relied heavily on information collected from individuals by the U.S. Bureau of the Census in its November, 1972, Current Population Survey. That survey included items dealing with voter registration and turnout, together with the usual demographic and background questions. From this Census survey, Rosenstone and Wolfinger selected a subsample of almost 8000 respondents, an average of slightly over 150 per state.[14] Recalling their hypotheses as stated above, it can be seen that a number of concepts had to be measured: (1) *the decision to vote*; (2) *time and energy (costs) required to vote*; and (3) *education*. Relying on the Census data, the operationalization of the variables "*vote*" and "*education*" by Rosenstone and Wolfinger was straightforward. These questions were asked of each respondent by the Census Bureau. "Vote" was defined as voting or not voting, "education" was measured as number of years of formal education. For these two variables the issues of concept operationalization were settled by the Census Bureau when collecting the data.

The concept "costs of voting" is obviously more difficult. Operationalizing this concept, Rosenstone and Wolfinger relied on several indicators of leniency of state registration laws. Included were measures of residency requirements, registration closing dates, places of registration, whether deputy registrars were allowed, hours the registration office was open, whether or not the registration office had evening and/or Saturday registration hours, whether absentee registration was allowed by mail, and number of years of nonvoting before purging names from rolls. All these variables were coded so as to measure time and energy costs to the potential voter. It was assumed, for example, that voting registration is facilitated (and therefore less "costly") in states establishing regular office hours and in those where registration offices are open after normal working hours or on weekends. These measures (and others) were used to operationalize the concept of time and energy (costs) required to vote.

[13] A similar point is made by Claire Selltiz et al., *Research Methods in Social Relations* (New York: Holt, Rinehart and Winston, Inc., 1959), p. 42.

[14] For a precise explanation of their procedures of sample selection, see Rosenstone and Wolfinger, "The Effect of Registration Laws on Voter Turnout," pp. 28–31.

Scaling as an Operational Tool

One technique often used by researchers in attempting to operationalize very abstract concepts is that of *scaling*. When a concept is so abstract (such as alienation or racial prejudice) that it cannot be adequately measured by reference to one indicator alone, several items may be used to provide a combined measure. The combination of those items selected to provide the measure is called the scale. In operationalizing the concept campaign participation, for example, one might ask respondents whether they voted, talked about the campaign, worked for a candidate, or gave money to a particular party or candidate. Based on answers to these four questions, respondents could be assigned a single score assumed to be an overall measure of campaign participation. Scaling techniques will be discussed in more depth in Chapter 4.

Again, it is stressed that all of these issues must be thoroughly considered before actually beginning the stage of data collection. Once the data have been collected, it is too late to worry about what items will be needed to properly operationalize the concepts involved.

Topic Selection:
Some Concluding Suggestions

The foregoing discussion should provide a framework within which the student can more rationally proceed with the sometimes difficult task of topic selection and with the evaluation of the probable successful completion of the project. Before concluding this chapter, some final suggestions for selecting a topic are in order.

Select the topic as early as possible. Everyone is familiar with the student who the day before Thanksgiving break, decides on a topic, rushes to the library, checks out the few remaining books in the area, finds that the paper simply cannot be prepared in 2 or 3 days, and returns to campus pleading with the instructor for a deadline extension of 1 or 2 weeks (to which the instructor reluctantly agrees provided that the student will accept a penalty of a lowered letter grade or two). This, of course, violates almost all the principles established in this chapter. Early topic selection ensures greater access to materials, more time to carefully formulate hypotheses, greater flexibility in data collection, and increased time for data analysis and report writing. This will almost always result in a better research project.

Select a topic of limited range. Beginning researchers typically will select a very broad topic and immediately find themselves overloaded with information. A student selecting the topic "differences between Democrats and Republicans," for example, would find hundreds of articles and books on various aspects of this topic published in the last few years alone. Clearly, this is too broad a topic to be managed in one semester. More appropriate would be the topic "issue differences between Democrats and Republicans" or even "contemporary domestic issue differences between Democratic and Republican voters." Selecting a narrow topic is not only more manageable, but is also likely to result in more interesting and certainly more definitive results.[15]

Do not neglect the possibility of replication. Replicating the works of others is a legitimate and very worthwhile exercise in scientific research. It would be appropriate to try to determine if voting patterns found by previous research in some other city would parallel voting patterns in your own city, or if political attitudes found in some other college would match political attitudes in your university. If similar results are found, you have provided additional confirmation to whatever theory or proposition is being tested. If differences are discovered, you can speculate on the reasons for these differences and suggest ways in which the theory may need to be altered.

Do not be afraid to abandon a topic if it becomes impossible to complete. A very common mistake is to hold on to a topic after it becomes obvious that the data cannot be collected, interviews will not be possible, materials are not available, or you simply discover that you are really not interested in that area. Early selection of a topic makes it possible to uncover these problems while there is still time to switch to another topic. It is much preferable to switch topics rather than turn in a poor paper along with a lot of excuses for a lackluster performance.

The early stages of the research project are complete. The researcher has a topic, is thoroughly familiar with the literature and the relationship of his or her topic to that literature, and has developed one or more testable hypotheses. Interest now turns to the sources of data and the methods by which the data can be collected.

Exercises

1. Referring to textbooks, political science journals, and your own interest areas, develop *three* possible research topics. Look up each of these topics in the *International Encyclopedia of the Social Sciences* and report some of the major problem areas and list some of the important reference works for each topic.
2. a. For each of the research topics developed in Exercise 1, apply the criteria for evaluation discussed in this chapter.
   b. Which of these potential topics appear most feasible and most manageable?
   c. Why is this so?
3. Selecting *one* of the research topics developed in Exercise 1 and relying on the various social science indexes and abstracts discussed in this chapter, thoroughly review the literature in this area. List the 10 books or articles that appear most

[15]A similar point is made by Herbert F. Weisberg and Bruce D. Bowen, *An Introduction to Survey Research and Data Analysis* (San Francisco: W. H. Freeman and Company, 1977), p. 223.

relevant to your particular area of interest and prepare a paragraph summary of each, listing hypotheses tested, sources of data, and findings.

4. a. For the research topic reviewed in Exercise 3, develop three possible research hypotheses of *your own*.

   b. What function would these hypotheses serve if you actually were able to carry out this research?

   c. Why is this so?

5. Review three empirical studies published in recent political science journals. For each study, report:

   a. The hypotheses being tested.

   b. The sources of information and data.

   c. The means of operationalizing concepts employed.

   d. The findings.

   e. The conclusions.

3

GATHERING INFORMATION

Data collection is always a fascinating phase of research, and this is particularly true in the case of political research. The collection of information often takes the student out of the library, out of the classroom, and into the "field" — the "real" world of politics. Here, the researcher may interview public officials, attend legislative sessions, examine public documents, talk with people about political matters, or simply trace public issues through newspaper sources. Through the collection and handling of information, the researcher begins to "feel" the actual excitement of politics and political behavior.

Even if the researcher decides to rely on data collected by others, assembling this information into usable form can still be a very creative experience. Considerable detective work will be required to sift through the many sources of available information (discussed below) to find just the right data for testing the hypotheses that have been developed. The researcher will often have to combine information from two or more sources, and the result will be a unique data set, tailored to the specific needs of the research situation. The researcher will be able to approach the issues and shed new light on a particular problem in ways that have never before been attempted.

In setting out to collect the needed information, two options are available: (1) the researcher may collect his or her own data; or (2) the researcher may rely on data collected by someone else. The decision between these strategies, as Jones has observed, is based on desired control and available resources.[1] Researchers with limited resources and those not requiring a great deal of control over the type of data collected or the conditions under which the data were collected probably will be content to rely on data collected by others. Students of comparative and international politics, because of the many

[1] E. Terrence Jones, *Conducting Political Research* (New York: Harper & Row, Publishers, 1971), pp. 83–84.

problems and complications of conducting research in these areas, may rely in most cases on information collected and supplied by others. A third factor influencing the strategy of data collection is also important. If the researcher is interested in an area where no reliable information is currently available, the only option is self-collection of data. Students of state and local politics, for example, often find themselves interested in issues pertaining to a *particular* locality (such as background characteristics of a city's council members, participation of local citizens in civic associations, and attitudes of public officials to issues of local concern) for which no body of systematically collected data is available. In instances such as these, there is no option. The researcher must collect his or her own data.

Whether one decides to personally collect data (sometimes called *primary data*) or to rely on that collected by others (often called *secondary data* analysis) the process can be made more productive and more rewarding by following a few established procedures, discussed next.

Self-Collection

A number of strategies present themselves to researchers who decide that data must be personally collected. These include historical and documentary search, experimental research, observational techniques, and survey research. While each of these techniques may provide useful data (indeed, in the actual research effort it is advisable to employ as many techniques of data collection as possible), the observational and survey methods will be most carefully examined below (documentary and experimental methods are more briefly treated in later sections). Using observation techniques, the researcher *observes behavior as it occurs*; using survey techniques, the researcher relies on the *reports of individuals* of their behavior or attitudes. Each of these data collection techniques has particular advantages and disadvantages.

Observation Techniques

Data are sometimes collected while the behavior that is of interest to the researcher is actually taking place. As an observer of events, the researcher may assume several roles, ranging from "complete observer" (where the researcher is completely divorced from the activity being examined) to "complete participant" (where the researcher is completely involved as an active participant).[2] An example of the former role would be that of the student of local politics collecting data while observing a session of a city council meeting; an example of the latter role would be the student of

[2] For a more complete discussion of these roles, see Nan Lin, *Foundations of Social Research* (New York: McGraw-Hill Book Company, 1976), pp. 206–209.

national party conventions who actually becomes an official delegate and collects data while attending one of the national conventions.

Regardless of the role assumed, the observation technique has one great advantage over any. other means of data collection: the researcher is observing behavior *as it actually happens*. The researcher does not have to rely on respondents' ability to remember events that occurred sometime in the past; events are recorded as they take place. Furthermore, a number of political events that are of interest to students of politics are open to the public and readily accessible. Included would be meetings of city councils, county commissioners, legislative committees, school boards, advisory committees, and the like.

On the other hand, observational techniques have several limitations which lessen their utility to political research. In the first place, many of the phenomena that are of interest to political researchers (such as alienation, political efficacy, and attitudes toward political issues) are not *directly* observable, and often the events that political scientists are interested in studying (riots, revolutions, and war, for example) cannot be predicted. Observational techniques typically require a considerable amount of skill and training. Access to situations that would be of interest (such as decision making at the White House) may be impossible, and the data generated from such observation are often difficult to quantify.

For these and other reasons,[3] observational techniques are not as often used in political research as in some other disciplines, such as anthropology and psychology. Still, some very productive examples of research having political or policy implications and relying partly or wholly on observational techniques are available. Examining the relationship between federal programs and city politics, Jeffrey L. Pressman gathered much of his data from his experiences as an aide to the mayor of the City of Oakland. Describing his research methodology, Pressman, says:

> The empirical basis for the study [is] drawn to a large extent from my experiences in — and observation of — the City of Oakland. From 1967 to 1971 I participated in the Oakland Project, a group of graduate students and faculty members at the University of California, Berkeley, who were engaged in a program of participant-observation in Oakland. As a member of the project, I worked in the office of the mayor from 1967 to 1969. During that time, I concentrated both my work and my observation on relations between federal and city agencies.[4]

The result of Pressman's research is an excellent study of the problems and limitations of local political leadership. Pressman was able to thoroughly

[3]For a thorough discussion of the advantages and disadvantages of observational techniques, see Claire Selltiz, Marie Jahoda, Morton Deutsch, and Stuart W. Cook, *Research Methods in Social Relations*, rev. ed. (New York: Holt, Rinehart and Winston, Inc., 1959), pp. 200–207.

[4]Jeffrey L. Pressman, *Federal Programs and City Politics* (Berkeley, Calif.: University of California Press, 1975), pp. 19–21.

investigate the images that local and federal officials have of each other and to relate the implications of federally set domestic policy for local politics and policy making. Pressman's experiences provided invaluable new insights for students of local politics and intergovernmental relations.

A second example of the use of the observation technique is Elliot Liebow's study of street-corner life in Washington, D.C.[5] In collecting his data, Liebow became an active participant in the lives of the small group of street-corner men who were the focus of his study. Describing the beginning stages of his research, Liebow states:

> From the very first weeks or even days [of the study], I found myself in the middle of things; the principal lines of my field work were laid out, almost without my being aware of it. For the next year or so... my base of operations was the corner Carry-out across the street from my starting point.[6]

On his second day in the field, one of Liebow's subjects told him, "Well, if you hang around here, you'll see it all." Liebow did hang around and if perhaps he did not see it *all*, his observations were to add immeasurably to our understanding of urban life. Originally prepared as a Ph.D. dissertation in anthropology, Liebow's account of life in the inner city has had important and long-lasting implications for domestic urban policy making.

The research by Pressman and Liebow are excellent examples of the use of observational techniques. All political researchers would be advised to thoroughly review their techniques, as these studies point out both the strengths and weaknesses of observational research. Each of these studies was concentrated in a single area (Oakland and Washington, D.C.). In a strict sense, the findings reported are applicable only to those localities and only to the particular time period of the studies. At the same time, these studies provide a depth of insight that could not be achieved using other techniques, and each has stimulated much additional research.

Observational techniques typically are classified as being *structured* or *unstructured*. Pressman's and Liebow's studies are examples of unstructured observation. As these studies demonstrate, using unstructured techniques the researcher does not attempt to manipulate the subjects or structure the research situation; participants are observed in their natural setting.

Sometimes, the researcher may actually set the agenda and assign roles. The nature of the research in this instance is said to be structured observation. A scholar of municipal politics might ask a group of students to participate in a mock city council meeting, or a student of international politics might ask a group of students to participate in a simulated session of the United Nations. In either case the researcher determines the rules, assigns

---

[5] Elliot Liebow, *Tally's Corner: A Study of Negro Streetcorner Men* (Boston: Little, Brown and Company, 1967).

[6] *Ibid.*, p. 237.

roles, and sets the agenda. The subjects are then asked to participate in a *simulated* decision-making situation, and the researcher observes the dynamics and the outcome of the decision-making process under a variety of circumstances. While such simulated exercises are artificial in the sense that "real" policy is not being made, the method still is observational and insightful results may be obtained.

The Survey

To the list of the limitations of observational techniques discussed above, one additional one should be mentioned. This is time. Observational techniques can be extremely time-consuming. Both Liebow and Pressman spent months in the collection of information for their studies. It is not unusual for an individual using this approach to devote a year or more to the data-collection stage alone.

While it is unquestionably true that such expenditures of time can sometimes reap rich rewards (as witnessed by the Pressman and Liebow studies), it is also true that few students can devote this amount of time to a single project. More expedient methods of data collection are required, and political researchers often turn to the survey technique.

The survey as a research technique has a second important advantage over observational methods. This concerns the issue of representation. Observational studies are generally limited to one area (one city, one neighborhood, one block); generalization to larger units is risky, at best. Using survey techniques, on the other hand, the researcher theoretically can include the entire universe in his or her study (all state legislators, city council members, or classmates), or at least can rely on a *sample* of respondents which, hopefully, is representative of the larger body. Thus the survey, which perhaps sacrifices the depth of information that can be gathered through observational techniques, is typically a less time-consuming method of data collection and the results are usually much more generalizable. Because of these important attributes, contemporary political research more often relies on the survey as a means of collecting information.

The survey is a means of data collection that relies on the verbal report of the respondent. Behavior is not actually observed; through questionnaires or interviews the respondent is asked to report on his or her behavior or attitudes.

An important issue in the use of survey techniques relates to the respondents' ability to respond accurately and the willingness to respond honestly. If behavior is not actually observed, how is the researcher to judge the validity of response? For most political research the issue of honesty probably need not be too great a concern. Researchers have found that most people seem willing to provide information as honestly and as accurately as possible. If a question arises in a particular instance, the answers of one respondent can be checked by collaboration with the answers of others. Also, some scales developed for social research include items designed to measure inconsistency or falsification in response.[7] But the major point to be made is that in most circumstances veracity of response will not be a major issue, and one need not devote a great deal of time to developing elaborate checks on response honesty.[8]

Of greater concern is the issue of the respondents' *ability* to accurately answer questions. In an interview study of over 80 members of presidential administrations from Truman through Carter, Stephen J. Wayne found that "In general, the respondents had vivid recall, often remembering in minute detail incidents that occurred 20 to 30 years ago."[9] Wayne's experiences notwithstanding, it is still true that respondents sometimes may not know answers to questions posed (such as, "What was your grandmother's party affiliation?"); may not have developed an informed opinion ("What is your opinion of the latest Middle East peace initiative?"); may not remember ("Which political party did you support in the 1964 Senate race?"); or simply may be unable to make accurate self judgments (questions dealing with racial and religious prejudice might fall into this category). In such instances the researcher can sometimes improve the accuracy of response by allowing the respondent additional time to answer. For example, the researcher interested in an in-depth study of generational voting patterns may ask the respondent to find out the voting behavior of his or her relatives and to supply that information at a later time. Or, the student of municipal budgeting might leave with the municipal finance officer a list of detailed budget questions and request a response in several days. No matter what tactics are used, however, some inaccuracies will inevitably result in survey research. Although precautions should be taken to minimize these risks, survey research proceeds with the assumption that most people respond honestly and acurately most of the time and that individuals, themselves, are in the unique position of

[7]The widely used 58-item Coopersmith Self-Esteem Inventory Scale, for example, includes 8 questions which are said to form a "lie scale." See Coopersmith Self-Esteem Inventory Scale, developed by Stanley Coopersmith and distributed by Self-Esteem Institute, San Francisco.

[8]In this regard, one area of particular concern to students of voting behavior deals with the validity of responses to questions of voting turnout and candidate preference. The American National Election surveys conducted by the Center for Political Studies at the University of Michigan consistently show an overreport of voting turnout and a slight tendency to exaggerate the party vote in the direction of the winning candidate. In 1964, for example, the percent of the sample reporting having voted in the national election of that year was about 15 percent higher than official turnout records. In a perceptive article, Aage Clausen demonstrates that because of certain differences between the population considered as eligible voters and the universe from which the samples are drawn, even these discrepancies are not as great as they may seem. See Aage Clausen, "Response Validity: Vote Report," *Public Opinion Quarterly*, 32 (Winter, 1968–1969), 588–606.

[9]Stephen J. Wayne, *The Legislative Presidency* (New York: Harper & Row, Publishers, 1978), p. xi.

being able to respond to questions dealing with their own attitudes and opinions. Several decades of survey research support this assumption.[10]

There are basically two types of survey techniques: *interviews* and *questionnaires*. In an interview situation the researcher asks the questions and records the responses. In the questionnaire format, subjects typically are asked to record their own responses to a prepared list of written items. The distinction between these two tools deserve further comment.

The Questionnaire

The questionnaire is a very important data-collection instrument for political researchers. Typically, the questionnaire will be delivered through the mail or, on occasion, hand-delivered. Compared with the interview technique, the questionnaire is much easier from the standpoint of the researcher. Questionnaires are less time-consuming and less costly. For the price of a postage stamp, information can be solicited from anyone almost anyplace in the world. Since questionnaires generally are standardized (i.e., the same questions are asked of everyone in the same order), they ensure uniform response patterns. Since questionnaires at least provide the appearance of anonymity, subjects may be more likely to honestly and accurately respond to sensitive topics. Questionnaires also pose less of an intrusion on respondents' time, and since they may be completed and returned at their convenience, responses received may be more thoughtful and accurate.

The questionnaire has one major disadvantage: unpredictability of responses. The researcher does not know who or how many will actually return the questionnaire. Thus the rate of return and possible biases in return are two very important issues to be considered in questionnaire research.

The Rate of Questionnaire Return. The issues of return rate and return bias are directly related. Typically, the higher the rate of return, the more confident can the researcher be that those who respond actually represent the total group. Since achieving a representative return is really the important issue, every reasonable effort to ensure a high rate of return must be made.

Because of the high volume of unsolicited and "junk" mail received by everyone in the United States today, it is easy for questionnaires to become lost, mishandled, or misplaced. Potential respondents find it much more difficult to refuse a request for a personal interview than to discard an impersonal letter received through the mail. Additionally, respondents who receive a personal appeal for an interview are likely to feel more important to the study. Knowing that the researcher is willing to give up an hour or so

[10]One of the best discussions of the problems arising in survey research is that provided by Claire Selltiz, Lawrence Wrightsman, and Stuart Cook, *Research Methods in Social Relations*, 3rd ed. (New York: Holt, Rinehart and Winston, Inc., 1976), pp. 292–330. The discussion above heavily relies on that presentation.

of time to gain the interview, the respondent is likely to believe (correctly) that his or her opinions are very important to the study's success. Compare this with the respondent receiving a survey through the mail who knows that the researcher is willing to spend only a few cents (the price of postage) to obtain his or her response. In this case, respondents understandably are more likely to discount the importance of their contribution and, consequently, response rates will be lowered. To achieve as high a return rate as possible, every aspect of the questionnaire must be carefully considered. This will include attention to be paid to the envelope, the cover letter, instructions, questionnaire length, clarity and simplicity in questionnaire wording, providing adequate range of response possibilities, follow-up letters, and a promise of results. Each of these is discussed below.

The Envelope. The envelope in which the questionnaire arrives is the respondent's first introduction to you and your study. Care should be taken to make this first impression a positive one. The evelope should be hand-addressed or typed personally for each respondent. Avoid using address labels (which give the impression of a mass-produced effort) and make every attempt to address envelopes to individuals (rather than "Occupant" or "The Mayor"). Unless financial resources are extremely limited, the researcher should use first-class (or even commemorative) postage stamps (rather than taking advantage of second-class postage rates). It is important that the respondent begin with a positive impression. If the envelope is not opened, the questionnaire will not be returned. Although you may be sending out hundreds of questionnaires, each recipient should feel personally identified with, and important to, the study.

The Cover Letter. The questionnaire will be accompanied with a cover letter that explains who you are, what the study is about, why and how the respondent was selected, why it is important for the results to return the questionnaire, and who is funding the study. If the study is part of a class project or a thesis effort, it is helpful to include a statement from the instructor or thesis advisor explaining the importance of the survey to the student's project. It is desirable to personally type cover letters for each respondent, but the volume of the mailing sometimes makes this impossible. The cover letter should assure the respondent of the confidential nature of the study — you will not identify names with responses. If it truly is an anonymous survey (the researcher is not able to identify people with responses), this should be mentioned as well. The cover letter should also include the researcher's name, address, and phone number. Respondents should be encouraged to contact the researcher if they have any questions.

The Instructions. Instructions for completing the survey will appear as part of the cover letter or, perhaps, separately. In either case, the instructions should encourage the respondent to expand on answers to questions on the back of the survey or, if desired, on a separate piece of paper.

The Questionnaire. Another major factor affecting return rates is the length of the survey instrument. Long and tedious questionnaires simply will not result in high response rates. The researcher must decide which are the most important questions to be asked and must be willing to eliminate others. Failure to do so may result in a return rate too low to be useful. As a general rule, it would be advisable to limit mailed questionnaires to a maximum of five pages. Even briefer questionnaires would be encouraged.

The questionnaire should be presented clearly and simply. Care must be taken to avoid double barreled questions: those that really ask about two issues in a single question. For example, the question "Would you favor the reduction of local taxes by placing a ceiling on the rate of property value assessments?" is really two questions. The researcher should first determine if the respondent favors a reduction in taxes (not even obvious answers should be assumed) and *then* should ascertain the respondent's feeling's toward accomplishing this by placing a ceiling on the rate of property value assessments. This might be accomplished as follows:

Question 1: Do you favor the reduction of local taxes in your area? (check one)
Yes____; No____; Uncertain____

Question 2: If you responded "yes" to the question above, would you favor accomplishing a reduction of taxes by placing a ceiling on the rate of property value assessments? (check one)
Yes____; No____; Uncertain____

In this manner, ambiguity in questions and response is greatly reduced.

When asking opinions, it is advisable to provide the respondent with a range of possible response options. That is, the researcher usually should avoid opinion questions offering only "yes" or "no" options. At a minimum an "uncertain" response (or some other suitable neutral response category) should be offered, and it is advisable to offer a range of response alternatives so that both direction and intensity of response can be assessed. For example, David Caputo and the author have conducted several questionnaire studies of municipal chief executive officers concerning their attitudes about various aspects of the general revenue-sharing program — a program annually returning billions of dollars to states and communities — as well as their attitudes toward a variety of other federally-directed urban programs.[11]

[11] See David A. Caputo and Richard L. Cole, *Urban Politics and Decentralization* (Lexington, Mass.: Lexington Books, 1974).

Sample questions from that survey demonstrating some of the variety of alternatives which may be offered are presented below.

We are interested in your overall evaluation of the general revenue-sharing program. In general, would you say that to date you are very satisfied, somewhat satisfied, somewhat dissatisfied, or very dissatisfied with the program?

| Very satisfied____ | Somewhat satisfied____ | Uncertain____ | Somewhat dissatisfied____ | Very dissatisfied____ |

Over the past several years, would you say that general revenue sharing has increased public interest in local politics and public affairs, decreased public interest, or has it had no effect at all in your city?

| Greatly increased public interest____ | Somewhat increased public interest____ | No effect____ | Somewhat decreased public interest____ | Greatly decreased public interest____ |

Given your knowledge of President Carter's urban policy proposals, what do you think their overall impact on the funds available to your city will be?

| Increase funds greatly____ | Increase funds somewhat____ | No effect____ | Decrease funds somewhat____ | Decrease funds greatly____ |

As in the examples above, a five-point response scale can be used. Seven-point or nine-point scales (or some other interval range) might be developed, but the important point is that using such response scales the respondent is provided several options and the researcher discovers both the *direction* and *intensity* of opinions.

An issue arises as to whether to rely on closed-ended or open-ended questions. *Closed-ended questions* (also called "fixed alternative" or "forced-choice" questions) are those, such as the examples above, which state the question and provide the array of possible responses. The respondent simply has to place a check or some other mark in the appropriate space. Minimum response effort is required.

Open-ended questions are those which ask the question but allow space for the respondent to answer in his or her *own words*. In the foregoing example dealing with the local tax issue, the second question could have been worded, "If you responded 'yes' to the question above, what tactics would you favor to bring about a reduction of taxes?" Suitable space would then be provided for the response.

Open-ended questions do not force a preestablished response set and allow the respondent to answer as he or she really feels. Often, responses will be generated which the researcher has not anticipated. This is especially useful in exploratory studies — those which are to precede a larger survey.

Closed-ended questions, on the other hand, are easier to code and analyze. More important to the success of the mailed questionnaire, they are faster to answer. The respondent need only place a mark in the appropriate space. In general, the student would be advised when relying on a mailed questionnaire to ask as many questions in a closed-ended format as possible. A few preliminary interviews will assist the researcher in phrasing the questions and in anticipating the range of possible answers. A very useful tactic, if space permits, is to present a closed-ended question but to follow this with a question to the effect: "Why do you feel that way?" or "Would you like to expand on your answer?" Adequate space would then be provided for the respondent to comment. In this manner, the advantages of the closed-ended questionnaire are preserved, and the researcher will have the benefit of longer answers from those finding the need and having the time to so respond.

Care should also be taken in the structure and placement of the questions. More general items should be placed early in the survey and items of similar focus should be grouped together. It is recommended as well that more personal items be placed near the end of the survey. Questions pertaining to age, sex, race, income, and so forth should be the last few items. Also, careful consideration of the respondent's feelings and sensitivities should go into the construction of these more personal items. It is more considerate, for example, to ask a person "What is the year of your birth?" than "How old are you?". Questions of a personal nature, indeed any questions that are not germane to the study, should not be asked.

Follow-up and Promise of Results. After waiting a sufficient period (two or three weeks), follow-up letters and questionnaires to those not responding may be called for. The follow-up letter should explain once again the nature of the study and should stress the importance of achieving a high response rate. Generally, two follow-up appeals will be sufficient to solicit responses from those who care to answer. The effort and time wasted from more appeals is usually not worth the few additional replies that might result.

Also assisting in boosting the return rate is the promise of a copy of the study's results. If at all possible, the researcher should promise a summary copy of the results as a means of expressing appreciation to those who respond. This promise should be fulfilled.

Although it is not always possible to state with precision the improvement in rates of return that result from the use of these techniques, Delbert C. Miller has provided some rough estimates.[12] According to Miller, use of follow-up

[12] Delbert C. Miller, *Handbook of Research Design and Social Measurement* (New York: David McKay Company, Inc., 1970), pp. 81–83.

questionnaires should increase the return rate by 40 per cent; inducements (such as promise of study results) should increase the return rate by 33 percent; briefer questionnaires should boost the total rate of return by 22 percent; and closed-ended questions should result, he says, in an increase of 13 percent. Although these are only estimates — actual return rates will vary from situation to situation — the student would be advised to carefully consider the possible impact of following (or not following) these guides when conducting mail surveys.[13]

Assessing Response Bias. Careful attention to the techniques discussed above should result in the largest possible rate of return. However, it should never be expected that everyone will reply, and it is always possible that those who do return the questionnaire may not accurately represent the population. Thus the sample may be biased, and this is really the critical issue in questionnaire research. It is sometimes argued that those feeling more strongly, one way or the other, about the issues being studied, and those who are better informed and higher educated, are more likely to respond.[14] To the extent that any discrepancy exists between the sample return and the universe of respondents, the validity of the entire study is jeopardized.

Techniques for improving the rate of return were discussed above, and the greater the rate of return, the more confident can the researcher be in the representativeness of the sample. Although there are no strict guidelines, it is suggested that a return of at least 35 to 40 percent should be sought. Serious questions of bias could be raised with any response rate that is much lower than this.[15]

Regardless of the return rate, the researcher should make every effort to determine and report whatever biases in the sample may be known or suspected. Very often in research utilizing questionnaires, some information about the population will be known. University officials will have some information pertaining to the characteristics of the entire student body (hometown, religious preference, academic major, year of studies); city, county, and state-wide demographic data (age, income, racial distribution, etc.) will be available from Census reports; various organizations, such as Congressional Quarterly, Inc., compile data on all Senate and House members (such as age, party affiliation, size of home district); the Republican and Democratic National Committees usually maintain some information pertaining to delegates attending the national conventions (age, sex, and

[13] For a recent and excellent review of the literature dealing with mail questionnaires and telephone surveys and suggestions for maximizing the response rate to both see, Don A. Dillman, *Mail and Telephone Surveys* (New York: John Wiley & Sons, 1978).

[14] For an introduction to this literature, see A. N. Oppenheim, *Questionnaire Design and Attitude Measurement* (New York: Basic Books, Inc., 1966).

[15] However, Charles Mayer and Robert Pratt found a return of 23.5 percent to very closely represent the population in their study. See "A Note on Nonresponse in a Mail Survey," *Public Opinion Quarterly*, 30 (1966–1967), 637–646.

race); and so on. The point to be made is that by matching known characteristics of the population to that of the sample returning the questionnaire, some indication of sample bias can be achieved.[16]

As an example, consider again the questionnaire studies of chief executive officers of large American cities (those over 50,000) conducted by D. A. Caputo and the author. In attempting to ascertain response biases, known characteristics of all 409 cities over 50,000 were compared with these same characteristics of the cities of the chief executive officers returning the surveys conducted in 1973 and 1974. Results of those comparisons are provided in Table 3.1.

Inspecting the information presented in Table 3.1, one can immediately judge the representativeness of the two questionnaire surveys, at least as far as these characteristics are concerned. It can be seen, for example, that the actual percentage of Negro population in all cities over 50,000 (12.6 percent) is slightly underrepresented in both questionnaire surveys. If in applying this technique, biases are found that may significantly affect the results, procedures are available which attempt to compensate for these differences.[17] Of course, this technique only provides some measure of what might be called

TABLE 3.1

Comparisons of Mean Characteristics of Cities Whose Officials Responded to Questionnaire Surveys with All Cities over 50,000

	All Cities over 50,000 (N = 409)	1973 Survey (N = 212)	1974 Survey (N = 216)
Population, 1970	186,120	184,506	221,882
City type 1 = Central City 2 = Suburb	1.4	1.4	1.3
Form of government 1 = Mayor/Council 2 = Council/Manager	1.6	1.6	1.7
% Population change, 1960–1970	24.4	33.9	24.1
% Population Negro	12.6	11.8	11.4
Foreign-born population	34,473	38,307	41,899
Mean income	$11,011	$11,103	$10,835

Source: David A. Caputo and Richard L. Cole, "City Officials and Mailed Questionnaires: An Investigation of the Response Bias Assumption," Political Methodology (Fall, 1977), 271–287.

[16]This assumes, of course, that the researcher is able to collect information on the same set of characteristics from both the sample and the population.

[17]See Lewis Mandell, "When to Weight: Determining Nonresponse Bias in Survey Data," Public Opinion Quarterly, 38 (1974), 247–252.

"demographic bias," and important attitudinal and opinion differences between the population and the sample may still exist. Still, this method provides at least some indication of sample representation.

The Interview

The interview is an alternative survey technique. Using interview procedures, the researcher personally asks questions of the respondents and personally records the answers.

The advantages and disadvantages of the interview are, in many respects, the opposite of those pertaining to the questionnaire. The interview process is usually more time-consuming and generally costs more money (especially if the researcher has to hire interviewers to assist in the process). The great advantage of the interview is that it almost always results in a higher response rate. People are often flattered to find that someone is actually interested in their opinions and attitudes. Even very busy people will generally find the time to meet with the researcher. Of course, the researcher will have to be flexible and will have to be willing to conduct the interview *at the convenience of the subject*. For this reason, those contemplating interview research should schedule the data-collection stage during a period when their time is relatively unencumbered.

Interviews have other advantages as well. The interview situation is more flexible in that difficult or confusing questions can be explained thoroughly before responses are solicited. Interviews allow for a depth of exploration impossible with quick questionnaires. Interviews allow the respondents to answer in their own words — responses are not forced into some preconceived pattern. Additionally, the researcher can be sure that the person he or she is interested in interviewing is actually responding. Questionnaires addressed to mayors or other officials can easily be shuffled off to an assistant.

Sometimes, the interview will follow an *unstructured format*. That is, the researcher may be interested in obtaining general background information on a particular topic and will not have specific and identical questions to ask of each respondent. Often, an unstructured format is used in preparation for the development of a more structured interview schedule or in developing a questionnaire.

More typically, interviews will follow a *structured routine*. That is, the same, or approximately the same, questions will be asked of each respondent, usually in the same order. The instrument relied upon by the interviewer to guide the interview is called the *interview schedule*. The interview schedule will list the questions to be asked and the order in which they are to be pursued. As in developing the questionnaire, a considerable amount of thought should be given to devising the interview schedule, and questions that are extraneous should be deleted.

The interview schedule may be highly structured. An example of one such interview schedule is that used by the Survey Research Center (SRC) of the

What is the highest grade of school or year of college you completed?

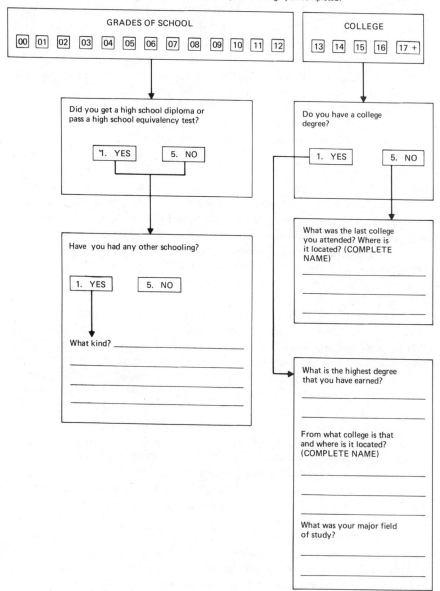

Figure 3.1
Measure of education used in CPS, 1978 American National Election Study. (Source: Survey Research Center, Institute for Social Research, The University of Michigan.)

Institute for Social Research, the University of Michigan. Consider the measure of respondent's education that the SRC included in its 1978 survey of a sample of the American electorate, shown in Figure 3.1. Interviews of this nature are highly directed. Interviewers are extensively trained and no deviations from the interview schedule are permitted. As shown in the example above, precise instructions are provided to carry the interviewer from item to item.

The degree of rigor utilized in the SRC interviews is necessary to ensure uniform response from the entire sample. However, the political researcher should remember that one of the great advantages of the interview technique is its flexibility. Typically, the interview schedule developed by an individual researcher will not be as structured and as inflexible as that used by national polling organizations such as the SRC. This is especially true when interviewing "elites" or other specialized segments of the population. In the process of conducting interviews, the researcher may find that some questions which were deemed essential are not so important and that questions which were not even considered are very significant. The researcher should take advantage of the fact that the interview, in contrast with the questionnaire, allows for alterations in the schedule that will maximize its utility as a data-collection instrument.

Lewis Dexter, a social scientist with considerable experience as an interviewer, has provided a set of instructions that should be helpful to those conducting interview research (especially of elites).[18] Among Dexter's suggestions are the following:

1. Always call or write for an appointment in advance of the interview. Don't just drop in.
2. Arrange the meeting at a time and place convenient for the interviewee. If possible, meet the respondent at his or her office.
3. Avoid interview situations of obvious distraction. The home may be one of these (children and pets weaving in and out), as well as the luncheon appointment (too much noise; note taking is impossible).
4. Explain at the beginning of each interview who you are, who sponsors the research, and what the project is about.
5. Begin the interview with more vague and general questions. More specific questions should be asked later.
6. Write up the notes on the interview as soon after it is completed as possible. When interviewing several individuals it is easy to confuse responses unless notes are prepared immediately.

Anyone contemplating interview research should carefully review Dexter's entire book, as it stands as the most complete and thoughtful guide to

[18] Lewis Anthony Dexter, *Elite and Specialized Interviewing* (Evanston, Ill.: Northwestern University Press, 1970).

interview techniques. To this list of suggestions should be added the following: Dress appropriately. The researcher should convey the impression that he or she is on a serious assignment, not stopping by on the way to the beach. Always show up on time. In fact, it is often useful to arrive early. One can learn a great deal about an organization from talking with secretaries, aides, and others who might be encountered while waiting, as well as from brochures and pamphlets that might be available for distribution. Try to receive permission to use a tape recorder. Most people do not mind being recorded, and the recorder guarantees an accurate transcript of each interview. Reluctant interviewees can usually be persuaded by assurances that the recorder will allow the interview to proceed at a faster pace (since you will not have to take notes) and that you will stop the recorder at any time the interviewee selects. This will satisfy most respondents, but, of course, the recorder should not be used if the subject refuses. If a recorder is to be used, always familiarize yourself with the machine and test the tape *before* the interview. The interviewer clumsily fumbling with a strange machine will find the interview situation deteriorating from the outset, and a defective tape can ruin the entire interview. *Always* send a thank-you note as soon after the interview as possible. Not only is this a matter of respect and courtesy, it facilitates the request for an interview by another researcher at some later time.

Comparing the Questionnaire and Interview Techniques

It can be seen from the foregoing discussion that the choice of survey technique is largely a cost/benefit decision. Those having a considerable amount of time and resources probably would opt for the interview. Since both time and resources usually are in short supply, political researchers rely heavily on the questionnaire. The questionnaire is a valuable tool and when used carefully can be a very productive source of information.

Regardless of the means selected for data collection, important decisions concerning sample selection remain to be decided. These are explored in the following section.

Sample Selection

Political researchers very often deal with situations in which all units in a population of interest *can be* included in the study. If the focus of analysis is large American cities or the 50 American states, or if the student is interested in congressional or United Nations voting behavior, or the American presidency, it typically will be feasible and desirable to collect information about all (or almost all) units (all cities, all states, all legislators, all presidents, and so forth). In cases such as these, the issue of sampling obviously is not a factor.

On the other hand, political researchers are also often interested in situations in which a complete enumeration of the population is impossible or nearly impossible. This is especially true in the area of voting behavior (where the population may be the entire electorate), but it is also true whenever the population size is large and information is difficult to collect. When the population size is too great for information to be collected on every unit, the researcher will have to be satisfied with studying a segment somewhat smaller than the total. This segment is called a *sample*. The sample is useful to the political researcher to the extent that it facilitates the collection of information and is representative of the entire population. Two major issues must be addressed when deciding to select for study a sample of the total population. One of these is the size of the sample, the other is the method by which the sample will be selected. While sampling theory is much too complex to be thoroughly examined here,[19] enough guidance concerning these issues can be provided to enable the researcher to confidently proceed with the sample-selection phase of the study.

Method of Selecting the Sample

Actually, many techniques for selecting a sample are available. The type of sample procedure utilized will vary from situation to situation.

For purposes of comparison with the more rigorous sampling techniques, consider what might simply be called the *convenient sample*.[20] As the label implies, the major criterion for selecting this sample is researcher convenience. You might pass out a survey to neighbors, friends, relatives, or classmates. You might stand in front of the student cafeteria and solicit opinions from those who pass. You might go to a shopping center on a Tuesday afternoon and interview anyone who is willing to take the time to respond. In all these situations, the selection process is more or less haphazard — people are included just because they are available and willing to cooperate. Slightly more rigorous than the convenient sampling technique are *judgment sampling* (in which the researcher attempts to evaluate and select those he or she judges to be representative of the population), and *quota sampling* (in which subjects are selected in proportion to their distribution in the whole population — 10 percent black, 50 percent women, and so forth).[21]

All of these *nonprobability sampling methods* can easily result in the selection of a sample that fails to represent the total population. The opinions of your friends, relatives, or those who shop on Tuesday afternoon may not accurately reflect the opinions of the broader community.

---

[19] See L. Kish, *Survey Sampling* (New York: John Wiley & Sons, Inc., 1965).

[20] Another term often used to describe this sampling technique is "haphazard sampling."

[21] For additional nonprobability sampling procedures, see Donald P. Warwick and Charles A. Lininger, *The Sample Survey: Theory and Practice* (New York: McGraw-Hill Book Company, 1975).

Probability sampling techniques have been developed so as to minimize the risks of drawing an unrepresentative sample. The risks can never be eliminated, *but at least these techniques allow the researcher to state the extent of probable error*. The probability sample is one drawn so that each element of the population has a known, and typically equal, chance of being selected. One type of probability sample is the *simple random sample*. One might conceive of a researcher placing the names of all 5000 students of a college in a single pile and from this pile drawing a sample of 500. Or, one might assign sequential numbers to each of the 5000 students and then select the sample of 500 by matching those numbers to 500 numbers selected from a table of random numbers. Or, one might rely on a computer programmed to perform such a task. In any case, the sample has been drawn so that the subjects are selected by chance and each has an equal probability of being selected. A variation on simple random sampling is known as *systematic sampling*. Here, the sample is drawn so that every kth person is selected (where k equals some number). In the example presented above, the researcher is drawing a 10 percent sample (500 out of 5000 students). The researcher might randomly decide to begin with the sixth person on the list and select for the sample every tenth student after that (students 16, 26, 36, etc.) This is a very convenient method of sample selection as long as there is no reason to suspect that a bias might result from the selection of every tenth student.

Beginning researchers, especially, would more than likely use one of the foregoing methods of probability sampling. Yet, there are more sophisticated methods used by professional polling organizations and those engaged in more elaborate research. These techniques are designed to produce more accurate samples, to ensure more adequate representation in the sample of various subsamples, or simply to reduce the costs and effort in large-scale sampling efforts.

Stratified sampling techniques break the population into important subtypes and then sample from each. In the example above, the researcher might first divide all 5000 students into those coming from central cities, those coming from suburbs, and those coming from rural areas (assuming that this information is available). Samples could then be drawn from each of these subtypes, with the result being that the sampling error on this variable (location of hometown) would be reduced almost to zero — the sample distribution on this variable would perfectly (or almost perfectly) match that of the population. The student body could be further stratified to reduce sample variation on other variables as well. *Disproportionate sampling techniques* are used when the researcher wishes to ensure adequate representation of a subgroup. The researcher may know, for example, that out of the population of 5000 students only 250 are from rural areas. A 10 percent sample of the 5000 would yield approximately 25 students from rural areas. If location of hometown is to be an important focus of the study, this would clearly be too few rural students for meaningful analysis. Using dispropor-

42

tionate sampling techniques, the researcher would intentionally oversample from the group of rural students. Perhaps 100 students could be drawn from this group and the remaining 400 could be drawn from the rest of the student body. Comparisons could then be made between groups, and weights could be applied to the nonrural sample to allow appropriate generalization to the entire student body.

Single-stage and multistage cluster sampling techniques are designed to reduce the cost of large-scale sampling operations. Using these techniques, the researcher samples by "clusters" before selecting individuals. That is, a student of community voting behavior might randomly select a group of neighborhoods in a particular city and then randomly select interviews from only those neighborhoods. Since the student's interviews would be clustered in particular neighborhoods (rather than randomly spread throughout the city), time and effort should be reduced. *Multistage cluster sampling* further extends this logic. A student of national voting behavior might select a cluster of communities, and from these randomly select a cluster of neighborhoods, and from these randomly select a cluster of blocks. In addition to saving time and effort, cluster sampling also relieves the researcher of having to obtain a complete listing of the population. All that is needed is a list of the elements to be included in the clusters (communities, blocks, etc.).[22]

Most students will probably never use these more sophisticated methods of sampling during their college careers. The techniques can be quite costly and time-consuming and are designed to achieve a degree of precision typically not required or expected in undergraduate or even graduate research. Yet, the student could profitably compare his or her sampling method with the probability sampling techniques, and every effort should be made to *approximate* the more sophisticated procedures. It should always be remembered that the more haphazard the sampling technique, the greater is the risk of drawing an unrepresentative sample. If generalizations to the population cannot be made without a degree of confidence, a question arises as to whether the research should be conducted in the first place.

Sample Size

One of the most often asked questions in survey research is how large a sample is required to carry out the study. The answer depends on several factors. One is the size of the population, a second is the variance in the population, a third is the amount of error in the sample judged tolerable, and the fourth is the degree of confidence the researcher wishes to have in generalizing from the sample to the population.

Common sense suggests that the larger the population, the greater is the needed sample size. A sample of 35 students from a class of 40 is more likely

[22]A brief but informative overview of multistage sampling techniques is provided in *Interviewer's Manual* (Ann Arbor, Mich.: Survey Research Center/Institute for Social Research, 1976), pp. 35–39.

to accurately represent the whole class than is a sample of 35 students likely to accurately represent the student body of 5000. Thus, increasing sample size reduces the probability of selecting an unrepresentative sample. However, it is very important to note that after a point, increasing the sample size has a relatively small impact on the accuracy of the sample selected. It will be shown below that even for a very large population a relatively high degree of accuracy can be achieved with a very small sample. The slight increase in accuracy that might result from doubling or tripling the sample size often is simply not worth the cost. Even national polling organizations with resources far outstripping most individual researchers rarely draw a sample of greater than 1500 to 2000 individuals.

Population variance is the second important factor relating to needed sample size. The greater the variance in the population, the greater the size of sample needed. To take an extreme example, if in a particular election *every* voter favored one candidate over the others and *all* voters intended to vote according to their preference, a sample of only 1 would be required to accurately predict the outcome of the election. Similarly, the sample size needed to accurately predict the outcome of an election is less in a situation in which one candidate enjoys an 80 to 20 percent ratio of support over the opposition than in an election in which one candidate leads the other by a support ratio of only 52 to 48 percent.

Thus, population size and population variance are important elements in determining the sample size needed. In actuality, however, these factors typically do not cause a great deal of worry. The difference between the sample size needed for a population of 1000 is not vastly different from the sample size needed for a population of 500,000 (assuming that other factors are held constant). Therefore, infinite population size is generally assumed. Since information on population variation is rarely available, *maximum* variance also is assumed. Thus, the two factors of population size and variance are generally considered constants in the sample-size formula; they typically will not be altered from situation to situation.

The important factors to be considered in determining size of needed sample are the extent of accuracy desired in predicting from the sample to the population and the degree of confidence that can be placed in this prediction. Of course, all researchers want to be very confident that the sample values closely approximate the population values. However, greater accuracy and greater confidence require increasing the sample size, resulting in additional time and monetary costs. Based on available resources, the researcher may be willing to accept a sample size that 95 times out of 100 will be expected to vary 5 percent or less from the population rather than a sample size that would be expected 99 out of 100 times to be accurate within 1 percent of the population. Again, available resources is a key criterion in reaching these decisions.

Given these factors, the calculation of the required sample size is relatively straightforward. First, the formula for estimating proportional sample error at the 95 percent confidence level is presented:

$$SE = \pm 1.96 \sqrt{\frac{p(1-p)}{n}}$$

Several comments about this formula are in order. First, SE represents the degree of expected proportionate sample error. This is the extent to which sample values would be expected to deviate from population values. The 1.96 value represents a Z score which, when used in conjunction with the concept of the normal curve, represents a confidence level of 95 percent. This means that the researcher can be confident that 95 out of 100 times the sample drawn will not exceed the error range (SE). The topics of the Z score and the normal curve will be discussed in Chapter 5. It is only noted here that a desired confidence level of 90 percent would require a Z value of 1.645 and a confidence level of 99 percent would require a Z value of 2.5758. The p in the formula represents the estimated population variance. Since, as discussed above, actual population variance is almost never known, maximum variance is assumed and the value is recorded as 0.5. The n represents the sample size. So, for a sample of 600 drawn from an infinitely large population, the extent of error expected at the 95 percent confidence level would be calculated as

$$SE = \pm 1.96 \sqrt{\frac{0.5(1-0.5)}{600}}$$
$$= \pm 0.04$$

It would be expected that for every 95 of 100 samples drawn, sample values would deviate from population values by no more than ± 4 percent.

Since we typically are more interested in estimating sample size desired, the formula becomes[23]

$$n = \left(\frac{1.96}{SE}\right)^2 (p(1-p))$$

where n = sample size needed
   p = assumed population variance
   SE = tolerable error

Assuming an error tolerance of 5 percent at the 95 percent confidence level,

---

[23] For brief but excellent discussions of sampling error and sample size, see Lin, *Foundations of Social Research*, pp. 159–162; Warwick and Lininger, *The Sample Survey*, pp. 90–95; and Dickinson McGaw and George Watson, *Political and Social Inquiry* (New York: John Wiley & Sons, Inc., 1976), pp. 364–368.

the size of the sample needed is

$$n = \left(\frac{1.96}{.05}\right)^2 (.5(1-.5))$$
$$= 384.16$$
$$= 385$$

READER NOTE: In calculating sample size, it is customary to round all values up to the next larger integer to avoid fractional cases.

For very large populations, a useful table summarizing various sample sizes required for varying degrees of error tolerance and confidence levels (assuming simple random sampling) is presented in Table 3.2. This table should provide a good idea of the sample size needed for differing error and confidence ranges. Two additional points need to be made. First, it always is a good idea to oversample. A researcher content with a 5 percent error tolerance at the 95 percent confidence level might well be advised to select a sample of 450 or so (rather than 385). The inclusion of additional cases, if selected without bias, increases the probable accuracy of the sample. More important, it is likely that for various reasons information will not be collected from *every* element of the original sample. Some people will refuse to respond, some will not be at home, some will have moved away, and so forth. Oversampling by 10 or 15 percent adds a degree of protection.

Second, it should be noted that these sample sizes are appropriate only for generalizing from the entire sample. If the research focus shifts to *subgroups* in the sample, these error and confidence ranges associated with the total

TABLE 3.2
Sample-Size Requirements for Varying Degrees of Error Tolerance and Confidence Levels

Error Tolerance (percent)	Confidence Levels	
	95 percent	99 percent
1	9,604	16,587
2	2,401	4,147
3	1,068	1,843
4	601	1,037
5	385	664
6	267	461
7	196	339
8	150	260
9	119	205
10	96	166

Source: Adapted and extended from Charles H. Backstrom and Gerald D. Hursh, *Survey Research* (Evanston, Ill.: Northwestern University Press, 1963), p. 33.

sample no longer apply. In selecting a sample size, care must be taken to ensure adequate numerical inclusion of the important subgroups to be analyzed.

Making Use of Available Data

Only a few years ago, the political researcher would have few alternatives to self-collection of data. There simply was very little systematically collected information available. Happily, this is no longer the case. Many government and private organizations collect, store, and release information at little or no cost. Today, in fact, researchers often have a difficult time just keeping abreast of the growing supply and sources of information available for analysis.

Those who specialize in particular areas will soon become familiar with the sources of data most useful to their own research, but for the beginning researcher the sheer quantity of data sources can seem overwhelming. Although it is not possible here to mention all the sources of data which political researchers find useful, a few of the major sources can be listed and briefly annotated. A personal inspection of these data sources is advised for a full appreciation of the richness and variety of the data therein contained.

General Sources of Data

Data Archives. All political researchers should be familiar with the major social science archives, most of which have appeared in the last couple of decades. These are organizations that specialize in the collection, storage, and dissemination of data, usually in machine-readable form. Among the major data archives are the *Bureau of Applied Social Research* (Columbia University), *The National Opinion Research Center* (University of Chicago), and the *Roper Public Opinion Research Center* (Yale (University).[24]

Perhaps the most important of the data archives is the *Inter-University Consortium for Political and Social Research* (ICPSR). Located at the University of Michigan, the *Consortium* (of which there are over 220 member universities and colleges) has since 1962 collected, processed, and distributed data in machine-readable form. Available from ICPSR are elite and mass attitudinal data, census records, election returns, international interaction information, and legislative records. Information in some or all of these areas is available for over 130 countries. For scholars of American politics, particularly American voting behavior, the Consortium's American National Election Studies, conducted every other year since 1952, provide the most detailed data base on the political attitudes and behavior of the American public available.

---

[24]A listing of many of the major political and social science archives is available from The Laboratory for Political Research, University of Iowa.

The Almanac of American Politics. Organized by state, *The Almanac of American Politics* (published annually by E. P. Dutton, New York) presents a summary of important political issues in each of the American states, followed by important state census data (population size, percent urban, median income, median education, etc.), information on each state's share of federal outlays and economic base, voter information (percent registered, mean voting age, employment profiles, ethnic group breakdowns), and biographical information on state governors, senators, and House members, including ratings for all senators and congresspeople by various rating organizations (including Americans for Democratic Action, COPE, Ripon Society, and Consumer Federation of America). *The Almanac* is an excellent quick source of information on American politics.

Census Data. The United States Bureau of the Census is the major data-collection agency in the United States. A wide variety of census reports are available, including the census of Agriculture, Population, Housing, Manufacturers, Transportation, Construction Industries, Selected Services, Wholesale Trade, Retail Trade, and Governments. For general information, the student of politics will find three Census publications of most use.

1. *Census of Population: General Population Characteristics.* This publication provides general race, sex, and household and family characteristics for each state, and within each state for cities, towns, and other places with populations over 50,000; 10,000 to 50,000; 2500 to 10,000; and 1000 to 2500; and for counties.
2. *Census of Population: General Social and Economic Characteristics.* This publication provides, for the same jurisdictions as noted above, social and economic data, including employment status, school enrollment, country of origin, income levels, percent below poverty line, mobility, and so forth.
3. *Census of Population: Detailed Characteristics.* This publication provides for states, large cities (100,000 and over), and standard metropolitan statistical areas detailed social and economic information dealing with such topics as race, ethnicity, mobility, school enrollment, marital status, employment status, disability, income levels, and poverty status.

Statistical Abstract of the United States. Another report prepared by the Bureau of the Census which will be found to be extremely useful is the *Statistical Abstract of the United States.* Published annually since 1878, the *Statistical Abstract* combines data from many government and private publications as well as from unpublished documents. The *Statistical Abstract* includes information on a wide range of topics. Among those of most interest to political researchers are population, health, education, law enforcement, federal government finances and employment, national defense, state and local government finances and employment, and elections. Although focusing primarily on the United States, the *Statistical Abstract* includes a section on comparative international statistics as well.

State and Local Data

Students of state and local politics will find three publications prepared by public interest groups especially useful. *The Municipal Year Book*, published annually by the International City Management Association (Washington, D.C.), provides a wealth of data on cities, most collected through questionnaire surveys of municipal officials. Information and analysis will be found dealing with administration, legislation, and judicial trends; employment; salaries; public services; and other municipal activities. The latest two *Year Books* (1977 and 1978) have included interesting international sections.

Equivalent to *The Municipal Year Book* at the county level is *The County Year Book*. Published annually since 1975 by the National Association of Counties and the International City Management Association (Washington, D.C.), *The County Year Book* provides information and analysis at the county level dealing with the areas of administration, legislation, and judicial trends, finance, employment, and services and administration. These data, too, are largely collected by means of mailed surveys.

At the state level, the student will find useful *The Book of the States* (Lexington, Ky.: The Council of State Governments). Published biennially, *The Book of the States* provides information and data (with brief analysis) for all states in the areas of constitutions and elections, legislatures, the judiciary, administrative organizations, finance, intergovernmental relations, and the major state services (education, transportation, health and welfare, etc.).

In addition to these publications, the researcher will find useful a number of special publications of the Bureau of the Census. Two of these are of special importance. The first, the *Census of Governments*, published every year ending in 2 and 7 (1972, 1977, etc.), provides data for the five major types of local governments — counties, municipalities, townships, school districts, and special districts — in the areas of government organization, number of elective offices, indebtedness, public employment, finances, school enrollments, retirement systems, and historical data.

The second, the *County and City Data Book*, published every 5 years as a supplement to the *Statistical Abstract*, provides selected data for all counties and cities over 25,000. Included is information dealing with population characteristics, education, labor force, income, housing, government finances, crime rates, manufacturing and trade, school services, and hospital care.

Four special publications by the Bureau of the Census will also be found useful: *City Government Finances; State Government Finances; County Government Finances;* and *Local Government Finances in Selected Metropolitan Areas and Counties* (providing information for the nation's 74 largest standard metropolitan statistical areas). These volumes, published annually, provide detailed financial information on sources of revenue, expenditures by function, and indebtedness for the respective jurisdictions.

Additionally, most states prepare and publish state statistical abstracts similar in content to the *Statistical Abstract of the United States,* described above. A current list of state statistical abstracts is presented in the *Statistical Abstract of the United States, 1978,* pp. 1008–1011.

Congressional, Executive, and Court Information

For students of Congress and the Executive, the two most important sources of information and data are the *Congressional Quarterly Weekly Report* (along with its companion, the annual *Congressional Quarterly Almanac*) published by Congressional Quarterly, Inc., Washington, D.C., and the *National Journal,* published weekly by the Government Research Corporation, Washington, D.C. *The Congressional Quarterly Weekly Report* provides an up-to-date weekly review of congressional activities. *CQ* reports votes on key issues in addition to a status review of major legislation and provides analyses of key legislative areas (including, as appropriate: energy; national security; health, education, and welfare; transportation; law enforcement; consumer affairs; and agriculture). The *Weekly Report* is indexed quarterly and annually.

The National Journal focuses on the White House and executive departments and agencies. Typically featured will be articles on the presidency, politics, the economy, the bureaucracy, and urban affairs. Each issue includes a feature called "Washington Update," which discusses important current political issues and the status of current legislation. The *National Journal* is indexed weekly and annually.

Two additional Congressional Quarterly, Inc. publications will be found especially useful for data dealing with Congress. One of these is *Congressional Roll Call.* Published annually, *Congressional Roll Call* presents a member-by-member survey and analysis of congressional votes. Included is a section discussing key House and Senate votes followed by analyses of important coalition voting patterns. These include what *CQ* calls the Conservative Coalition; Presidential Support Opposition; Voting Participation; North–South Split; Party Unity; Bipartisanship; and Freshman Voting. This publication is an invaluable source of information and analysis for voting on key congressional issues.

Another important *CQ* publication is the *Guide to Congress* (1976). The *Guide* presents a comprehensive historical and contemporary overview of Congress, including chapters dealing with the origins and development of Congress, powers of Congress, congressional procedures, Congress and the electorate, pressures on Congress, and qualifications and conduct of members. The appendix to this volume, alone, provides a wealth of information and data, including a biographical listing of every member of Congress from 1789 to 1976, together with their party affiliation and dates of service.

Students of Congress will find additionally useful the *Biographical Directory of the American Congress, 1774–1971*. This volume, compiled under the direction of the Joint Committee on Printing and published as Senate Document No. 92-8 (92nd Congress, 1st Session), presents a paragraph-length biography of every member of the U.S. Congress. The paragraphs usually comment on early education, family occupation, military career, dates of congressional service, honors and distinctions received, other public offices held, and birth and death statistics. An updated biography of congressional members can be found in the *Congressional Directory* (published annually by the U.S. Government Printing Office, Washington, D.C.). A final biographical source which students of Congress might find helpful is the *Congressional Staff Directory* (published annually since 1959 by Charles B. Brownson). This volume presents biographical information on House and Senate staff personnel.

A Census publication of interest to congressional scholars is the *Congressional District Data Book*. This volume presents much the same information as that in the *County and City Data Book*, aggregated by congressional district. Also presented is a congressional district map for each state, together with census data concerning all major cities in each district and the recent voting history of each district.

Students of the Supreme Court and the Presidency do not enjoy access to the wealth of information readily available to those interested in Congress. However, some publications, in addition to the National Journal, will be found useful. Four of them are listed below.

Guide to the U.S. Supreme Court (Congressional Quarterly, Inc., Washington, D.C., 1979). Students will find this to be the most comprehensive and authoritative review of the Supreme Court, its members, and important court cases that is available in a single volume. Included are sections dealing with the origin and development of the Supreme Court, the role of the court in the U.S. federal system, pressures on the court, biographies of all members of the court (from John Jay to John Paul Stevens), and a survey of the court's major rulings since 1790.

Facts About the Presidents, by Joseph Nathan Kane (H.W. Wilson Company, New York, 3rd ed., 1974) provides biographical and historical information on U.S. Presidents (Washington through Ford), including facts dealing with parents and siblings, education, party affiliation, political careers, and cabinet and court appointments. Wide-ranging miscellaneous information on each president is included. What student of the presidency could rest comfortably in ignorance of the knowledge that the first asteroid named for an American President was Hooveria, or that the initial "S" in President Harry S. Truman's name has no special significance and is not an abbreviation of any name, or that William McKinley was the first President to use the telephone for campaign purposes?

The Biographical Directory of the United States Executive Branch, 1774–1971, edited by Robert Sobel (Westport, Conn.: Greenwood, 1971), provides brief sketches of the careers of all cabinet members, as well as of all presidents and vice-presidents during this period.

The Weekly Compilation of Presidential Documents (General Services Administration, Washington, D.C.), published every Monday, contains texts of presidential statements, interviews, nominations, appointments, messages, and other presidential materials released by the White House during the preceding week. The volume is indexed semiannually.

Voting, Elections, and Public Opinion Data

Two publications will be found particularly useful as sources of election data. The first of these is *America Votes*, by Richard Scammon and (since 1976) Alice McGillivray, published since 1956 for each biennial election by (since 1966) Congressional Quarterly, Inc., Washington, D.C. *America Votes* presents the results of (1) presidential primaries, (2) state-by-state election returns for presidential and senate races by county, (3) state-by-state congressional election returns by congressional districts, (4) results of state party primaries and party run-off elections, and (5) historical state voting profiles since 1946. Also included is a brief analysis of each election year.

The second major source of election information is *Guide to U.S. Elections* published by Congressional Quarterly, Inc., Washington, D.C., 1975. Relying largely on the Historical Archive of the ICPSR, this publication presents state-by-state election data for all major political offices from 1824 to 1975. Included are data on political parties, presidential elections, Senate and House elections, and a special section on southern primaries.

Three additional sources will be found helpful to students of elections and voting patterns. Svend Peterson's *A Statistical History of the American Presidential Elections* (New York: Frederick Ungar Publishing Co., 1963) presents presidential election statistics from 1787 to 1960. In compiling this information Peterson relied on many and varied sources, including the National Archives and newspaper files at the Library of Congress. For each election the volume contains state-by-state results of electoral votes and popular votes for all candidates. For all the states Peterson also lists votes by party for presidential contests. W. Dean Burnham's *Presidential Ballots, 1836–1892* (Baltimore, Md.: The Johns Hopkins Press, 1955) is a rich source of information for presidential elections during this period. Burnham provides state-by-state returns for presidential elections during this period, including (1) county-by-county party control, (2) county-by-county popular vote, and (3) state electoral vote. Richard Scammon's *America at the Polls: A Handbook of American Presidential Election Statistics, 1920–1964* (Pittsburgh, Pa.: University of Pittsburgh Press, 1965) presents a statistical history of presidential elections from the election of President Harding in 1920 to President Johnson in 1964. For each election, the publication includes state and county figures for total vote, party breakdown, pluralities, and percentage of total votes for Republican and Democratic candidates.

Scholars of voting behavior will also find useful the following national election studies, all available through ICPSR: United States (1948–1978); Argentina (1963); Australia (1967); Brazil (1960); Canada (1965, 1968, 1972, 1974); Chile (1958); Great Britain (four waves of studies: 1963, 1964, 1966, 1970); France (1958); Germany (several studies available from 1953 to 1972); Israel (1969); Japan (1961, 1967); The Netherlands (three-wave panel study: 1970–1973, 1967, 1971); Norway (1957, 1965); Sweden (1960, 1964); and Switzerland (1972).

Students of public opinion will find most convenient *The Gallup Opinion Index* (published monthly since 1965 by the American Institute of Public Opinion, Princeton, New Jersey). Each month the *Index* reports results of the Institute of Public Opinion's surveys of samples of the American public (1500-person sample) on wide-ranging domestic and international issues. In the September, 1978, issue, for example, are reported results of questions dealing with attitudes toward the Middle East, possible Republican and Democratic presidential choices, capital punishment, and UFO sightings. These topics may not all be of equal interest to political scientists, but each is usually conveniently broken down by various descriptive characteristics (such as sex, race, education, and party preference). A useful feature is the reporting of trends when the same question has been asked on repeated occasions.[25]

International and Comparative Data

Students of international and comparative politics perhaps do not enjoy the variety of and accessibility to sources of data as do students of American politics. Here, newspapers, magazines, journals and other similar materials may represent a large component of data sources. Some familiarity with the language or languages of the nations to be studied may be helpful or even essential. Still, many useful sources of statistical information are readily available. Some of the most important of these are listed below.

Statistical Yearbook. Published annually by the United Nations, the *Statistical Yearbook* presents country-by-country data in such general categories as population, manpower, agriculture, industrial production, manufacturing, energy, trade, consumption, finance, housing, health, and education.

Demographic Yearbook. Also published annually by the United Nations, the *Demographic Yearbook* presents country-by-country data in such areas as

[25] For a review and a critique of many of the data sources mentioned above, as well as of others, see Edward R. Tufte, "Political Statistics for the United States: Observations on Some Major Data Sources," *American Political Science Review,* 71 (March, 1977), 305–314.

marriage, divorce, birth and death rates, and other general population characteristics.

The Europa Year Book. Published annually since 1926 by Europa Publications Limited, London, and appearing since 1960 as a two-volume set, *The Europa Year Book* lists country membership in international organizations. For each country, the publication also provides data dealing with such topics as language, religion, recent history, economic affairs, social welfare, and education. For most countries information is also provided on their constitutions, form of government, party system, and government leaders. Details of finance, press matters, radio and television, trade and industry, tourism, and university affairs are included as well.

The International Almanac of Electoral History. Thomas T. Mackie and Richard Rose's work, *The International Almanac of Electoral History* (New York: The Free Press, 1974), provides a rich source of electoral information for those western industrial societies conducting competitive elections regularly since the end of World War II. Data are provided for 23 countries, including Australia, Canada, Germany, Japan, United Kingdom, United States, France, Italy, and Finland. For each country, the evolution of the electoral system and franchise laws are described, a list of political parties is presented, election results are presented giving the total numbers and percentage for each party, and the number and percentage of seats won by each party are listed. This publication represents a very useful source of data, especially for students of comparative electoral patterns.

European Historical Statistics, 1950–1970. Prepared by Brian R. Mitchell, *European Historical Statistics* (New York: Columbia University Press, 1975) presents a variety of statistical information for European countries, including that dealing with climate, population, labor force, agriculture, industry, trade, transportation and communications, finance, and education.

The International Year Book and Statesman's Who's Who. Compiled by Robert M. Bradfield and published annually by Kelly's Directories Limited (Kingston upon Thames, England), this volume presents a brief country-by-country overview, including information pertaining to constitutions and government, the party system, local government, the legal system, and data dealing with such varied topics as population, birth and death rates, finance, communications, and education. Also included is a brief biographical sketch of statesmen of the world.

Statistical Abstract of Latin America. This annual publication, edited by James W. Wilkie and published by UCLA Latin American Center Publications (Los Angeles), presents geographic, social, socioeconomic, economic, and trade statistics for the Latin American countries.

A series of data sets available through ICPSR will also be of special interest to students of international and comparative politics. The *World Handbook of Political and Social Indicators* (assembled by Bruce Russett, Karl Deutsch, Hayward Alker, and Harold Lasswell) features data for 141 countries, dealing with various social, political, economic, and demographic indicators. Most data are from the 1961–1963 period. The *World Handbook of Political and Social Indicators, II* (assembled by Charles Taylor and Michael Hudson) consists of data for 136 countries, including indicators of population size, communications, education, culture, economics, and politics for the four base years of 1950, 1955, 1960, and 1965. The *Cross Polity Survey* (assembled by Arthur S. Banks and Robert B. Textor) features data for 115 countries, including indicators of economics, demography, political modernization, and interest articulation. *The Cross-National Time Series, 1815–1973* file (assembled by Arthur S. Banks) consists of longitudinal national data for 167 nations. Included are data dealing with demographic, social, political, and economic topics. The *Civic Culture Study* (compiled by Gabriel Almond and Sidney Verba) consists of basic political attitudinal and demographic data on respondents from five countries (Germany, Italy, Mexico, the United Kingdom, and the United States) collected in 1959 and 1960. A series of studies conducted between the years 1974 and 1976 under the direction of Jacques-Rene Rabier and Ronald Inglehart provides a wide variety of information on respondents from ten European countries. Included in the *Euro-Barometer* studies are data dealing with respondents' attitudes toward community goals, personal and environmental situations, European unification, regional development, status of women, consumers, poverty, and standard of living along with standard demographic information.

Additionally, students of comparative politics, and especially comparative electoral politics, will benefit from a series of studies of elections and electoral behavior of selected democratic countries recently published by the American Enterprise Institute for Public Policy Research (Washington, D.C.). Included in AEI's publication list are studies dealing with Great Britain, Japan, France, Australia, Canada, Denmark, Norway, Sweden, and Italy. Studies of Germany, Israel, Ireland, Spain, India, and Greece are planned or in progress.

In addition to the more general sources listed above, it should be noted that many countries prepare yearbooks presenting a variety of useful data. Although it is not possible here to discuss each of these yearbooks, typically these publications will be most complete and most reliable for western industrialized countries, less regular in publication for developing countries, and less reliable for communist countries. Regardless, students should be familiar with these publications in their own particular areas or countries of interest.

Content Analysis

When relying on such data sources as newspapers, biographical directories, presidential papers, magazines, letters, diaries, minutes of meetings,
transcripts, and other nonstatistical archival and documentary records, a
systematic means of condensing and organizing for analysis and manipulation such information is necessary. The process by which this is done is
called *content analysis*. Content analysis has been defined as "...any
systematic reduction of a flow of text, that is, recorded language, to a
standard set of statistically manipulable symbols representing the presence,
the intensity, or the frequency of some characteristics relevant to social
science.[26]

Although not used with great frequency in political research, content
analysis nevertheless has had many interesting and significant applications.
One of the more fascinating and well-known applications of the technique in
political research is Mosteller and Wallace's attempt to identify the authorship of twelve of *The Federalist Papers*, numbers 49 to 58, 62, and 63. Starting
with a set of essays known to have been written by Hamilton and a set known
to have been written by Madison, Mosteller and Wallace were able to identify
certain words and frequency of word use discriminating between the two
authors. For example, Madison was much more likely to use the word "by,"
Hamilton was more likely to use the word "to." Hamilton frequently used the
word "upon," Madison almost never used it. Comparing such words and
their frequency of use with the twelve disputed papers, the authors concluded
that Madison was extremely likely to have written all of the twelve disputed
Federalist Papers, with the possible exception of number 55, and even there
the evidence yields 80 to 1 odds in Madison's favor.[27]

The symbols to be examined by use of content analysis may be said to be
either *programable* or *semantic*.[28] Programable units are units, such as words,
terms, and characters, which are readily identifiable. Here, the researcher may
simply count the frequency of occurrence of a certain word (and perhaps
other words having the same connotation) or combination of words in
particular passages. While tedious, this process is relatively unambiguous
and, in fact, computer programs are available to assist in the process.[29]

Semantic units are those having themes — the message which the source is
intending to convey. Such messages may be found in sentences, paragraphs,

---

[26]John Markoff, Gilbert Shapiro, and Sasha Weitman, "Toward the Integration of Content
Analysis and General Methodology," in David R. Heise, ed., *Sociological Methodology, 1975*
(San Francisco: Jossey-Bass, 1974), 1–58. Students interested in the topic of content analysis
should consult the extensive list of references supplied by these authors.

[27]See: Frederick Mosteller and David L. Wallace, *Inference and Disputed Authorship: The
Federalist* (Reading, Massachusetts: Addison-Wesley, 1964).

[28]The terminology used here follows that of Lin, *Foundations of Social Research*, 217–219.

[29]See: Philip J. Stone, et al., *The General Inquirer* (Cambridge, Massachusetts: M.I.T. Press,
1966).

or entire passages. Here, the process of coding is quite difficult and considerable care must be taken to ensure common agreement among all coders. It might even be necessary for one set of coders to duplicate the work of another. Any discrepancies between the two sets of coders then would have to be resolved.

Content analysis, then, is used to assist in the analysis of nonstatistical information. It may be found most useful in the analysis of documentary, newspaper, or archival records as discussed above.[30]

Some Concluding Thoughts

With the exception of topic selection, no phase is more important to systematic political research than is data collection. The quality of the data collected will have considerable bearing on the success of the entire project. Considerable care must be taken to assemble data of the highest possible quality.

At the same time, as this chapter has made clear, the selection of data-collection techniques is to a large extent a function of time and resources. An individual scholar, with limited time and money, simply cannot match the skills and resources of the professional data-collecting organizations mentioned in this chapter. It is for this reason that use of existing data is so strongly advised. Not only will this save considerable time, but the data available almost certainly are superior to that which most individuals, in a short time period, can assemble.

On the other hand, self-collection of data is one of the truly exciting phases of social science research. As the opening paragraph of this chapter suggested, it is out in the field that one really begins to gain a feeling for and an understanding of politics and political behavior. Collecting your own data also allows for maximum creativity in research design and topic selection — your interests and imagination are not confined by the limitations of someone else's data.

With caution, then, the student is encouraged, at least on some occasion, to design a project calling for self-collection of data. In doing so, it should be remembered that no analytic technique can compensate for poorly collected and assembled data. Considerable thought must go into the data-collection stage, and every reasonable precaution must be taken to collect data of the highest quality. Nothing is so critical to the achievement of an effort both satisfying to the researcher and of value to the broader academic community.

---

[30]For an interesting and recent application of computer-assisted content analysis to the study of soviet politics see Charles D. Cary, "A Technique of Computer Content Analysis of Transliterated Russian Language Textual Materials: A Research Note," *American Political Science Review*, 71 (March, 1977), 245–251.

Exercises

1. Discuss *three* research situations in which *observational techniques* for collecting data might appropriately be employed. In each situation, describe difficulties that might arise in collecting information and how these might be handled.
2. a. Review three political science works (books or articles) using observational techniques as the sole or primary source of data collection.
   b. What data-collection difficulties did the authors of these studies encounter?
   c. How were they resolved?
3. a. For a research topic of interest to you, develop a questionnaire that could be administered to a relevant sample of individuals. Include in your questionnaire at least three *background questions* (such as age, education, and sex), three *opinion questions* ("What do you think about _____?"), and three *knowledge questions* ("Name one senator from your state", etc.).
   b. Which of these items are best presented as open-ended and which are best presented as closed-ended questions?
   c. Why is this so?
   d. Evaluate each question in terms of (1) ease of responding; (2) type and amount of information possibly solicited; and (3) ease of analyzing.
4. a. Administer the questionnaire developed in Exercise 3 to at least 10 respondents.
   b. On the basis of this experience, how would you alter your instrument in preparation for mass administration?
   c. List the reasons for your answer to part (b).
5. a. Assume that the questionnaire developed in Exercise 3 is to be mailed to a sample of 1500 residents of your hometown. What techniques might be used to achieve as high a rate of return as possible?
   b. Why is the return rate a factor to be considered in mailed surveys?
6. a. Develop and discuss a research situation in which the *interview* might be the most appropriate means of data collections.
   b. Why in this situation is the interview the most appropriate mode of data collection?
   c. What precautions might you take to maximize the benefits of the interview?
   d. What situations would you try to avoid?
7. a. Assume that your class is to conduct a research study dealing with a sample of students from your university and that you have been assigned the task of selecting the sample. Discuss some of the issues that you must consider in drawing the sample, including the method of sample selection you would recommend and the factors important to determining the size of the needed sample.
   b. What should you report to the class concerning inferences about the entire student body that can be drawn appropriately from the sample you will select?
   c. Why is this so?
8. a. In your own principal area of research interest, find and report on three sources of existing data that you believe to be most helpful.
   b. What are some of the problems you find with existing data sources in your field of interest?
   c. How are these being remedied? (Consult your librarian.)

4

DATA STORAGE, PROCESSING, AND MEASUREMENT

Having collected a set of data, the researcher's attention is now directed to the assembling, storing, and processing of such information and to the issues of data measurement. These topics are discussed in this chapter.

Data Assembly and Storage

After the researcher has collected the information or has found an appropriate source of information, the data must be assembled in a manner permitting and facilitating analysis. In some instances, the analysis may be performed manually, taking information directly from the questionnaire, survey schedule, or some other source. This is especially true if the number of cases is small (say less than 100) and the amount of information collected on each case is relatively limited. In situations such as these, the researcher may perform the desired analytic tasks with a desk calculator.

Today, however, it is more often the case that the researcher will want to store the gathered information in a manner permitting analysis with electronic data-processing equipment. Computers, which are readily accessible to most students at most colleges and universities, greatly speed the processing and analysis of data. The development in the past few years of various packaged statistical programs (to be discussed below) permits very sophisticated computer-assisted analysis of data by those having only the most basic programming skills. Also, the increasing deployment of remote terminal devices permitting easy researcher/computer interaction at locations other than the computer installation renders the computer an even more convenient tool.

Even if the researcher has a small set of data and does not plan to apply complex statistical analysis, consideration may still be given to assembling the information in a manner that would permit computer analysis. This is because data made ready for computer analysis can be much more conveniently and permanently stored and such information is much more easily transferred from one location or one researcher to another.

Thus, before proceeding to the actual analysis stage, the researcher will probably want to assemble the collected data in a form permitting computer processing. This means that the data will be stored on a medium such as punchcards, magnetic tapes, or magnetic disks which can be "read" and compiled by the computer. Kenneth Janda has outlined the advantages of storing data on punchcards. In general, these advantages apply to whatever storage medium is selected. The advantages of such storage, Janda says, are speed, convenience, neatness, accuracy, permanency, flexibility, and reproducibility.[1] Questionnaires and surveys can be lost, misplaced, torn, or destroyed. Information stored on cards, tape, or disk is more secure, easier to process, and amenable to more complex analytic procedures. The researcher, then, should be thoroughly familiar with the procedures for assembling and storing data.

The Punchcard

Data may be placed on a storage medium (card, disk, tape) through several routes. At many installations, it is possible to enter data directly to a disk storage device through a remote terminal facility. However, probably the most commonly used means of storing data is by use of punchcards. Data that are punched on cards can be analyzed directly from the cards themselves, or the cards can be used to transfer the data to even more convenient and permanent modes of storage (such as magnetic tape and disk).

Most beginning researchers will first place their information on cards. An example of a blank punchcard (containing no information) is presented in Figure 4.1. It can be seen that the standard punchcard consists of 80 columns and 10 (0 to 9) numeric rows. Data are almost always stored on cards in the form of numbers, but letters and symbols are sometimes used. Two unnumbered rows (designated as positions 11 and 12) are present for punching letters and symbols.

Up to 80 columns of information on each case (each voter, city, state, nation, etc.) can be stored on each card. If more space is needed to record the information for each case, the researcher simply uses additional cards until all information has been recorded. Two, five, 10, or even more cards may be needed to contain all the information for each case.

The column spaces are used to represent variables and may be utilized in whatever manner most convenient to the researcher. It is only mandatory that the same columns be selected to represent the same information for all

[1]Kenneth Janda, *Data Processing*, 2nd ed. (Evanston, Ill.: Northwestern University Press, 1969), p. 7.

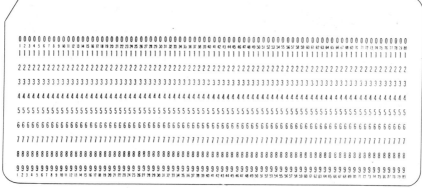

Figure 4.1
A blank punchcard.

cases. Thus, if column 50 is designated as the column in which party identification is to be located, this column must be used to record party identification for all respondents.

The process of punching information on cards is known as *keypunching.* Through the use a keypunch machine — a device with a keyboard similar to a typewriter except that it is used to punch holes in cards rather than print images on paper — information is recorded on the punchcard. The keypunch simultaneously punches holes in the columns and prints this same information at the top of each appropriate column. The printed information is only for the visual convenience of the researcher; the computer "reads" only the punched holes.

The transfer of data from surveys, questionnaires, or other sources to cards is one of the most common causes of error in empirical research. The computer will read and analyze whatever is punched in the appropriate columns. If keypunching mistakes are made, these may never be revealed by the analysis. Usually, then, it is to the advantage of the researcher to hire a trained and experienced keypuncher who will both punch the information onto cards and "verify" that this has been done accurately. This will minimize keypunching errors (although some can be expected to persist).

The Codesheet

Information can sometimes be transferred directly from a questionnaire or survey to the punchcard. If the researcher has carefully prepared the survey instrument so that the keypuncher (who probably will be totally unfamiliar with the study) can easily determine the coding scheme, information can be punched directly from the survey instrument. The survey presented in Figure 4.2 is prepared so that the keypuncher can work directly from the survey itself. It can be seen that the keypuncher is provided precise instructions for placing the information on cards. In column 1 of each card, the keypuncher is to punch a 1 or a 2, depending on which response is

Column Number:

1. Respondent's Sex: 1

    1. Male _____

    2. Female _____

2. Respondent's Race: 2

    1. Black _____

    2. White _____

    3. Spanish _____

    4. Asian American _____

    5. Other _____

3. Respondent's Party Identification: 3

    1. Democrat _____

    2. Republican _____

    3. Independent _____

    4. Other _____

4. Respondent's Education: _____   4–5

    (code actual years of education)

Figure 4.2

Example of a survey permitting direct transference of information from survey to punchcards.

marked; in column 2 a number, from 1 to 5, is to be punched corresponding to respondent's race; and so forth.

More often it is the case that preliminary processing of the data will be required before keypunching is possible. This is especially true if the survey contains open-ended questions, such as those described in Chapter 3, which have to be carefully analyzed and coded before punching can proceed. Here the data are first transferred to a *codesheet*.

A codesheet is a sheet of paper having 80 columns (corresponding to the 80 columns on a punchcard) and several rows. Each row corresponds to one punchcard. If in a particular study all the information for each case (say each individual) could be coded in 80 columns or less, each row of the codesheet would represent one case. If more than 80 columns are required for each case, the coder proceeds to each subsequent row of the codesheet until all information for each case has been recorded. It is almost always true that each case will be given a distinct identification number and this number will be coded as well (usually in the first or last several columns). *Coding*, then, is the process of assigning numbers to all possible responses to all questions or items.

An Example

All of this will become much clearer by reference to an example. Suppose that the researcher has collected some fiscal and political information on the American states. From those sources discussed in Chapter 3, such as *The Book of the States* and the *Statistical Abstract of the United States*, the researcher may have assembled for each state a set of information pertaining to per capita revenue, per capita expenditures, and party affiliation of state house and senate members. This information might be transferred to a codesheet, as shown in Figure 4.3. The figure illustrates several important points about the preparation of codesheets. First, it can be seen that for each state the same information is coded in the same columns. Columns 1 and 2 are consistently used for ID, columns 4 to 7 are consistently used to code per capita revenue, and so forth. As discussed above, it is essential that this practice always be followed. The amount of column space assigned to any variable is equal to the *largest* value for that variable. In the example above, four column spaces are allotted to "other" per capita expenditures, even though only the State of Alaska required this many columns. It can be seen as well that all variables (ID, revenue per capita, etc.) are separated by a single blank column. this is optional and is used only for the visual convenience of the coder. Also, it is noted that the variables are entered into the columns so that the units' position of each variable is recorded in the extreme right column; blank spaces are positioned in the left columns and are interpreted by the computer as zeros. These are called "right-justified" fields and all variables should always be so recorded. For example, in the State of Arkansas it can be seen that there was only one Republican state senator in 1978. This is indicated by placing a "1" in column 43. Had the "1" been placed in column 42, the computer would have interpreted this as 10 Republicans.

The information on the codesheet is then transferred to punchcards. Figure 4.4 illustrates the information presented on the codesheet punched onto cards. Having been punched onto cards, the data now are ready for analysis or for transfer to other storage devices. In the above illustration only 58 columns were required to code all the information of interest for each state. Thus, only one card was needed for each state (since a single card consists of 80 columns). As previously discussed, if more than 80 columns are necessary for each case, then more than one card per case will be required. In such an instance the first card for each case is known as "deck 1," the second as "deck 2," and so forth.

The Codebook

With the information punched onto cards, the researcher may proceed directly to the data-analysis stage. Usually, however, the researcher will want first to prepare a *codebook*. The codebook serves the researcher as a road map serves a motorist. That is, the codebook tells the researcher the precise location of each variable in the data set. For a small set of data (such as that

	ID	REVENUE PER CAPITA	EXPENDITURES PER CAPITA – 1975						SENATE – 1975			HOUSE		
			TOTAL	EDUCATION	HIGHWAYS	WELFARE	HEALTH	ALL OTHER	DEMOCRATS	REPUBLICANS	TOTAL	DEMOCRATS	REPUBLICANS	TOTAL
ALABAMA	01	827	827	327	97	83	90	230	34	0	35[a]	103	2	105
ALASKA	02	2291	2782	855	415	128	82	1301	12	8	20	25	15	40
ARIZONA	03	1024	1029	447	110	42	69	361	16	14	30	22	38	60
ARKANSAS	04	760	728	289	116	79	63	180	34	1	35	95	5	100
WISCONSIN	49	1101	1091	461	124	151	71	284	22	11	33	66	33	99
WYOMING	50	1388	1371	589	253	51	119	359	12	18	30	29	32	62[a]

Figure 4.3

Example of a codesheet (Source of data: 1977 Statistical Abstract of the United States and The Book of States, 1978–79.) [a]note: both Alabama and Wyoming had one legislator not affiliated with either of the major parties. Columns 59–79 not shown.

64

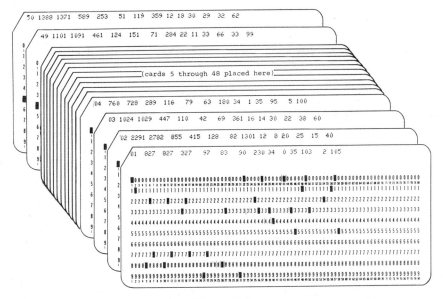

Figure 4.4
The information presented in Figure 4.3 punched onto punchcards.

illustrated in Figure 4.3), the codebook may be only one page in length or, in fact, may not be necessary at all (the codesheet can in effect serve as the codebook). For larger sets of data, a codebook is essential. The codebook for the University of Michigan's Center for Political Studies (CPS), 1976 American National Election Study, available through ICPSR, is over 500 pages in length. The section of that codebook dealing with respondent's party identification is reproduced in Figure 4.5.

| ① VAR 3168 | ② R'S PARTY ID:R/I/NO/OTR/D | ③ MD+GE 8 |
| ① REF 3168 | ④ LOC 336 WIDTH 1 | ⑤ DK 5 COL 64 |

⑥ Q D1. GENERALLY SPEAKING, DO YOU USUALLY THINK OF YOURSELF AS A REPUBLICAN, A DEMOCRAT, AN INDEPENDENT, OR WHAT?

⑨	⑧	⑦
663	1.	REPUBLICAN
820	2.	INDEPENDENT
228	3.	NO PREFERENCE
19	4.	OTHER
1133	5.	DEMOCRAT
5	8.	DK
3	9.	NA

Figure 4.5
Section of CPS 1976 American National Election Study dealing with respondent's party identification. Circled numbers are not included in the codebook but are used for reference in the following text. Frequencies shown are based on weighted sample size of 2,871.

For every variable, it can be seen that this particular codebook indicates (1) the variable and reference numbers assigned to each variable in the study; (2) an abbreviated variable name; (3) the designation of missing data (in this case, code values greater than or equal to 8 are designated as missing data — those which the researcher will probably want to exclude from the analysis); (4) the location and width of this variable when stored on magnetic tape in the OSIRIS format; (5) the deck and column location of this variable when stored on cards or on tape in card image; (6) the text of the original question; (7) the code value for each response; (8) the response possibilities; and (9) the number of people selecting each response. Such information is not only helpful, for a data set containing almost 1000 variables (as is the case with the 1976 American National Election Study) it is essential.

Computer Operations and Packaged Programs

When using the computer, two general options may be available. Most computer installations permit operation in what is called *batch mode*. This means that the researcher provides all at one time a set of instructions to the computer by means of punchcards or, perhaps through a remote terminal device (discussed below). Some time later, output (analysis) is received from the computer, usually in the form of "hard copy" — analysis presented on paper, cards, or tape. At some installations, researchers will be allowed to submit their cards (data and instructions) directly to a *card reader* and retrieve their own results from the *printer*. At others, hired operators will perform these tasks.

The second option for computer use is called the *interactive mode*. Here, usually through use of a remote terminal, the researcher interacts directly with the computer and receives results immediately (or almost immediately). Some terminals look like teletype machines, some look like typewriters, but increasingly, terminals are of the cathode-ray-tube variety (CRTs). CRTs look like television screens attached to a typewriter-like keyboard. Instructions are entered through the keyboard, displayed on the screen, and output then comes back to be printed on the screen (usually, the researcher can command that the output be written on paper or another medium). When terminals are used, the researcher will interact with the computer by means of an editor language, which usually looks very much like normally written English. Many editor languages are available and their use varies greatly from installation to installation.

When using the computer to analyze data, the user will submit to the computer his or her data set, together with a set of instructions for the statistical manipulation of that data set. These instructions may be prepared in one of a number of computer languages, perhaps the most popular being

Fortran. Preparing a set of instructions in Fortran or another computer language is known as *programming*. Many political researchers are quite skilled in computer programming and, indeed, many Ph.D.-granting political science departments allow doctoral candidates to substitute highly developed programming and statistical skills for knowledge of one of the more traditional foreign language requirements.

On the other hand, many political researchers are not sophisticated computer programmers. For these, as mentioned above, the use of the computer in conjunction with data analysis has been greatly facilitated by the development of a number of packaged statistical programs. These programs are called "packaged" because they include several preprogrammed statistical routines most often used by social and political researchers. In using these programs, the researcher needs to know very little about the mechanics of computer programming. All he or she needs to do is to select from the package the particular subroutine that is to be applied to a set of data. Using the instructions contained in the *user manual* accompanying the packaged program, the researcher selects the appropriate subroutine and directs the computer to apply that set of statistics to the data being analyzed.

Using one of the packaged programs known as SPSS (to be discussed below) the two commands

```
FREQUENCIES     GENERAL = INCOME, AGE
STATISTICS      ALL
```

will generate frequency distributions (to be discussed in Chapter 5) for the variables "income" and "age," listing the absolute and percent frequencies for each level of income and age, as well as the following statistics for each variable: mean, standard error, median, mode, standard deviation, variance, kurtosis, skewness, range, minimum score, and maximum score. Clearly, these packaged programs simplify the programming stage of data analysis.

Several of these packaged programs are presently available.[2] Large computer centers will probably have most or all of these available for general use, and most computer centers will have their own specialized programs as well. The researcher should be thoroughly familiar with that which is available at his or her computer facility. The most widely used of the packaged programs include the following:

The Biomedical Computer Programs (BMD). Developed at the University of California at Los Angeles, BMD was one of the first of the packaged

---

[2]For a brief introduction of many of these package programs, see: Richard W. Moore, *Introduction to the Use of Computer Packages for Statistical Analyses* (Englewood Cliffs, N.J.: Prentice-Hall, Inc., 1978). An interesting introduction to the use of the computer in research with specific reference to the OSIRIS program is presented in Judith Rattenbury and Paula Pelletier, *Data Processing in the Social Sciences with Osiris* (Ann Arbor, Mich.: Survey Research Center/Institute for Social Research, 1974).

programs to achieve wide distribution. Among the subroutines in the BMD package of most interest to political researchers are simple data description, general plot including histogram, cross-tabulation, *t* program, correlation and regression, discriminant analysis, factor analysis, canonical correlation, and various time-series routines.

OSIRIS III. Developed at the University of Michigan, principally through the efforts of the Institute for Social Research, OSIRIS III assists in all phases of data preparation, organization, and analysis. OSIRIS III contains almost 60 subprograms, including those designed to perform the following routines: univariate and bivariate tables, scatter plot, frequencies, correlation and regression, analysis of variance, factor analysis, Guttman scale, cluster analysis, and various multiple analysis tasks.

Statistical Package for the Social Sciences (SPSS). SPSS is, perhaps, the most convenient and well documented of the various packaged programs. Development of SPSS initially began in 1965 at Stanford University and has continued for the past several years at the National Opinion Research Center (University of Chicago). Later versions of the package have been prepared by Norman H. Nie, C. Hadlai Hull, Jean G. Jenkins, Karin Steinbrenner, and Dale H. Bent. According to the user manual accompanying the latest version, SPSS is now being used at over 600 installations. Among the subprograms available in SPSS are frequencies, cross-tabulation, simple and multiple correlation and regression analysis, analysis of variance, discriminant analysis, factor analysis, and scalogram analysis. Additionally, SPSS offers several convenient options for data transformation and manipulation.

Statistical Analysis System (SAS). SAS was developed by Anthony Barr and James Goodnight of the Department of Statistics, North Carolina State University. Rapidly gaining in popularity and acceptance, SAS performs such analyses as plotting values, calculation of means, regression, analysis of variance and covariance, discriminate analysis, time-series analysis, factor analysis, Spearman's rank-order correlation, frequency tables, and the Guttman scale routine.

The availability of such packaged programs, it should be obvious, has greatly eased the task of computer utilization in political and policy research. The researcher does not have to know how a computer works or even very much about how to prepare a computer program. With the aid of the accompanying manuals, the researcher in just a short time can become "expert" in the use of one or several of the packaged programs. These programs, then, can be used to generate the most complex and sophisticated of statistical analysis.

However, a price is to be paid for this luxury. In the first place, the researcher is limited to the routines contained in the packaged program. It might be the case that a researcher wishes to apply a statistical test or a variant of a statistical test not included in the packaged program available at his or her installation. However, this is increasingly unlikely, as each of the programs described above is constantly improved and updated. More important is the issue of the researcher's *understanding* of the underlying assumptions of the statistic being applied. The extraordinary ease with which the most complex statistics can now be applied to a set of data makes it even more important that the researcher understand when and under what circumstances the various statistics may be appropriately used. The researcher must be thoroughly familiar with his or her own data and with the appropriate classification of statistics that can be applied — *the computer does not make these decisions.* These issues are central to the conduct of systematic research and are discussed in more detail throughout the remainder of this book. Prior to this discussion, an examination of the nature and measurement of data is in order.

Variables and Values

We have been using the term "variable" in several different contexts; it is time now to examine this term more closely. Variables are empirical terms having two or more values. Sex, party identification, years of education, age, annual income, and race are all examples of variables often used in political and social research. Variables that may vary by magnitude (more than, less than, higher than, lower than, etc.) are called *quantitative variables*; those which vary by attributes are called *qualitative variables.* Age and education are examples of quantitative variables; sex and party identification are qualitative variables. Both types are often used in political research. Variables may also be distinguished according to the number of values they may assume. Some variables are dichotomous and take on only two values. Sex is an example of a dichotomous variable, so is employment status defined as employed or unemployed, and so is race defined as white or nonwhite. Some variables may take on several values (such as social class, party identification, and education); others may have a range of values almost equivalent to the size of the population (such as income).

Three classifications of variables will be referred to at several junctures in this text. *Dependent variables* are those we are trying to explain, understand, or predict. *Independent variables* are those we are using to assist in our explanation, understanding, or prediction of the dependent variable. *Control variables*, as will be explained more fully in Chapter 8, are those assisting in more clearly defining the relationship between the independent and dependent variables. It should also be understood that the terms independent, dependent, and control are situationally defined. A variable considered to be the independent variable in one study may be taken as the dependent variable in another. One researcher may be interested in the effects of alienation (taken as the independent variable) on political behavior; another may be interested in those demographic factors associated with political alienation (taken as the dependent variable).

Levels of Measurement

Coding, as discussed above, is the process of assigning numbers to represent values of variables. This is an important stage in the research process. Research could proceed without assigning numbers to all variables (party identification could be labeled simply "Democrat," "Republican," "Independent," or "Other") but the assignment of numbers greatly facilitates the analysis process. At the same time, it is clear that the numbers assigned to particular classifications of data cannot all be manipulated in the same way. We know that assigning a 1 to the Protestant category of religion, a 2 to the Catholic, and a 3 to the Jewish is not to imply any particular ordering among those categories. Numbers can be used in several different ways. Sometimes they can be used only as convenient labels for categories of variables; sometimes they can be used to rank or order categories of variables; sometimes they can be used to specify the distance or interval between categories of variables. It is essential that the student distinguish among these several levels of measurement, since the various analytic techniques discussed in the following chapters are designed to be applied to specific levels of measurement.

Nominal Measures

Nominal measures are those which simply attach numeric labels to various categories of variables. Numbers in this instance are assigned to categories of variables simply as a convenient means of classification. Symbols other than numbers could be used, but numbers facilitate analysis with electronic data-processing equipment. Many examples of nominal measures are available in political research. When assigning to the variable "religion" the value of 1 for all Protestants, 2 for all Catholics, 3 for all Jews, and 4 for all Others, the researcher has developed a nominal measure of religious preference. Sex, party identification, region of the country, nationality, race, and college major are typical examples of nominal variables. Numbers that are assigned to categories of nominal measures do not show order or distance; they only classify.

The important point about numbers assigned to categories of nominal variables is that they be *mutually exclusive* (no case can be assigned to more than one category) and that they be *exhaustive* (all cases are assigned to one of the categories). The selection of numbers assigned to the categories is

70

arbitrary. Protestants could be assigned the number 1, 5, or 20; it makes no difference (as long as different and distinct numbers are assigned to Catholics, Jews, and other religious preferences).

Ordinal Measures

Ordinal measures are those which not only classify but also reflect a ranking (or an ordering) among the assigned values along some characteristic or property. Ordinal measures, then, indicate positioning — a higher number may indicate "more than," "greater than," or "more likely than" a lower value. Socioeconomic status when categorized as working class, middle class, or upper class would be considered an ordinal scale. If the numbers 1, 2, and 3 were assigned to the various values of socioeconomic status, individuals assigned a 3 are defined as having a higher value on this scale than those assigned a 1 or a 2. In Chapter 3, those questionnaire items which measured attitudes of local officials to various aspects of the general revenue-sharing program were all ordinal scales. Another example of an ordinal scale is the measure of liberalism-conservatism used by the Center for Political Studies in its American National Election Studies. That question, as asked in the 1978 survey, is presented in Figure 4.6.

Ordinal measures thus indicate degrees of difference but do not represent equivalence of interval difference. In the example of the liberalism-conservatism measure, a 7 is a more conservative response than a 6, but we do not know *how much* more conservative. The difference between a 6 and a 7 may not be equivalent to the distance between a 5 and 6, and indeed, the distance between a 6 and a 7 may not be the same even for any two people. However, ordinal measures can be compared, and statements of "greater than," "more than," and the like are appropriate.

Interval and Ratio Measures

Interval measures are those for which properties of a variable not only can be ranked or ordered, but where the distance between those rankings is exact and constant. Interval measures not only position and categorize phenomena, they indicate the extent of difference between values. Income,

We hear a lot of talk these days about liberals and conservatives. Here is a seven-point scale on which the political views that people might hold are arranged from extremely liberal to extremely conservative.

1	2	3	4	5	6	7
Extremely Liberal	Liberal	Slightly Liberal	Moderate, Middle of Road	Slightly Conservative	Conservative	Extremely Conservative

Where would you place yourself on this scale, or haven't you thought much about this?

Figure 4.6

CPS measure of liberalism – conservatism. (*Source:* CPS, 1978 American National Election Study.)

education, temperature, and age are examples of interval measures. *Ratio measures* (rarely achieved in the social sciences) are those which in addition to having all the properties of interval measures, have a natural "zero" point. Properties such as weight, time, and length can be measured at the ratio level.

In political science, it is often said that most measures are of the nominal or ordinal variety. Still, much of our data is at least interval in nature. Such information as population, gross national product, voting turnout, and revenue and expenditure data could all be measured at the interval level. Even data that clearly are nominal may be transferred into metric-level measurement by conversion to percentages, when this is appropriate. The researcher might measure religion as percent Catholic, Protestant, Jewish; party identification might be measured as percent Democrat, Republican, and Independent; and so on. It is advisable to use the highest-level classification scheme possible. Higher-level measures permit much more sophisticated analysis, as the following chapters will make clear.

Indexes and Scales

It was mentioned in Chapter 2 that one technique helpful in the operationalization of concepts is that of *scaling*. Actually, the researcher will find scaling techniques helpful for several reasons. In the first instance, it is true that scales often can assist in the measurement of very complex concepts. Concepts such as alienation, racial prejudice, and political activism may be too complex to be adequately measured by reference to a single item. Several items designed to measure the various dimensions of these concepts might be included on a survey and the combined responses to these items would be said to form a scale of alienation, racial prejudice, or political activism.

Second, scales may be used in an attempt to develop higher-level measures of a particular concept. Scales may be used to develop ordinal or even interval-appearing level measures.

Scales are also efficient means of summarizing information. A survey might include several items designed to measure self-esteem, political activism, or levels of political information. Analyzing each separate indicator might be tedious and repetitious; combining the items into a single scale of self-esteem, political activism, or political information might be a preferable way to present the information.[3]

For these reasons, then, the topic of scaling is important to systematic political research. Very simple scales can be constructed using only one statement or item. The Center for Political Studies in its 1978 National

[3]One of the best brief discussions of scaling and the reasons for scaling is presented in Earl R. Babbie, *Survey Research Methods* (Belmont, Calif.: Wadsworth Publishing Company, Inc., 1973), pp. 253–278. The discussion above, as well as that which follows, relies heavily on Babbie's presentation.

Recently there has been a lot of talk about women's rights. Some people feel that women should have an equal role with men in running business, industry, and government. Others feel that women's place is in the home.

1	2	3	4	5	6	7

Equal
Role

Women's
Place in Home

Where would you place yourself on this scale, or haven't you thought much about this?

Figure 4.7

Women's rights scale. (*Source:* CPS, 1978 American National Election Study.)

Election Study asked respondents the question shown in Figure 4.7. This item is considered to be a women's rights scale. Respondents indicate that they are more or less in favor of equal roles for women and men.

More generally, scales are thought of as composite measures formed by combining scores or answers to two or more items. Scaling can be defined here as those "techniques . . . employed in combining one or more measurements in order to form a single score that is assigned to each individual."[4] The most often used of these techniques are discussed below.[5]

Index Construction

A crude form of scaling is that which might simply be called *index construction*. Actually, the words "index" and "scale" are used almost interchangeably in the literature. As used here, an index refers to assigning scores based simply on the combined response to two or more items *assumed* to be related. Scaling techniques, as will be discussed below, are used to empirically demonstrate a hierarchical ordering of items.[6]

As an example of index construction consider the campaign activity items asked by the Center for Political Studies in its American National Election surveys. In its national survey, the CPS asks respondents whether they participate in a number of campaign activities. The questions are usually phrased as follows:

[4]Claire Selltiz, Lawrence S. Wrightsman, and Stuart W. Cook, *Research Methods in Social Relations,* 3rd ed. (New York: Holt, Rinehart and Winston, 1976), p. 400.

[5]For an excellent review and presentation of the most often used scales in political research, see John P. Robinson, Jerrold G. Rusk, and Kendra B. Head, *Measures of Political Attitudes* (Ann Arbor, Mich.: Institute for Social Research, 1969).

[6]For further elaboration, see Babbie, *Survey Research Methods,* pp. 254–255; and E. Terrence Jones, *Conducting Political Research* (New York: Harper & Row, Publishers, 1971), p. 33.

Interviewer Checks One:

1. During the campaign, did you talk to any people and try to show them why they should vote for one of the parties or candidates?　　Yes___;　No___

2. Did you go to any political meetings, rallies, funding-raising dinners, or things like that?　　Yes___;　No___

3. Did you do any (other) work for one of the parties or candidates?　　Yes___;　No___

4. Did you wear a campaign button or put a campaign sticker on your car?　　Yes___;　No___

5. Did you give any money to a political party or candidate this year?　　Yes___;　No___

In constructing an index of participation in campaign activities (excluding voting), one might assign a score of "1" to each "yes" response and a "0" to each "no" response and sum the results for each individual. Using the SPSS package of statistical programs, this could be accomplished with the following procedure:

```
COMPUTE          CAMPART=TALK + MEETING + WORK +
                 BUTTON + MONEY
```

where

CAMPART = index of campaign participation
TALK, MEETING, WORK, BUTTON, MONEY = each individual's score on each of the five items of campaign activity.

Combined in this manner, scores on this index of campaign activity would range from 0 (those participating in none of the activities listed) to 5 (those participating in all activities).[7]

Constructing indexes, it can be seen, is very simple; however, the major disadvantages of this technique are also obvious. First, it is difficult to know how to weight the various components of the index. In the example above, all items have equal weight; however, it might be sensible to assign more importance to some items (such as contributing money) than to others. The decision as to how weights are to be assigned, if at all, is left largely to the individual researcher.

[7] A scale of political participation based on a similar set of questions first was developed by Angus Campbell et al. in *The Voter Decides* (Evanston, Ill.: Row, Peterson, 1954). For an analysis of responses to such a campaign activity scale over time, see Sidney Verba and Norman H. Nie, *Participation in America* (New York: Harper & Row, Publishers, 1972), pp. 248–264.

Another problem of index construction lies in the interpretation of scores other than the highest and lowest values. In the example above, a 0 indicates participation in none of the listed activities and a 5 indicates participation in all, but how are the scores 1, 2, 3, or 4 to be interpreted? A score of 3, for example, could be achieved through participation in several different combinations of activities, but it is not apparent just which items were combined to achieve this score. Most important, perhaps, is the fact that we have no way of knowing whether the components of this index are really interrelated — that is, does each item really measure campaign participation or are other dimensions being tapped as well? Giving money to a party or a candidate, for example, might be as much a measure of affluence as a measure of campaign activity. Thus more elaborate scaling techniques are required.

Likert Scaling

The *Likert scaling technique* in reality is a more sophisticated means of index construction.[8] But, unlike the procedure described above, the Likert technique provides some empirical justification for item inclusion. Assume that the researcher wants to construct an index of domestic liberalism. Briefly stated, the steps in Likert scale construction are as follows:

1. The researcher assembles a large number of questions (perhaps 50 items or more) which he or she believes tap the dimension of domestic liberalism.
2. Possible responses to each item so selected are ordered on a continuum indicating intensity of feeling (such as from strongly agree to strongly disagree, or strongly favor to strongly disapprove). Usually, this is a five-point response continuum (such as strongly agree, agree, uncertain, disagree, strongly disagree), with the middle score reserved as a "no opinion" or "uncertain" response category. However, a continuum of seven, nine, or more responses is possible.

    Each response to each question is assigned a score value. A response of "strongly agree" may be assigned a score of 5 and a "strongly disagree" response may be assigned a score of 1. It is important that scores are assigned to questions in a *consistent* manner. If the answer considered to be most conservative to one question is assigned a score of 1, all most-conservative responses must be assigned the score of 1. The scoring scheme is not revealed to the respondent.
3. The researcher then selects a sample of respondents believed to be representative of the group to which the index is to be administered. If the researcher were attempting to construct a scale to measure domestic liberalism of the elementary and secondary school popu-

---

[8] See Rensis Likert, "A Technique for the Measurement of Attitudes," *Archives of Psychology*, 22 (1932), 1–55. See also the excellent discussion of the Likert technique in Babbie, *Survey Research Methods*, pp. 269–270.

lation, this sample might consist of schoolchildren. All the items that have been selected for possible index inclusion are then administered to the sample.

4. Based on their answers to these questions, each respondent is assigned a total score. If the researcher has assembled 50 questions designed to measure domestic liberalism and the most liberal response to each question is assigned a score value of 5 and the most conservative is assigned a score value of 1, any individual's *total* score could range from 250 (most liberal) to 50 (most conservative) and any individual's *average* score could range from 5.0 to 1.0.

5. Based on their total scores, the sample subjects are then divided into groupings. For items measuring liberalism, the sample might be broken into quartiles: the 25 percent with the most liberal scores, the 25 percent next most liberal, the 25 percent next most liberal, and the 25 percent with the most conservative scores.

6. Each item on the original list of 50 is then separately evaluated and those found to best discriminate between the upper quartile of scores (in this example the most liberal respondents) and the lower quartile (in this example the most conservative respondents) are selected for inclusion in the final index.[9]

If, for example, the weighted mean score of the most liberal quartile on the first question were found to be 3.5 and the weighted mean score of the most conservative quartile were found to be 1.5, the difference would be 2.0. For each item in the scale, this difference is known as the *discriminative power* of the item. If the difference in weighted mean scores between the most liberal and most conservative quartiles on the second question were found to be only 0.5, it would be concluded that the first question better discriminates between liberal and conservative respondents. The researcher might apply more rigorous difference of means tests (such as those to be discussed in Chapter 9) to distinguish between the items. But the point is that items having the greatest mean difference are assumed to best discriminate among those to whom the index is to be administered, and those questions are selected for inclusion in the final index.

The Likert technique can be criticized on the grounds that there is no way to determine if the items finally selected to comprise the index really do measure the concept of interest (in the example above, domestic liberalism); and because of its obvious reliance on the selection of extreme items, the Likert technique may not be able to satisfactorily distinguish between more moderate respondents. Still, the technique does provide a more rational basis for item selection, is relatively quick to apply and administer, and does

[9] Those desiring more rigorous criteria might select the top and bottom 40 or 50 percent for item evaluation.

provide a range of alternative responses to each question.[10] For these reasons, the Likert technique is widely used in political research.

One recent example of the use of the Likert technique is provided by Thompson and Browne's study of urban bureaucratic responsiveness to the hiring of minorities. The authors wanted to develop a scale of attitudes toward minority hiring which was to be administered to a sample of urban personnel management officials. According to the authors: "In order to measure commitment to hiring minorities, [we] solicited the advice of a panel of personnel experts and subsequently devised a set of eight Likert items. These items are designed to measure the degree to which officials believe that government should seek out and employ minorities where these groups suffer from underrepresentation in the public bureaucracy."[11] The personnel management officials were asked to indicate their extent of agreement with the following items selected by Thompson and Browne to comprise this scale:

1. That the government should make a special effort to advertise job vacancies in the minority community.
2. That minorities should receive preference where minority and white applicants are of equal ability and minorities are underrepresented on a department's work force.
3. That government has a responsibility to recruit members of disadvantaged groups.
4. That government employers are *not* placing too much emphasis on affirmative action.
5. That special committees of minority leaders should be set up to make recommendations to improve hiring.
6. That government should at times hire a minority applicant even if there is a more competent white one who wants the job.
7. That where minorities are underrepresented, consideration should be given to hiring only minorities until they attain adequate representation.
8. That public agencies should establish hiring targets for racial minorities and timetables for obtaining them.[12]

In constructing the final Likert-type scale, it is important that responses to the items selected be varied so that (in the case of liberalism, for example) the very liberal responses are not always those in agreement with each statement and conservative responses are not always in disagreement (or vice versa).

---

[10]A review of the advantages and disadvantages of the Likert method may be found in Selltiz et al., *Research Methods in Social Relations*, pp. 418–419.

[11]Frank J. Thompson and Bonnie Browne, "Commitment to the Disadvantaged Among Urban Administrators: The Case of Minority Hiring," *Urban Affairs Quarterly*, 13 (March, 1978), 355–378.

[12]*Ibid.*, p. 361.

The questions should be presented, in other words, so that agreement sometimes indicates a liberal response and sometimes indicates a conservative response. This is to prevent respondents from falling into what is known as a *response-set* pattern — simply selecting the same responses for each item without thoroughly considering each question. In their survey, Thompson and Browne reversed three of the items in their minority hiring scale so that positive responses did not always indicate a favorable attitude to minority hiring.

Thurstone Scales

A number of methods were developed by Louis Thurstone in his attempts to develop scaling techniques resulting in scales that more clearly possess interval properties. These techniques are variously known as the methods of *paired comparisons, equal-appearing intervals,* and *successive intervals.*[13] Although each method cannot be described in detail here, the general procedure for the equal-appearing interval method is as follows:

1. The researcher selects a large number of items possibly measuring the dimension being examined (liberalism, prejudice, alienation, etc.).
2. A large number of judges (50 or more) are asked to sort these statements into several piles (usually 7 or 11), ranging from those most favorable to the dimension being examined to those most unfavorable.[14]
3. Each statement is assigned a score equivalent to its mean (sometimes median) position in the various groups. If 25 of 50 judges placed the first statement in the first pile and 25 placed it in the second pile, its score would be 1.5.
4. Statements that receive widely diverse pile placements are discarded. If for example, 10 judges place the third statement in the first pile, 10 place it in the third grouping, 10 place it in the fifth pile, 10 place it in the seventh pile, and 10 place it in the eleventh grouping, the statement probably should be discarded as being too ambiguous.
5. From the remaining items, the researcher selects a set evenly spread along the various points on the continuum.

When the Thurstone scale is administered, respondents are asked to indicate whether they agree or disagree with each statement (each of which has

[13] See Louis Thurstone, "The Method of Paired Comparisons for Social Values," *Journal of Abnormal and Social Psychology,*" 21 (1927), 384–400; Louis Thurstone, "A Theory of Attitude Measurement," *Psychological Bulletin,* 36 (1929), 221–241; and Louis Thurstone and E. J. Chave, *The Measurement of Attitude* (Chicago: University of Chicago Press, 1929).

[14] The terms "favorable" and "unfavorable" are used only for convenience. The piles could be representative of liberal to conservative, trusting to alienated, prejudice to tolerant attitudes, and so forth.

been assigned a score according to the procedure outlined above). Of course, the value assigned to each item is not revealed to the respondents, and respondents' total scores are calculated as the mean value of the statements to which they agree.[15]

The advantage of the Thurstone technique is its presumed achievement of an interval (or at least an interval-appearing) scale. A number of problems are also associated with the technique. The selection of judges may have a biasing influence on the assigning of scale values. Judges from differing backgrounds may rate items differently. Also, since scale scores are calculated as the mean or median of the value of those items agreed to, the same score on the scale may represent different attitudinal dimensions. That is, the same score may be achieved by those responding differently to differing questions.[16]

Techniques are available that may assist in minimizing the problems listed above. Perhaps the principal reason for the technique not being used as much today as when it was first introduced is due simply to the cumbersome and time-consuming procedures required. In proportion to the amount of effort involved, the results have not been shown to be clearly superior to those obtained by the Likert procedure.[17]

Guttman Scaling Techniques

All the above mentioned techniques share one common problem. They can provide no assurance that the items selected to comprise the scale all actually measure the same dimension. In our example given above of constructing an index of campaign activity, it was noted that the same score — 1, 2, 3, or 4 — could be achieved through several different combinations of response. As it stands, there is no way to determine from these index scores if the same score is tapping identical or different dimensions of campaign activity. A score of 2 achieved through contributing money and working for a candidate may denote a degree of activism and campaign commitment different from a score of 2 achieved from talking to someone (such as a spouse) about the election and placing a bumper sticker on the car. Some indication of whether the scale items are measuring a single dimension (i.e., are unidimensional) is clearly desirable. The Guttman routine attempts to provide this measure.[18]

The Guttman technique begins by ordering potential scale items according to the degree of difficulty assumed to be associated with responding positively to each item. According to the logic of the Guttman technique, if the scale

[15] For an excellent exploration of the Thurstone technique, see Nan Lin, *Foundations of Social Research* (New York: McGraw-Hill Book Company, 1976), pp. 413–417.

[16] These and other objections are discussed in Selltiz et al., *Research Methods in Social Relations*, p. 416.

[17] As argued by Lin, *Foundations of Social Research*, p. 192.

[18] See Louis Guttman, "A Basis for Scaling Quantitative Data," *American Sociological Review*, 9 (1944), 139–150; and Louis Guttman, "The Basis of Scalogram Analysis," in Samuel A. Stouffer et al. (eds.), *Measurement and Prediction* (Princeton, N.J.: Princeton University Press, 1950), pp. 60–90.

that has been developed really is unidimensional, it would be expected that individuals responding positively to the more difficult items would also respond positively to the less difficult items. For purposes of illustration, assume that the researcher has ranked the campaign activity items mentioned above in order of difficulty and that six individuals have been asked whether they participated in the various activities. The distribution of answers to these questions might appear as shown in Figure 4.8.

In Figure 4.8, a distribution is observed that is said to be perfectly unidimensional. As such, any individual's answer to each participation item can be predicted with complete accuracy from knowledge of that person's total score. Knowing that individual 4 received a score of 2, the researcher also knows which activities this person participated in (talking and wearing a button or placing a sticker on the car) and which he or she did not participate in. The researcher is then able to *reproduce* each individual's answers to each question knowing each individual's total score. Of course, it almost never would be the case that a scale would achieve 100 percent reproducibility, as in the simplified example above. More likely, there will be a number of *error responses*, responses that deviate from the expected pattern. If in the example above, the fifth individual had responded "yes" to wearing a button or placing a sticker on the car but "no" to talking about the election, this would be considered one deviation or error from expected unidimensionality. The ratio of these error responses to the total number of possible responses, known as the *coefficient of reproducibility*, provides one criterion for judging the unidimensionality of a set of scale items. The coefficient of reproducibility (CR) is calculated as

$$CR = 1 - \frac{\text{number of errors}}{\text{total number of responses}}$$

where the total number of responses is equal to the total number of cases times the total number of scale items.

more difficult ◄─────────────────► less difficult

Individual:	Give Money?	Work for a Candidate?	Go to Meetings?	Wear Button or Place Sticker on Car?	Talk?	Scale Score:
1	Yes	Yes	Yes	Yes	Yes	5
2	No	Yes	Yes	Yes	Yes	4
3	No	No	Yes	Yes	Yes	3
4	No	No	No	Yes	Yes	2
5	No	No	No	No	Yes	1
6	No	No	No	No	No	0

Figure 4.8
Illustration of unidimensionality.

80

A second criterion for evaluating a Guttman scale, known as the *coefficient of scalability*, is essentially a measure of how much the scaling routine actually improves reproducibility over that which would have been expected simply by reference to the marginal totals of responses for each item. Although absolute standards have not been established, it is recommended that a coefficient of reproducibility of at least 0.90 or 0.95, and a coefficient of scalability of at least 0.60, should be achieved.[19] If, in the original evaluation of potential scale items, either coefficient is below the recommended level, the scale can often be improved by dropping items.

An interesting use of the Guttman procedure is provided by Jules Wanderer's construction of an index of severity of urban riots.[20] Based on his analysis of 75 riots and civil–criminal disorders that took place in the United States during the summer of 1967, the items selected to comprise such a scale were found to be as shown in Table 4.1.

As is the case with all the scaling techniques discussed in this section, the Guttman routine is not without its critics. One of the problems of the Guttman procedure is that it is applied ex post facto. That is, the test is

TABLE 4.1
Guttman Scale of Riot Severity

Items Reported for Each City	Percent of Cities (N = 75)	Scale Errors	Scale Type
1. No scale items (no acts of disorder)	4	2	8
2. Vandalism	19	10	7
3. The above + interference with firemen	13	3	6
4. All of the above + looting	16	3	5
5. All of the above + sniping	13	7	4
6. All of the above + State Police called	7	4	3
7. All of the above + National Guard called	17	11	2
8. All of the above + law officer or civilian killed	11	2	1
Total	100	42	

$$CR = 1 - \frac{42}{515} = 0.92$$

Source: Adapted from Jules J. Wanderer, "An Index of Riot Severity and Some Correlates," *The American Journal of Sociology,* 74 (March, 1969), 503.

[19]For a quick but thorough discussion of all elements of the Guttman procedure, see the discussion presented by Norman H. Nie et al. in the SPSS *User Manual* (New York: McGraw-Hill Book Company, 1975), pp. 528–533.

[20]Jules J. Wanderer, "An Index of Riot Severity and Some Correlates," *The American Journal of Sociology,* 74 (March, 1969), 500–505.

applied to a set of data after the data have been collected. Even if the items meet the suggested criteria for one set of individuals, there is no assurance the same items will form an acceptable scale for another group. Thus the researcher desiring a scale meeting the criteria necessary for unidimensionality must evaluate the items of that scale with every administration.[21]

Multidimensional Scaling

Political researchers are increasingly interested in the topic of multi-dimensional scaling. This topic is much too complex to be explored in this text, but it should be noted that here the research focus shifts from the attempt to find a set of items that form a single-dimensional scale (as was the case when applying the Guttman technique) to the determination of the *variety of dimensions* that may exist in a given set of data. Having collected information on the public's rating of presidential candidates, it might be of interest to determine the various dimensions of candidate evaluation in the mass public. Two political scientists, in fact, analyzed the public's evaluation of 12 candidates for President in 1968.[22] Two principal dimensions of candidate evaluation in that year were found. One, the authors concluded, corresponded "to the [traditional] partisan issues which divided the old left and the old right." The other was said to represent the "new issues which divide the new left and the new right, issues which are not linked to the partisan attachments of an earlier generation."[23] Multidimensional techniques, then, can be used to more accurately reveal underlying structures and patterns, to assist in the comparison of different groups, and to aid in the identification of items that separately might appropriately be used to construct scales.[24]

Reliability and Validity

A final consideration in the development of appropriate measures concerns the issues of *reliability* and *validity*. To be useful, measuring instruments should be both reliable and valid. Measures are *reliable* to the extent that the same individual achieves identical (or nearly identical) scores on repeated administrations of the measure. Measures are *valid* to the extent that they

---

[21] For more penetrating criticisms of the Guttman routine, see John P. Robinson, "Uses and Abuses of Guttman Scaling," paper presented at the annual meeting of the *American Sociological Association*, August, 1968; and Carmi Schooler, "A Note of Extreme Caution on the Use of Guttman Scales," *American Journal of Sociology*, 74 (November, 1968), 296–303.

[22] Herbert F. Weisberg and Jerrold G. Rusk, "Dimensions of Candidate Evaluation," *American Political Science Review*, 64 (December, 1970), 1167–1185.

[23] *Ibid.*, p. 1179.

[24] For an excellent introduction to multidimensional scaling, see Joseph B. Kruskal and Myron Wish, *Multidimensional Scaling*, Sage University Paper Series on Quantitative Applications in the Social Sciences, 07–11, (Beverly Hills, Calif.: Sage Publications, 1976).

really reflect the actual activity or behavior that is being studied. As an example, a measure of alienation is said to be reliable if the same individuals receive approximately the same scores on repeated testing, or if individuals having similar levels of alienation receive similar scores. A measure of alienation is said to be valid if it really is measuring alienation and not some other trait.

Reliability is a reflection of stability, dependability, and consistency in measurement.[25] It is assumed that any individual's score on some measure is a result of that individual's "true" position on the concept being measured (alienation, prejudice, campaign activity, for example) plus an "error" component. Error may be caused by any number of factors, including those relating to the inadequacy of the measuring instrument. Reliability, in essence, is a function of this error component of any individual's or any group's score. The greater the variation in total score attributable to error, the less reliable is the measure.

A number of techniques are available for estimating the reliability of a particular measure. Using the *test–retest method of estimating reliability*, the researcher simply administers the same test to the same group on more than one occasion. The correlation between the scores on the different administrations is said to be the measure of reliability. The higher the correlation between the sets of scores, the more reliable is the measure. Although the test–retest method provides a measure of reliability, it has two obvious limitations. Administering the same test to the same individuals may influence their scores, and "real" changes in attitude may take place from one test administration to another which would serve to lower the correlation (thus giving the appearance of an unreliable test) even though the reliability of the measure may not have been affected at all.

The *split-half method* of estimating reliability actually splits or divides an original scale into two or more subscales. Each subscale is administered to a group of individuals, and the average difference among the obtained scores is said to be a measure of test reliability. If the scores on one subscale deviate from the scores on a second subscale by an average of 5 percent the split-half reliability would be said to be 0.95 (1.0 minus 0.05). A score of 0.90 or higher is considered acceptable evidence of a reliable scale.

Validity refers to whether the measuring instrument actually measures that which it purports to measure. The determination of validity is more important than determining reliability. A measure that is valid would have to be reasonably reliable, but a reliable measure (one producing the same scores on repeated administrations) may not be valid (it may actually be measuring unknown properties). Measurement validity is very difficult to establish, especially in the social sciences. If "true" positions on the variable of interest were known, validity could be directly assessed (simply by comparing such

[25] For an excellent discussion of reliability, see Fred N. Kerlinger, *Foundations of Behavioral Research*, 2nd ed. (New York: Holt, Rinehart and Winston, Inc., 1973), pp. 442–455.

scores with known positions). Since true positions are almost never known, validity can only indirectly be estimated by reference to other relevant indicators.[26]

Face validity refers to whether in the subjective judgment of the researcher or a team of judges assembled by the researcher, the scale appears to measure the full range of the phenomenon of interest. *Empirical validity* refers to the congruence between results obtained from the measure and some other evidence of the phenomenon. Instruments designed to measure campaign activity should distinguish between those who actually are active and those who are not. If it is found that some measure of political activity does not distinguish between those who are known activists and those who are not, the measure's validity is questionable. This is another way of saying that to be valid the measure should be predictive.

Often, however, the researcher is interested in concepts that are too abstract to be compared with empirical behavior. This might be the case with such concepts as alienation, political trust, political efficacy, and so forth. In instances such as these, the researcher may have to rely on theory and reasoning rather than on empirical verification for measuring validity. As Selltiz et al. have put it, "The propositions under investigation may form a highly complex deductive web...."[27] *Construct validity*, as this procedure is called, attempts to logically relate the various strands of such a theoretical web. In so doing, the researcher might compare the results of measures that, theoretically, should be related. It would be expected that measures of civil rights attitudes would correlate with measures of welfare attitudes, or that measures of conservatism would correlate with measures of candidate preference. Of course, perfect congruency is not obtained or expected, but the notion is that, if the underlying assumptions are correct, some congruence should result if the measures are indeed valid.

Techniques of establishing reliability and validity are obviously not perfect. Evidence relating to validity is especially difficult to obtain. In establishing validity, the instrument should appear to the researcher or a team of judges to measure what it proposes to measure (face validity), it should be predictable in that it correlates with empirical evidence (empirical validity), and its predictions should make theoretical sense (construct validity). Not all of these criteria can be applied in every case, but the important point is that all possible evidence should always be considered.[28]

---

[26] As argued by Selltiz et al., *Research Methods in Social Relations*, p. 170.

[27] *Ibid.*, p. 173.

[28] For an excellent critique of category scaling techniques and an argument for applying magnitude scaling techniques designed to achieve interval level data in political science situations, see Milton Lodge and Bernard Tursky, "Comparisons Between Category and Magnitude Scaling of Political Opinion Employing SRC/CPS Items." *American Political Science Review*, 73 (March, 1979), 50–66.

Concluding Comments

This chapter has introduced the student to the use of the computer in political and policy research. It obviously has not been possible here to thoroughly explore all the advantages of computer-assisted research, but at least it is hoped that any initial fears that the student may have harbored regarding the computer have been substantially allayed. It is true that the computer is a very complex and complicated machine. But it is also true that the recent development of packages of statistical programs (such as those mentioned in this chapter) have opened the world of the computer and its analytic power to researchers who have only the most elementary knowledge of electronic data processing and computer programming. It would be expected that future advances will extend even further the computer's accessibility and the political researcher's reliance on electronic data-processing equipment.

Yet the real message of this chapter is that this great and marvelous tool must be used with caution and reason. Essentially, the computer will analyze whatever is fed into it. The computer does not ask if hypotheses have been clearly developed, if information has been appropriately collected, if concepts have been adequately operationalized, if data have been properly coded and measured, or even if the research is worth pursuing. All these decisions (and many more) must be made by the human researcher. The programming slogan "garbage in/garbage out" could not be more appropriate. The quality of output is determined by the quality of input, not by the sophistication of the computer.

Having been relieved of the mechanical burdens of data processing, manipulation, and calculation, the student can sometimes forget that the human element is still an integral part of political research. The systematic researcher will use the computer as a tool assisting in the research process but will not neglect the many and important decisions that still must be made apart from the computer and all its wizardry.

Exercises

1. a. Visit your university computing center and/or your department's data laboratory. Locate the keypunch and (if appropriate) remote terminal areas.
   b. Inquire as to the proper mode of submitting and receiving jobs from the computer and the typical length of "turnaround time" (time from submission of a job to receiving output from the computer).
   c. Discover how much assistance your computer center provides to computer users and the location and hours of such assistance.
   d. Find out which, if any, of the social science data archives your university subscribes to and the availability of such data for *your* use.
   e. Discover the variety of packaged programs available for use at your center and the location of documentation for each package.

2. a. In your own area of interest and from the sources of available data discussed in Chapter 3, select a small number of cases (15 to 20 cities, states, presidents, nations, etc.) and for each case compile information on five or six variables.
   b. Place this information on a codesheet (available at the computer center or university bookstore).
   c. Transfer your information to punchcards.
3. a. For Exercise 2, prepare a codebook for this set of data.
   b. What important elements should a codebook contain?
   c. Why are the elements listed in part (b) necessary in a codebook?
4. a. With permission from your instructor and appropriate approval of your computer center, apply one of the packaged programs to the data set compiled in Exercise 2 to produce a frequency distribution for each variable.
   b. Report the results of this analysis.
   c. Comment on the utility of the computer and the packaged program for political research as revealed in this assignment.
5. a. For the data set compiled in Exercise 2, discuss the types of variables collected and coded.
   b. Which (if any) are quantitative and which (if any) are qualitative?
   c. Which might most appropriately be considered independent and dependent variables and under what conditions might this ordering change?
   d. What are the levels of data (nominal, ordinal, interval) of your variables, and why is this consideration important to any subsequent research you might attempt?
6. a. For any area of political research of interest to you, develop five questions that might be used to form an index of some concept in that area.
   b. Under what circumstances would such an index be desirable?
   c. What are some of the potential problems in developing an index or a scale in this manner?
   d. What techniques might be applied to refine the index so constructed?

5

DESCRIBING AND SUMMARIZING DATA

Having completed the often lengthy and usually tedious process of collecting, coding, and keypunching information, the researcher is ready to begin the process of data analysis. This is often the most exciting phase of the research process. The pace quickens as the computer begins to generate printout, as gross patterns that have been obscure begin to reveal themselves, and as the researcher begins to receive the first hints of whether the data appear to substantiate his or her initial expectations. It is here that the political researcher begins to sense the excitement of "discovery" — a thoroughly invigorating and stimulating intellectual experience shared by all scientists.

At this early stage of data analysis, the researcher usually will want to begin by examining and describing in summary fashion the information that has been collected. Having spent a considerable amount of time among the trees, the researcher is anxious now to step back and begin to comprehend the whole forest. Sometimes, in fact, the data-analysis stage may end at this point. Sometimes our interest extends no further than aggregate description. Having obtained a sample of the American electorate, for example, the researcher may simply be interested in discovering what *proportion* voted in the most recent presidential election, the *distribution* of party preferences among the sample, and the *average* amount of time devoted by each individual to political affairs. Examining all 50 American states, the political scientist may be interested in determining the *typical* length of state constitutions, the *mean* salary paid to legislators, and the job held most *frequently* by individuals before being elected governor. A student of urban politics might be interested in finding the *variation* of mean income levels among America's largest 100 cities, or the *proportion* of these same cities experiencing a mayoralty election turnout of 50 percent or more.

In each of these examples, we have emphasized such terms as "typical," "proportion," and "variation"; in each instance, the researcher is interested only in making summary statements about the group being examined. To repeat an important point, this may be the extent of the data analysis needed. Summary information such as this may be all that is required for the task at hand. Since only one variable at a time is being examined (percent voting, party identification, etc.), the category of methods used in such analysis is called *univariate analysis.*

In summarizing and describing distributions of single variables, the researcher may want to examine frequency or percentage distributions, measures of central tendency, measures of dispersion, and shape and form of the distributions. Beginning students are probably most familiar with frequency presentations and the application of measures of central tendency (such as the mode, median, and mean); however, all of these measures are useful, as will be discussed in this chapter. Since the proper application of these measures is dependent on the level of data being examined (nominal, ordinal, or interval), it might be useful for the student to review those sections in Chapter 4 that deal with this topic before proceeding.

The Frequency Distribution and Graphic Presentations

One of the first steps in analyzing and reporting information often is the construction and presentation of frequency distributions of the variables of particular interest. The *frequency distribution* refers to a tabulation of data according to the important categories of those variables of interest to the researcher. A frequency distribution of age, for example, refers to the listing of the numbers of individuals assigned to each age category. A frequency distribution of party identification refers to the listing of the number of individuals assigned to each category of party identification.

The general format for the presentation of a frequency distribution might appear as shown in Table 5.1. As the table indicates, in presenting a frequency distribution, the researcher begins by listing each category of the variable to be examined, presents the number of observations (frequencies) assigned to each category, calculates the total number of observations for the variable, and generally presents the proportion or percentage of frequencies falling into each category. When examining nominal data (as discussed in Chapter 4), such as sex, race, or party identification, the researcher may present these categories in any reasonable order. When examining ordinal data, such as socioeconomic status, the researcher will present the data in order from the "lowest" to the "highest" (or vice versa) scale categories. When examining interval data, such as age or income, the researcher will also present the data in ordered fashion but, in addition, may want to group the data according to

Table 5.1
General Format for the Frequency
Distribution .

Category	Frequency	Proportion (or Percent[a])
A	f(A)	f(A)/N
B	f(B)	f(B)/N
C	f(C)	f(C)/N
D	f(D)	f(D)/N
E	f(E)	f(E)/N
	Total N	

where A, B, C, D, E=categories of the variable
$f(A)$ through $f(E)$=number of observations in each category
N=sum of frequencies in all categories
$f(A)/N$ through $f(E)/N$=number of observations in each category divided by the total number of observations

[a]The proportion multiplied by 100 yields the percent. Also useful is a *cumulative distribution* which shows for each frequency or percentage category the number or percent of cases in that *and all preceding categories.*

Table 5.2
Frequency Distribution of the Population of the
United States by Age in 1980 (projected)

Age	Frequency (in thousands)	Percent	Cumulative Percent
Under 5 years	17,927	8.0[a]	8.0
5–13	30,197	13.5	21.5
14–17	15,763	7.0	28.5
18–21	17,117	7.6	36.1
22–24	12,346	5.5	41.6
25–34	36,172	16.1	57.7
35–44	25,721	11.5	69.2
45–54	22,698	10.1	79.3
55–64	21,198	9.5	88.8
65 and over	24,927	11.1	99.9
Total	224,066	99.9	

Source: Statistical Abstract of the United States, 1978.
[a]Here, and generally throughout this text, percents are rounded to the nearest tenth. When rounding, the total percent will often vary slightly above or below 100, as is the case here.

meaningful categories. A distribution showing frequencies, percents, and cumulative percents of the population of the United States grouped according to various age categories is presented in Table 5.2.

Table 5.3
Liberalism-Conservatism Distribution of Sample
of the American Public, 1976

Reported Views	Frequency	Percent
Extremely liberal	29	1.9
Liberal	147	9.8
Slightly liberal	177	11.8
Moderate, middle of the road	562	37.3
Slightly conservative	283	18.8
Conservative	257	17.1
Extremely conservative	51	3.4
Total	1506	100.1

Source: 1976 American National Election Study. The study was conducted by the Center for Political Studies of the Institute for Social Research, the University of Michigan and released through the Inter-University Consortium for Political and Social Research. Throughout, this study will be cited as: CPS, 1976 American National Election Study.

As another example of a frequency distribution, consider the responses of a sample of the American electorate to a measure of liberalism-conservatism. In its 1976 survey, the Center for Political Studies asked its respondents to place themselves on a seven-point continuum ranging from "extremely liberal" to "extremely conservative." The frequency distribution of these responses is presented in Table 5.3.[1] As indicated, of the 1506 people responding to this question, 29 (or 1.9 percent) considered themselves "extremely liberal," 147 (or 9.8 percent) considered themselves "liberal," and so forth.

An extension of the frequency distribution occurs when the researcher wishes to present his or her findings in graphic form. Often, graphs are a more convenient means of data presentation because a rapid visual examination of the presentation can reveal important characteristics of the data. When dealing with nominal or ordinal data, the data may be presented as a *bar graph*. As such, bars (which may be displayed horizontally or vertically) are drawn for each category of the variable in a manner so that the height (or length) of the bars represents the number of cases (frequency) for each category. Figure 5.1 presents the data considered in Table 5.3 in bar graph format. The visual advantage of data presented in bar graph format is obvious. One can see immediately that, in this instance, the largest number of respondents consider themselves to be "moderate," and smaller numbers consider themselves to identify with the remaining categories of liberalism and conservatism.

[1] Here and generally throughout this text when using data from the 1976 CPS American National Election Study, analysis is based on the unweighted sample size of 2248. These examples, then, are for the purpose of illustrating techniques and concepts, and results obtained should not be generalized to the voting population of the United States.

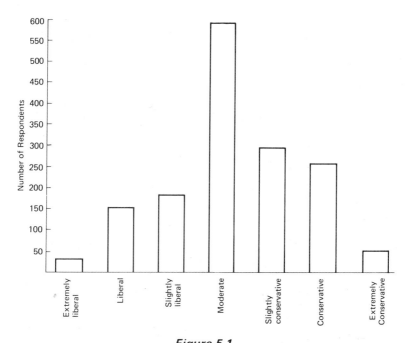

Figure 5.1

Liberalism–Conservatism distribution of sample of the American public, 1976. (*Source:* CPS, 1976 American National Election Study.)

When constructing a graph of interval data, the bars of such a graph are not separated and the resulting figure is called a *histogram*. The height of the bars of a histogram are proportional to the frequencies of each category, and the width of the bars are proportional to the size of each interval. Interval data can also be presented graphically by connecting the mid points of the top of each bar of a histogram with a solid line. The resulting graph, with bars removed, is known as a *frequency polygon*. Figure 5.2 illustrates a frequency polygon (dashed line) superimposed on a histogram (typically, of course, only one of these will be presented). The data represent the number of U.S. cities over 100,000 having a percent black population in 1970 falling into the intervals illustrated. From the graph, the number of cities falling into each interval can be inferred (for example, 23 cities had a black population comprising from 0 to 5 percent of the total population in 1970). The vertical axis could have been presented in percents rather than frequencies, in which case the graph would be called a percentage polygon. Again, the advantages of graphs, such as bar graphs and histograms, are in their ease of interpretation and assistance in comparing categories of variables.

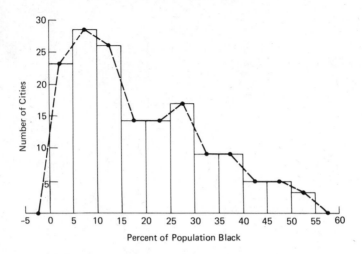

Figure 5.2

Histogram and frequency polygon of percent of population that is black in U.S. cities over 100,000, 1970, excluding Washington D.C. (Source: Statistical Abstract of the United States, 1978, pp 24–26.)

> *READER NOTE: The frequency polygon line need not be extended beyond the range of actual observations, but when extending each end of the frequency polygon to the base line (as is the case in Fig. 5.2), it is recommended that the graph be extended to intersect the horizontal axis at the midpoints of the vacant intervals on both ends of the distribution. This preserves equivalence of area under both the frequency polygon and the histogram.*

Measures of Central Tendency: The Mode, the Median and the Mean

Frequency distributions and graphs greatly assist in the description and understanding of variables, but the researcher often wishes to present his or her findings in a still more convenient fashion. Any report dealing with more than just a few variables would soon become quite unwieldly if reliance were solely on the presentation of charts and frequency distributions. Also, the researcher may desire more convenient measures for *comparing* characteristics of differing populations or subsets of a population (such as Democrats and Republicans, high- and low-income families, whites and nonwhites). In such instances, measures of central tendency (discussed below) and measures of dispersion (discussed in the following section) will be useful.

The Mode

For nominal data, the mode is a convenient measure of central tendency. Simply put, the *mode* is that category of a variable having the largest number

92

Table 5.4
Party Identification of Sample of the
American Public, 1976

Category	Frequency	Percent
Republican	535	23.9
Independent	637	28.4
No preference	170	7.6
Other	15	0.7
Democrat	885	39.5
Total	2242	100.1

Source: CPS, 1976 American National Election Study.

READER NOTE: Strictly speaking, the category of a variable having the largest number of observations (in Table 5.4, Democrat) is the mode; but it is common to label a distribution having two pronounced categories as bimodal and one having several pronounced categories as multimodal. If all categories have equal numbers of cases any category can be said to represent the mode, or, more often, it will be said that the distribution has no unique modal value. When reporting the mode, then, it is important to inspect the actual data and to apply that terminology which most accurately represents the distribution.

of observations. In its 1976 American National Election Study, the Center for Political Studies asked respondents to indicate their party identification. The responses to that question are presented in Table 5.4, where it can be seen that the modal party preference for this sample is Democrat.

The Median

A measure of central tendency used in conjunction with a distribution of ordinal data is the median. The *median* is defined as that value dividing the distribution into two groups of equal size in such a manner so that the value of

Table 5.5
Hypothetical Distribution of Scores to
Racial Tolerance Scale

Student	Score	Student	Score
1	7	10	4
2	7	11	3
3	7	12	3
4	6	13	2
5	6	14	2
6	5	15	2
7	5	16	1
8	4	17	1
9	4		

the median is no greater than the scores of half the cases nor no smaller than the scores of half the cases. For a distribution ranking cases from those lowest to those highest in value, the median is the score of the middle case if the number of cases is odd. If the number of cases is even, the median is the value of the two middle cases if these cases are tied; it is the value halfway between these two when they are not tied. As an example, assume that a political science student has administered a scale of racial tolerance to 17 classmates. The distribution of scores ranging from 1 (least tolerant) to 7 (most tolerant) might appear as shown in Table 5.5. In this example, the score of student 9 is the median: 4. This value is no greater than half the distribution (those 8 students whose scores range from 4 to 7) and no smaller than half the distribution (those 8 students whose scores range from 4 to 1).

Had student 17 not been included in this sample, there would be no middle case. In such situations, the median falls halfway between the two middle cases, in this case between students 8 and 9. Here, the median would still be reported as 4. If student 17 had not been included in the sample and the score of student 8 had been 5, the median would have been reported as 4.5.

The Mean

For interval data the *arithmetic mean* (or, simply, the *mean*) is the most often used measure of central tendency. The mean is operationally defined as the sum of all scores divided by the total number of cases. The mean is generally symbolized as $\bar{X}$, and the formula used to calculate the mean is defined as

$$\bar{X} = \frac{\Sigma X}{N}$$

where
$\quad \bar{X} = $ mean
$\quad \Sigma X = $ sum of all scores
$\quad N = $ total number of observations

READER NOTE: Often in the chapters that follow the symbol Σ will be used. This symbol, the Greek capital letter sigma, means to sum or to add. It simply is a shorthand way of saying, "add the following." ΣX, as used in the formula above, means to add all observations of that category of observations known as X.

Although the formula for the mean is simple and easily understood, it is important to note that the calculation has the algebraic property that the sum of the deviations of each score from the mean will equal zero. That is, if we subtract the mean from each score and add the results, the sum will be zero. This important characteristic will be discussed in later chapters.

A researcher interested in the mean annual income of 20 families selected for study simply totals the annual income for each family and divides the sum by 20. The result is the mean annual income for the group.

As another example, assume that the researcher is interested in examining the salaries paid by states to their governors and in comparing these salaries by regions. Table 5.6 shows the annual salaries of the governors of each of the 50 states (as of late 1977), the mean gubernatorial salary of each of the several regions calculated according to the formula for the mean, and the mean compensation for all 50 states (also calculated according to this formula). This table illustrates several important properties of the mean. First, it can be seen that presented in this fashion, mean scores assist in comparing different groupings. We can tell at a glance that the mean gubernatorial compensation of the Middle Atlantic region is higher than the mean for any of the other regions and that, on the average, the states of the Mountain region provide the lowest salary for their governors.

Also, these data indicate the impact that a few deviant cases can have on the mean score — a property known as *skewing* (this concept will be discussed further in a later section). When such extreme cases are present, the utility of the mean as a measure of typicality is diminished. Consider the Middle Atlantic region. There it can be seen that the gubernatorial salary of Delaware is far out of line with the other states in that region. Had Delaware not been included in this region, the mean annual compensation of these governors would have been calculated as $72,000. The actual mean income for this region ($62,750) is thus skewed by the inclusion of Delaware. Similarly, the state of Texas, with a gubernatorial compensation considerably higher than any of the other states in the Southern region, may be said to skew the mean for the entire region in a higher direction. In using and reporting mean scores, then, it is necessary to consider the effect that highly deviant cases may have on these scores and to consider the appropriateness of other measures of central tendency (such as the median), which may not be so sensitive to extreme cases.

Table 5.6 can be used to illustrate another important point. The researcher could average the mean scores of each of the eight regions, the result being the mean *regional* gubernatorial compensation. But, because of unequal frequencies in each region, this figure of $45,850 (not shown in Table 5.6) is not equivalent to the mean score for *all* 50 states (shown to be $44,739). The first score ($45,850) is known as the *unweighted mean* and may be the appropriate measure to calculate if the researcher is, in fact, interested in the mean regional annual compensation of governors. But, if the focus is to be on the mean annual compensation of all 50 states, and if this figure is to be derived from regional groupings, the *weighted mean* must be calculated. In this case, the weighted mean would be derived by weighting all regions by their respective number of states before calculating the mean. This is easily done, as illustrated in Table 5.7. The weighted mean is thus equivalent to the mean of the entire group of 50 states (see Table 5.6).

All of this is to say, in conclusion, that in calculating and reporting measures of central tendency (and, indeed, all statistical measures), it is

95

Table 5.6
Annual Compensation of Governors, Aggregated by Region

Region	Annual Salary	Region	Annual Salary
New England		Oregon	46,128
Connecticut	$42,000	Washington	55,000
Maine	35,000	Alaska	52,992
Massachusetts	40,000	Hawaii	50,000
New Hampshire	36,454	Mean	$50,644
Rhode Island	42,500		
Vermont	39,000		
Mean	$39,159	Solid South	
		Alabama	$29,995
		Arkansas	35,000
Middle Atlantic		Florida	50,000
Delaware	$35,000	Georgia	50,000
New Jersey	65,000	Louisiana	50,000
New York	85,000	Mississippi	43,000
Pennsylvania	66,000	North Carolina	45,000
		South Carolina	39,000
Mean	$62,750	Texas	69,100
		Virginia	50,000
East North Central		Mean	$46,110
Illinois	$50,000		
Indiana	37,000	Border states	
Michigan	57,250	Kentucky	$35,000
Ohio	50,000	Maryland	25,000
Wisconsin	49,920	Oklahoma	42,000
Mean	$48,834	Tennessee	50,000
		West Virginia	50,000
West North Central		Mean	$40,400
Iowa	$55,000		
Kansas	35,000	Mountain states	
Minnesota	58,000	Arizona	$40,000
Missouri	37,500	Colorado	40,000
Nebraska	40,000	Idaho	33,000
North Dakota	27,500	Montana	35,000
South Dakota	32,000	Nevada	40,000
		New Mexico	40,000
Mean	$40,714	Utah	40,000
		Wyoming	37,500
Pacific and external		Mean	$38,188
California	$49,100		

Mean annual compensation for all 50 states=$44,739 (rounded)

Source: The Book of the States, 1978–79.

96

Table 5.7
Calculation of the Weighted Mean

Region	Regional Mean $\bar{X}$	×	Number of States f	=	f$\bar{X}$
New England	$39,159		6		$234,954
Middle Atlantic	62,750		4		251,000
East North Central	48,834		5		244,170
West North Central	40,714		7		284,998
Pacific and external	50,644		5		253,220
Solid South	46,110		10		461,100
Border states	40,400		5		202,000
Mountain states	38,188		8		305,504
Total			50		$2,236,946

$$\text{weighted mean} = \frac{\$2,236,946}{50}$$

$$= \$44,739 \quad \text{(rounded)}$$

important (1) to have a firm idea of the questions to be answered, and (2) to be thoroughly familiar with the data being analyzed. The choice of which statistical measure to apply will be largely dictated by these concerns.

Measures of Dispersion

Although measures of central tendency are extremely helpful in identifying important trends among an array of data,[2] it should be obvious from the preceding discussion that some measure of the *deviation* from the average or typical is also needed. Measures of central tendency are likely to more accurately reflect the actual values of all members of a distribution when the data are closely grouped about the central values. Conversely, measures of central tendency are less likely to accurately reflect the actual values of all members of a distribution that is heavily skewed in one direction or the other, or if the data are widely dispersed. For this reason, measures of dispersion are a useful tool for a more complete understanding of a distribution of values.

[2]One of the principal limitations of measures of central tendency and, indeed, statistical analysis in general is that while the techniques may tell us something about *groups* of cases, they almost never can be used to provide definite predictions about *individual* cases. Thus, the researcher must be especially careful in the use and interpretation of statistical results. Statistical techniques may demonstrate trends, they may provide guides; but they should never be used to reach certain conclusions regarding individuals. The beginning student would be advised to review in this regard Morris Kline's, *Mathematics: A Cultural Approach* (Reading, Mass.: Addison-Wesley Company, Inc., 1962) and especially his section dealing with the use and limitations of statistical analysis (pp. 613–635).

Several of the most important measures of dispersion for the various levels of data are considered next.

The Variation Ratio: A Measure Useful with Nominal Data

The *variation ratio* (*v*) is a simple-to-calculate and easy-to-understand measure of variation for nominal data.[3] In essence, *v* tells us the extent to which the mode satisfactorily represents a particular frequency distribution. The general formula for *v* is

$$v = 1 - \frac{\text{number of cases in the modal category}}{\text{total number of cases}}$$

Inspecting this formula, it can be seen that if *all* cases fell in the modal category (i.e., if in a distribution of religion every individual happened to be classified as Protestant), *v* would be calculated as 0. From this it can be inferred that the *lower* the *v* score, the *more* representative is the mode of all cases.

As an illustration, consider the distribution of religion by region as revealed in the 1976 CPS American National Election Study. These data are presented in Table 5.8. It can be seen from the information in the table that the mode is a better representation of religion in the South (in this case, Protestant) than is the modal religious category for any other region. The variation ratio also shows that the mode is a less satisfactory summary of all religious categories in the Northeastern states than for any other region. Put another way, the Northeastern respondents were more varied in their religious affiliations. The researcher would want to be very cautious in

Table 5.8
Distribution of Religion by Region of the Country

| Religion | Region | | | |
	Northeast	North Central	South	West
Protestant	192	442	576	195
Catholic	220	149	102	78
Jewish	31	13	1	7
Total	443	604	679	280
$v = $	$1 - \dfrac{220}{443}$	$1 - \dfrac{442}{604}$	$1 - \dfrac{576}{679}$	$1 - \dfrac{195}{280}$
$v = $	0.503	0.268	0.152	0.304

Source: CPS, 1976 American National Election Study.

[3]As discussed in Linton C. Freeman, *Elementary Applied Statistics* (New York: John Wiley & Sons, Inc., 1965), pp. 40–43.

reporting the mode (in this case, Catholics) as being representative of the religious affiliation of all northeasterners in this sample.

Other measures of dispersion useful with nominal data have been developed. One of these which is particularly useful is the *index of qualitative variation* (IQV) developed by Mueller, Schuessler, and Costner.[4] The IQV provides an *overall* index of heterogeneity and does, therefore, present somewhat of a better summary description of the data than the statistic *v*. However, IQV is more difficult to calculate, and in most instances *v* is a satisfactory measure of dispersion for nominal data.

The Range: A Measure Useful with Ordinal Data

A simple measure of variation, useful when data are ordered or ranked, is known as the *range*. The range measures the distance between the highest and lowest values of a distribution: the smaller the range, the more accurate or representative of all values of the distribution is the median score.

In our example of the median, we presented a hypothetical distribution of scores of 17 students on a scale of racial tolerance ranging from 1 (least tolerant) to 7 (most tolerant). The median in that example was found to be 4 and the range is 6 (highest minus lowest score). Assume that in a second sample of 17 students, responses to the same seven-point scale were arrayed as shown in Table 5.9. In this instance the median still is 4, but the range (in this case also 4) indicates greater homogeneity in responses of the second group of students.

While simple to calculate and while certainly useful as a measure of dispersion, the range suffers from the obvious problem of being totally influenced by extreme values (the highest and lowest scores of a particular

Table 5.9
Hypothetical Distribution of Scores to
Racial Tolerance Scale

Student	Score	Student	Score
1	6	10	4
2	6	11	4
3	6	12	3
4	5	13	3
5	5	14	3
6	5	15	3
7	4	16	2
8	4	17	2
9	4		
	range (6–2) = 4		

[4]See John Mueller, Karl Schuessler, and Herbert Costner, *Statistical Reasoning in Sociology* (Boston: Houghton Mifflin Company, 1970), pp. 174–179.

distribution). In cases where only one or only a very few cases are actually assigned the highest or lowest possible values, the range may provide a misleading impression of variation. For this reason, a variety of other measures of the range of ordinal data have been developed. All of these essentially, are designed to eliminate extreme cases from consideration. The decile range (symbolized as d), for example, calculates the range over the middle 80 percent of the data (eliminating the extreme highest and lowest 10 percent of the cases). Even more restrictive measures of the range have been developed.[5] When the distribution is skewed by a few extreme cases, the other measures will probably provide a more accurate reflection of variance. Still, the simple range, as described above, remains the most-often-used measure of dispersion for ordinal data.

The Mean Deviation, Variance, and the Standard Deviation: Measures Useful with Interval Data

A measure of dispersion of somewhat greater utility than the range and useful when the data are interval is the *mean deviation*. The *mean deviation* is calculated by taking the difference between each observation and the mean, summing these deviations (ignoring negative signs, which would result in a sum of zero), and dividing by the total number of observations. Arithmetically, the mean deviation is expressed as

$$\text{mean deviation} = \frac{\Sigma |X_i - \bar{X}|}{N}$$

where X_i = each observation
$\bar{X}$ = mean of all observations
N = total number of observations
$|\ \ |$ = absolute difference (ignoring signs)

Table 5.10 illustrates the calculation of the mean deviation for the 1976 presidential voting turnout for the Northeastern states. It can be concluded that on the average, the voting turnout among registered voters in each Northeastern state in 1976 deviated from the mean turnout for all Northeastern states by 3.89 percent. The mean deviation is a helpful measure of dispersion because of its ease in calculation and interpretation. However, tests that ultimately are much more useful — especially when used in conjunction with more advanced statistics — have also been developed. Because of their greater theoretical utility (as will be explained below) these other tests are more likely to be used as measures of dispersion of interval data.

[5]See Mueller et al., *Statistical Reasoning in Sociology*, pp. 154–155, for a brief discussion of some of these.

Table 5.10
Percent of Registered Voters in Northeastern States Voting in 1976 Presidential Election

State	Percent Voting, X	$|X - \bar{X}|$
Maine	68.4	9.5
New Hampshire	76.7	1.2
Vermont	71.1	6.8
Connecticut	85.5	7.6
Rhode Island	78.2	0.3
New York	79.5	1.6
New Jersey	82.5	4.6
Pennsylvania	78.2	0.3
Massachusetts	81.0	3.1
Total		35.0

mean $(\bar{X}) = 77.9$

mean deviation $= \dfrac{35.0}{9}$

$= 3.89$

Source: Statistical Abstract of the United States, 1977.

Variance and the Standard Deviation

A second measure of interval level dispersion based on the mean variation is the mean-squared deviation — more commonly known as the *variance*. The formula for the calculation of the variance looks very much like the formula for the calculation of the mean deviation:

$$\text{variance} = \frac{\Sigma(X_i - \bar{X})^2}{N}$$

where X_i = each observation
$\bar{X}$ = mean of all observations
N = total number of observations

Rather than taking the absolute difference between each observation and the mean, ignoring the sign, as was the case when calculating the mean deviation, the variance squares these differences, sums the squares, and divides the sum by the total number of cases. In the case of voting turnout in the Northeastern states, illustrated in Table 5.10, the variance is found to be 25.47. The lower the variance, the more accurately does the mean represent all the scores of all cases in a distribution of interval-level data. However, the variance is not often reported as a measure of dispersion; it is more often used in conjunction with more advanced statistical tests. In later chapters the concept of variance will be explored in much greater depth.

The *standard deviation* is probably the most used measure of dispersion for interval-level data. It provides a powerful summary statistic, as will be discussed later in this chapter. The formula for the standard deviation is

$$\text{standard deviation} = \sqrt{\frac{\Sigma(X_i - \bar{X})^2}{N}}$$

where X_i = each observation
$\bar{X}$ = mean of all observations
N = total number of observations

READER NOTE: Statisticians typically distinguish between the variance and standard deviation (as well as other statistics) calculated for a population and for a sample of a population. Symbolically, the values for the variance and standard deviation of a sample *are presented, respectively, as s² and s. For population data, these values are symbolized as σ² and σ. Additionally, when calculating the variance and standard deviation for sample data, most modern statisticians prefer the quantity* n − 1 *(where* n = *sample size) as the denominator in order to achieve an unbiased population estimate. For large sample sizes, this alteration obviously will have little impact on the score produced; for small sample sizes, especially, this correction factor should be employed.*

Again considering the 1976 presidential voting turnout in the Northeastern states, the standard deviation is found to be 5.05. As a general rule, the standard deviation of a distribution may be *estimated* to be $\frac{1}{5}$ of the range. Because the range in this case is 68.4 to 85.5, we could have estimated s as $\frac{1}{5}$ of 17.1, or 3.42. Obviously, this estimated standard deviation deviates from the true value (5.05); however, this shorthand procedure may be used when a quick estimate is needed.

Unlike the mean deviation (found for this same example to be 3.89), the standard deviation is not easily interpretable. It is when we consider the standard deviation in terms of the normal curve that the utility of the measure becomes apparent.

The Coefficient of Variation

Prior to a discussion of the normal curve, one final measure of dispersion needs to be discussed. This is the *coefficient of variation*, used when the researcher wishes to compare the dispersion of two or more groups about their respective means. If the mean score for each group were exactly the same, the standard deviation would serve this purpose. If the means are different (as most often will be the case), a comparison of standard deviation scores alone might be misleading. A standard deviation of 3.3 for a group whose mean score on a particular variable is 5.0 would have a different interpretation than a standard deviation of 3.3 for a group having a mean score of 25.0 on this variable. That is, in the first instance the standard deviation of 3.3 would indicate a considerable amount of spread about the mean; in the second instance, the standard deviation of 3.3 would indicate a group more homogeneously grouped about the mean. The coefficient of variation is used to compare differences of this nature and is symbolized by

$$V = s/\bar{X}$$

where V = coefficient of variation
s = standard deviation
$\bar{X}$ = mean

For the two cases mentioned above, the coefficient of variation for the first group (mean of 5.0, standard deviation of 3.3) is 0.66. For the second group (mean of 25.0, standard deviation of 3.3), the coefficient of variation is 0.132. Again, the *lower* the coefficient of variation, the *greater* is the homogeneity of the group.

Shape of the Distribution

In addition to measures of central tendency and dispersion, distributions can be considered in terms of their *shape*. We noted above that the shape of a distribution can be revealed by connecting with a solid line the midpoints of the top of each bar of a histogram. The resulting shape will obviously be a function of the original frequency distribution. Distributions having large proportions of cases with scores above the mean will take on different shapes from those having large proportions of low scores or those having a large proportion of scores "clustering" close to the mean.

Three possible shapes are depicted in Figure 5.3. The first two shapes presented in the figure are said to be *skewed*; this means that in both instances there are more extreme scores in one direction or the other. In the first instance, there are more extremely low scores; the distribution in this case is said to be *negatively skewed*. It can also be seen here that the mean is pulled in the direction of the lower scores. In the second shape, there are more extremely large scores and the distribution is said to be *positively skewed*. In a positively skewed distribution, the mean is pulled in the direction of the higher scores.

The third shape is said to be *symmetrical*. In such a distribution an equal number of cases fall on each side of the curve and the mean, median, and mode will coincide. Thus it is apparent that in reporting measures of central tendency, the shape of the distribution is a factor to be considered. For distributions that are highly skewed, in one direction or the other, the mean may present a distorted image of the distribution. In such instances, the median or mode may be a more accurate measure, even though the mean might otherwise be appropriate.

103

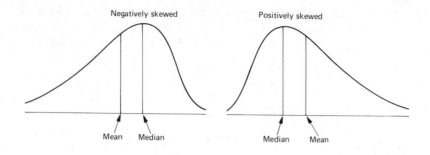

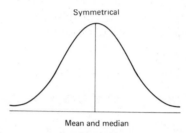

Figure 5.3
Some possible shapes of frequency distributions.

The Normal Curve

A special type of symmetrical distribution is known as the *normal curve.*[6] The normal curve is a distribution having the properties of being unimodal, symmetrical, and having equivalent mean, median, and mode scores. Another property of the normal curve is that a constant proportion of cases will lie between the mean and a distance from the mean defined in units of standard deviation.

It is the latter characteristic of the normal curve that is most useful to researchers. Figure 5.4 illustrates the areas of the normal curve defined in units of standard deviation. As shown, in a normal distribution approximately 34.13 percent of all cases can be found within an area of 1 standard deviation greater than the mean and an equal proportion are found to lie within an area of 1 standard deviation less than the mean. Thus slightly over 68 percent of all cases in a normal distribution can be expected to lie within 1 standard deviation (plus or minus) of the mean. Similarly, over 95 percent of all cases can be found within 2 standard deviations (plus or minus) of the mean, and practically all cases (over 99 percent) will fall within 3 standard deviations (plus or minus) of the mean.

---

[6]A special type of the normal curve is one with a mean of zero and a standard deviation of 1.0. Such a distribution is known as the standard normal curve.

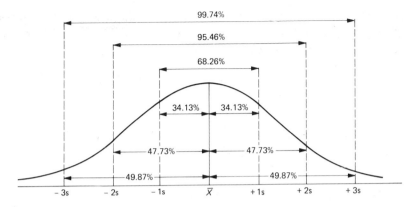

Figure 5.4
Areas under the normal curve.

In this manner, the standard deviation used in conjunction with the normal curve becomes an extremely important tool for data evaluation. Assume, for example, that the public's rating of a particular presidential candidate on a scale of from 0 (very negative) to 100 (very positive) is normally distributed with a mean of 50.0 and a standard deviation of 15. We are now in a position to conclude that about 68 percent of the public assigns this candidate a rating between 35 and 65 (± 1 standard deviation from the mean) and that over 95 percent of the public assigns the candidate a rating between 20 and 80 (± 2 standard deviations from the mean).

It is useful to think of frequency distributions in political and social research as approximating a normal curve. This is especially true when considering distributions of sampling statistics, to be discussed in Chapter 9. The properties of the normal curve become immensely useful in interpreting the nature of data, and, in fact, many distributions in the political and social sciences do approximate normality.

The Z Score

We also might be interested in estimating the proportion of the public assigning the candidate a rating of between 50 (the mean) and 75. This can be accomplished by calculation of the Z score (sometimes called the *standard score*), the formula for which is

$$Z = \frac{X - \bar{X}}{s}$$

where X = any proportionate distance (score) of any observation we wish to estimate
$\bar{X}$ = mean
s = standard deviation

105

The Z score tells us the number of standard deviations that the score lies above or below the mean. Applying the formula to the situation presented above, we see that the score is found to be

$$Z = \frac{75 - 50}{15}$$
$$= 1.67$$

In this instance, we find that the score of 75 is 1.67 standard deviation units greater than the mean.

We know, from our discussion of the normal curve, that 34.13 percent of the cases lie between the mean and one standard deviation above the mean, and that 47.43 percent of the cases lie between the mean and 2 standard deviations above the mean. Since we find that the rating of 75 is 1.67 standard deviation units above the mean, we know that the proportion of the public assigning the candidate a score of 50 to 75 is somewhere between 34.13 and 47.43 percent.

Tables have been developed which allow rapid interpretation of the Z values. One such table is shown in the Appendix (Table A, p. 261). To use this table, find the first two digits of the Z value presented in the leftmost column (in this case, 1.6) and the third digit as presented in the column headings. For a Z score of 1.67 we find the value to be 4525, which means that 45.25 percent of the public has assigned the candidate a rating of between 50 and 75. Had the Z score been 1.43, we would conclude that 42.36 percent of the public rated the candidate between these two scores. If we had wished to determine the proportion of the public assigning the candidate a rating of from 0 to 75, we simply would have added 0.50 to the Z value obtained above (0.4525), since the normal curve assumes that 50 percent of the population will lie on either side of the mean. Thus we would conclude that 95.25 percent of the public would rate the candidate from 0 to 75.

As a final illustration of the normal curve and the use of the Z score, assume that one is interested in finding the proportion of the public assigning the candidate very high and very low scores. For some reason we may be interested in knowing the proportion of the public assigning the candidate a score of 80 or higher and 20 or less. Such an interest would be illustrated in Figure 5.5.

To calculate this proportion, first we would find the proportion assigning the candidate a score of 50 to 80 and then *subtract* this total from 0.50 (since, again, it is assumed that 50 percent of all cases fall on the positive side of the mean). Since the same proportion of cases are assumed to rate the candidate a score of 80 to 100 as 0 to 20 (because, by definition, this is a normal curve), we then only need double this score to find the total proportion rating the candidate at both extremes. This is accomplished in the following manner:

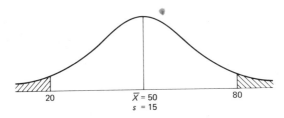

Figure 5.5
Normal curve, with emphasis on both ends of the curve.

$$Z = \frac{80 - 50}{15}$$

$$= 2.00$$

Returning to our table of Z values presented in the appendix Table A, it can be seen that 47.73 percent of the cases fall between the mean value of 50 and the rating of 80. Thus only 0.0227 (0.50 − 0.4773) of the public gives the candidate a rating of 80 or above. Doubling this to account for the proportion of the public assigning the candidate a score of 20 or less, we find that 0.0454 (or less than 5 percent) of the public assigns the candidate a highly positive or a highly negative score. Such information might be of interest not only to the political researcher but also to the candidate, who may value an image of appealing to a wide spectrum of the public without raising intense levels of feeling (either positive or negative) among the voters.

Summary

This chapter has examined some of the important ways of describing single variables.[7] A frequency distribution can be constructed showing numbers of cases per category, percentages, and proportions. Measures of central tendency (such as the mode, the median, and the mean) can be used to describe the average characteristics of a group. Measures of dispersion (such as the variation ratio, range, mean deviation, variance, standard deviation, and coefficient of variation) can be calculated showing the extent to which the distribution varies from the typical. Used in conjunction with the normal curve, the standard deviation can be used to estimate the proportion of cases falling within a certain distance of the mean.

All of these techniques assist in describing and understanding distributions. However, these techniques do not, in themselves, reveal *relationships* that

---

[7] It should be noted that many of the formulas presented in this chapter, as well as elsewhere in this text, are *definitional formulas*. Often *computational formulas*, which are less tedious to apply and which reduce the risk of computational error, can be employed.

may exist among variables. Often it is the discovery or measuring of relationships that is of central concern to the political analyst. We turn to this issue in the next chapter.

Exercises

1. In its 1976 American National Election Study, the Center for Political Studies reported the following responses to the question, "Is your religious preference Protestant, Roman Catholic, Jewish, or something else?":

Protestant	1405
aNontraditional Christian	64
Roman Catholic	200
Jewish	52
Other religions	38
No preference	128

aIncludes Unitarian, Mormon, Quaker, and other religions.

a. Prepare a frequency distribution for this set of data, showing the total number of cases in the distribution and the proportion and percent of cases falling in each category.
b. What measure of central tendency would be most appropriate to report along with this distribution? Why? What would this be in this instance?
c. What measure of dispersion would be most appropriate to calculate in conjunction with this distribution? Why? What is the value of this measure in this instance?
d. Discuss this distribution by reference to the measures of central tendency and dispersion calculated above. How do these measures assist in understanding this distribution?

2. In its 1976 American National Election Study, the CPS asked its respondents to rate the federal government and local governments in terms of how good a job these units of government were doing for the country. Frequency responses to these questions were as follows:

Rating		Federal Government	Local Governments
(Very poor job)	0	54	55
	1	12	23
(Poor job)	2	223	197
	3	128	136
(Fair job)	4	918	597
	5	173	199
(Good job)	6	237	436
	7	11	56
(Very good job)	8	15	34

a. construct a bar graph for both of these distributions.

b. Construct a frequency polygon for both distributions.

c. What do you believe would be the appropriate measures of central tendency and dispersion to report for these distributions? Why?

d. What do the graphs prepared above reveal about these distributions? Discuss.

3. In its 1976 American National Election Study, the CPS asked its respondents to rate George Wallace on a "feeling thermometer" ranging from 0 (very unfavorable) to 100 (very favorable). The means and standard deviation for white, black, Southern, and non-Southern respondents are shown below:

	Mean	Standard Deviation
White	46.7	26.3
Black	29.9	26.0
Southern	52.7	26.9
Non-Southern	42.9	26.2

a. On the basis of the mean scores and standard deviations, what can be said about the comparative evaluation of George Wallace by whites and blacks; by southerners and non-southerners?

b. For the white sample, calculate the proportion of cases assigning Wallace a rating of between the mean score and 80. What proportion of white respondents assigned Wallace a rating of 80 or less?

c. For the black sample, what proportion assigned Wallace a score of from 40 to 50? What proportion of the black sample assigned Wallace a score of 50 or higher?

6

EXAMINING RELATIONSHIPS: BIVARIATE TESTS FOR NOMINAL AND ORDINAL DATA

Measures useful for summarizing and describing single variables (such as those discussed in Chapter 5) play an important role in the conduct of systematic research. The student of politics will obviously be interested in such information as the variation in voting turnout among the American states, the proportion of Democratic congresspersons supporting a Democratic president's proposed legislation, the degree of political activism among the public, and the frequency of presidential veto of legislation. Information such as this, systematically collected and accurately reported, is essential to the informed political observer.

However, the political scientist is generally more interested in establishing *relationships* among variables. As a rule, the political scientist will want to discover factors *associated with* voting turnout, congressional voting patterns, political activism, and presidential veto of legislation. Put another way, the scientist is interested in establishing *predictive relationships* among variables. We want to know the extent to which knowledge of one variable assists in understanding another.

Sometimes, the researcher may be interested in discovering *patterns of relationships* among variables. Will it be found that legislators voting "yes" on a particular set of issues also tend to vote "yes" on another set? Are individuals who are liberal on issues concerning busing of schoolchildren and government aid to minorities also liberal on the issues of gun control and rights of the criminally accused? Is the electorate's evaluation of specific public officials related to the electorate's more general evaluation of political institutions? In each of these instances, the researcher is interested in discovering patterns of relationships among a set of data. In a more formal sense, the researcher may be interested in discovering interrelated items that may be used to form *scales* (as discussed in Chapter 4) of liberalism, cynicism, and other political attitudes.

More often, the scientist is interested in establishing relationships in his or her attempt to contribute to an understanding of the "causes" of certain phenomenon. Since the ultimate design of science is the establishment of causal relationships among variables, the discovery of *predictive relationships* is an important *first* step.

Even in the "hard" sciences, where rigorous control is possible, it is debatable whether undisputed causal laws ever can be found. Certainly, many obstacles exist to the development of causal relationships in the social sciences. Still, the first step in establishing such relationships is discovering predictive relationships among variables. If we find one variable useless in predicting another, and if controlling techniques (discussed in Chapter 8) confirm the absence of a relationship, then we can at least conclude that *no causal* relationship exists between the two. In this chapter, we examine those techniques useful for establishing relationships among two nominal or ordinal variables. In the next chapter, we examine tests of association for two interval variables. Since in each instance two variables are being examined at the same time, the category of methods used in such analysis is called *bivariate analysis*.

The Nature of Association

When we speak of two variables as being associated or related to one another, we are saying that knowledge of one variable assists in understanding or predicting another. As discussed in Chapter 4, the variable which we are interested in understanding or predicting is called the *dependent* variable. The variable that we are using to predict with is called the *independent variable*. The better able we are to predict the dependent variable from a knowledge of the independent variable, the stronger is the association between the two.

Most (but not all) tests of association for linear (or straight-line) relationships in use today range from a score of 0.0 to 1.0 (in the case of ordinal- and interval-level tests the scores range from -1.0 to $+1.0$). In all instances, the closer to 1.0 (in either a positive or negative direction), the stronger is the relationship; the closer to 0.0, the weaker is the relationship. A score of 1.0 (rarely, if ever, achieved in social science research) would indicate what is called a perfect relationship; knowledge of values of the independent variable would allow us to predict, without error, values of the dependent variable.

We will see in Chapter 8 that even strong associations can be deceiving. Sometimes what appears to be a strong relationship between two variables is actually caused by the confounding influences of one or more additional

111

variables. The scientist must eliminate as many of these potentially confounding variables as possible before concluding that a strong association between the two variables he is interested in actually does exist. For the moment, however, our concern is with establishing the initial relationship between the independent and dependent variables.

Tabular Presentation

When dealing with nominal or ordinal data, relationships are usually presented in tabular form. By convention, the variable considered to be the independent variable is symbolized as X and the dependent variable is symbolized as Y. The data should be presented so that the categories of the *independent variable* sum to 100 percent. The sums of each column are called the *column marginals*, and the sums of each row are called the *row marginals*. The format for such a table, assuming both variables to have only two values (low and high), could be presented as shown in Table 6.1.

This tabular example should be studied carefully, as it presents a general format for table presentations. It is stressed that for proper interpretation, the categories of the independent variable should total 100 percent. As a general rule, tables are easier to read and interpret if the independent variable is arrayed as the columns of the table. When the data are ordinal, it is conventional to assign lowest numerical codes to lowest values (a low social status score would be assigned a lower numerical code than would a high social status score, for example). Cells A through D represent all possible

Table 6.1
Dependent Variable (Y) by Independent Variable (X)

Dependent Variable, Y	Independent Variable, X		Row Marginals
	Low X Value	High X Value	
Low Y Value	Cell A — All cases scoring low on both X and Y variables	Cell B — All cases scoring high on X variable and low on Y variable	Total cases scoring low on Y variable (cells A+B)
High Y Value	Cell C — All cases scoring low on X and high on Y variable	Cell D — All cases scoring high on both X and Y variables	Total cases scoring high on Y variable (cells C+D)
Column Marginals	Total cases scoring low on X variable (cells A+C)	Total cases scoring high on X variable (cells B+D)	Total cases in table (cells A+B+C+D)

combinations of lower and higher values of variables X and Y (for nominal data, of course, "low" and "high" numerical codes are used only for the purpose of classification). All cases having low scores *both* on variable X and on variable Y would be assigned to cell A. All cases having high scores on the X value and low scores on the Y value would be assigned to cell B, and so forth. The total number of cases falling in all four cells, as well as the total marginal figures, add to the total n — the total number of cases in the table.

It should be intuitively obvious from an inspection of Table 6.1 that the *greater* the proportionate number of cases that fall in the diagonal cells, the *stronger* will be the relationship between the two variables. If a higher proportion of cases falls in cells A and D than in cells B and C, a relationship exists of the nature that higher values of the independent variable are related to higher values of the dependent variable (as one increases in value, so does the other). Conversely, if a higher proportion of cases falls in cells B and C than in cells A and D, a relationship exists such that higher values of the independent variable are associated with lower values of the dependent variable. It is convenient to refer to the diagonal associated with cells A and D as the *main diagonal* and that associated with cells B and C as the *off diagonal*. The more cases that fall on either diagonal, the stronger the relationship. If all cases are fairly evenly apportioned among all cells, very little relationship exists among the variables.

An example helps clarify these points. Assume that the researcher is interested in examining the relationship between income and education (measured as ordinal data). Perhaps it is expected that higher levels of education are associated with higher income levels. Relying on data supplied by the 1976 CPS American National Election Study, the resulting frequency distributions for education and income, both coded here as "low" or "high," are presented in Table 6.2. It can be seen from the frequency distributions that larger proportions of the respondents reported high education and high income levels (as these were coded for this example), but of course *this says nothing about the possible relationship between income and education*. The high-income respondents indeed may also be high-education respondents, or they may not. Frequency distributions alone will not reveal relationships, but cross-tabulation procedures may.

Using the SPSS packaged program, this could be accomplished by the following command:

CROSSTABS   TABLES = INCOME BY EDUC

where   INCOME and EDUC are designated as variable names for the
         variables income and education

For the sample taken from the 1976 CPS American National Election Study (shown in Table 6.2), a cross-tabulation such as that shown in Table 6.3 would result. Presenting the data in this manner, it can be seen immediately that

Table 6.2
Frequency Distributions of Education and Income

	Frequency	Percent
Education		
Low (less than 12th grade)	636	30.7
High (12th grade or higher)	1439	69.3
Total	2075	100.0
Income		
Low (less than $10,000 (annual income)	950	45.8
High ($10,000 annual income or higher)	1125	54.2
Total	2075	100.0

Source: CPS, 1976 American National Election Study. For this table, education has arbitrarily been coded as low (less than 12 grades of education) or high (12 grades of education or more), and income has arbitrarily been coded as low (less than $10,000 annual income) or high ($10,000 annual income or more).

some type of relationship does exist between income and education. Most of the cases lie on the main diagonal. In this example, this means that most respondents with low education also reported low income (72.8 percent), and that most of those reporting high education also reported high income (66.2

Table 6.3
Income by Education, 1976

Dependent Variable ↓ INCOMEª	Independent Variable ↓ EDUCATIONª		Row Marginals ↓
	Low	High	Total
Low	463 (72.8%)	487 (33.8%)	950
High	173 (27.2%)	952 (66.2%)	1125
Total ↑ Column Marginals	636 (100%)	1439 (100%)	2075 ↑ Table Totals

ªSee the text for an explanation of income and education codes.

114

percent). Thus knowledge of a respondent's education assists in predicting respondent's income — we have discovered a relationship.

Table 6.3 also helps to illustrate another point important to all social science research. The relationship between education and income is not perfect. Some respondents reporting low education also reported high income (27.2 percent), and some reporting high education also reported low incomes (33.8 percent). Thus other factors must be associated with income: education is not the only determinant. In thoroughly understanding income levels, the researcher would want to find all other factors associated with income and to specify the precise nature of the relationships among all these independent variables. However, for now it can be said that one factor associated with income has been found, and the analyst would want to determine the magnitude or strength of this relationship.

Of course, strength of association could be conveyed simply by reporting the percent of cases falling in each category. But for large tables, especially, this would be very tedious both for the researcher and the reader, and a variety of statistical tests of association have been developed for rapid summation of such information. These tests and the conditions under which each is appropriate are discussed in the remainder of this chapter.

Tests of Association for Nominal Data

The Phi (ϕ) Coefficient

If both independent and dependent variables are nominal and dichotomous (i.e., each has only two values), a test of association often used is that known as the phi (ϕ) coefficient (sometimes called the "point correlation coefficient"). The *phi coefficient* has the advantages of being easily understood, easy to calculate, and identical in value to the widely used Pearson correlation coefficient (to be discussed in Chapter 7) and to the τ_b coefficient (discussed in a later section) in a dichotomous situation.

Referring to the cell labels shown in Table 6.1, the formula for the phi coefficient is as follows:

$$\phi = \frac{AD - BC}{\sqrt{(A + B)(C + D)(A + C)(B + D)}}$$

The phi coefficient measures the concentration of observations on either diagonal.

As an example of phi, consider the data presented in Table 6.4. It can be seen from the table that a relationship does exist between voting patterns in 1972 and 1976, most of the cases are concentrated on the main (A–D) diagonal. Again, the strength of this relationship could be reported simply by reference to percents (74.1 percent of those voting for Nixon in 1972 voted for

115

Table 6.4
Candidate Choice in 1972 by Candidate Choice in 1976

1976 Candidate Choice	1972 Candidate Choice		Total
	Nixon *A*	McGovern *B*	Total
Ford	514 (74.1%)	45 (12.6%)	559
Carter	180 (25.9%) *C*	313 (87.4%) *D*	493
Total	694 (100%)	358 (100%)	1052

Source: CPS, 1976 American National Election Study.

Ford in 1976, and so forth). Or, the single phi statistic could be used to summarize this relationship. For this table, phi would be calculated as follows (refer to the formula):

$$\phi \frac{(514)(313) - (45)(180)}{\sqrt{(559)(493)(694)(358)}}$$

$$= \frac{160{,}882 - 8100}{261{,}668}$$

$$= 0.584$$

The interpretation of the actual magnitude of the correlation coefficient will be discussed later. Based on the phi coefficient, however, it could be concluded that a substantial relationship exists between candidate choice in 1972 and candidate choice in 1976.

The Lambda Asymmetric and Symmetric Coefficients

The phi coefficient discussed above is a quick and useful way to gauge the strength of a particular relationship. Phi is deficient, however, in that it is used only in the special case of a dichotomous relationship,[1] and because it lacks an intrinsic meaning of its own (a ϕ of 0.60 can only be said to be stronger than a ϕ of 0.59 and weaker than a ϕ of 0.61).

The *lambda statistic* is a useful statistic for measuring the strength of relationships between nominal categories of data. Unlike phi, lambda (symbolized as λ) can be used for a table of any size (the independent and

[1]An extension of phi for an $r \times c$ (any size) table is Cramer's V. However, V still lacks an operational meaning.

dependent variables may have any number of values); and, it is directly interpretable. Lambda ranges in value from 0.0 to +1.0.

The lambda coefficient is based on the notion of *proportionate reduction of error*.[2] In essence, lambda allows us to answer the question: How much can the error in predicting values of the dependent variable be reduced, knowing the values of the independent variable? A lambda value of 0.37 would mean that we are able by reference to the independent variable to reduce by 37 percent our errors in predicting values of the dependent variable. It is this direct interpretation that makes lambda such a useful statistic.

In practice, lambda may be used as an *asymmetric* (directional) or *symmetric* (nondirectional) statistic. As an asymmetric statistic, lambda is used when the direction of a relationship is being predicted. When used in an asymmetric sense, lambda is usually symbolized as λ_a. As a symmetrical statistic, lambda may be used when the direction of a relationship is unknown or cannot be predicted, as when examining the relationship between husbands' and wives' party affiliation (in this case it may make sense to argue that some mutual accommodation takes place, but it would be very difficult to prove that one spouse has more influence than the other[3]). Lambda in the symmetrical sense may be symbolized simply as λ.

By way of illustration, consider the frequency distribution of party identification as reflected in the 1976 Center for Political Studies Survey presented in Table 6.5. If we were asked to individually predict the party identification for each of the 1659 respondents, knowing no other information but the distribution presented above, we would predict Democrat for each respondent. We know from the data presented that the modal category

Table 6.5
Distribution of Party Identification, 1976[a]

Party Identification	Number of Respondents	Percent of Respondents
Democrat	718	43.3
Independent	492	29.7
Republican	449	27.1
Total	1659	100.1

Source: CPS, 1976 American National Election Study.
[a]For purposes of illustration, all responses other than those reported above were deleted.

[2] See Linton C. Freeman, *Elementary Applied Statistics* (New York: John Wiley & Sons, Inc., 1965), 71–78 for a discussion of the lambda coefficient.

[3] Actually, some interesting research on this very point is available. Paul Beck and M. Kent Jennings suggest that wives are somewhat more likely to change their party preference in the direction of their husbands' than vice versa. See their article, "Parents as Middle-Persons in Political Socialization," *Journal of Politics*, 37 (February, 1975), 83–107.

Table 6.6
Respondents' Party Identification by Fathers' Party Identification:
Cell Frequencies

Respondents' Party Identification	Fathers' Party Identification			
	Democrat	Independent	Republican	Total
Democrat	601	27	90	718
Independent	251	88	153	492
Republican	123	20	306	449
Total	975	135	549	1659

Source: CPS, 1976 American National Election Study.

is Democrat and that, by definition, more cases fall in this classification than in either of the other two. We also know that in predicting Democrat for everyone we would make 941 errors (total number of non-Democrats). Still, no other category would generate as high a percent of successful predictions as Democrat — we are assured of 718 (43 percent) correct predictions.

Suppose, then, that additional information concerning partisan choice is provided. It might be suspected that father's partisan choice has an impact on respondent's party identification. Relying on information provided by the 1976 CPS American National Election Study, Table 6.6 shows the relationship between fathers' and respondents' partisan choice. Provided with this information on fathers' partisan choice, we now are in a position to more accurately predict respondents' partisan choice. If we are told that a respondent's father is a Democrat, we would predict that the respondent would also be a Democrat (since this is the modal partisan choice for all respondents whose fathers were Democrat). Similarly, we would predict all respondents whose fathers are Independent to be Independents and all whose fathers are Republican to be Republicans.

By proceeding in this fashion, we will still make a number of errors. We will mistakenly classify 374 respondents whose fathers were Democrats, 47 respondents whose fathers were Independents, and 243 respondents whose fathers were Republican. These are respondents who deviate from each modal category of fathers' partisan choice. In all, using fathers' partisan choice as an aid in predicting, we will still make a total of 664 errors (the total number of respondents whose partisan choice differed from their fathers). Recalling that we would have made 941 errors in predicting partisan choice only on the basis of the distribution of respondents' party identification (Table 6.5), we have reduced by 277 the total number of errors in prediction knowing fathers' partisan choice. Lambda is a summary statistic which tells us proportionately the extent of error reduction.

The formula for lambda can be thought of as

$$\lambda_a = \frac{\text{amount of error reduction}}{\text{amount of original error}}$$

For Table 6.6, lambda would be calculated as

$$\lambda_a = \frac{941-664}{941}$$

$$= 0.294$$

Interpreting this coefficient, it would be said that knowledge of fathers' partisan choice (the independent variable) reduces by 29.4 percent the error in predicting respondents' party selection (the dependent variable). It is this intrinsic interpretation which gives lambda its distinctive advantage over a measure of association such as phi.

A somewhat more convenient formula for calculating lambda is the following:[4]

$$\lambda_a = \frac{\Sigma f_i - F_d}{N - F_d}$$

where

$$f_i = \text{largest (modal) frequency for each value of the independent variable}$$

$$F_d = \text{largest (modal) frequency found among the marginal totals of the dependent variable}$$

$$N = \text{total number of cases}$$

For Table 6.6, lambda according to this formula would be calculated as

$$\lambda_a = \frac{(601 + 88 + 306) - 718}{1659 - 718}$$

$$= \frac{995 - 718}{941}$$

$$= 0.294$$

In those instances when the researcher is not assuming a directional relationship among the data, the symmetrical lambda will be the appropriate statistical test. The symmetrical lambda is interpreted as the proportionate amount of prediction error in both variables which can be reduced from a knowledge of the values of each variable. The computational formula for

[4]As presented in Freeman, *Elementary Applied Statistics*, p. 74.

symmetrical lambda is

$$\lambda = \frac{\sum f_r + \sum f_c - (F_r + F_c)}{2N - (F_r + F_c)}$$

where

f_r = largest (modal) frequency occurring in each row

f_c = largest (modal) frequency occurring in each column

F_r = largest (modal) frequency occurring in the row marginals

F_c = largest (modal) frequency occurring in the column marginals

N = total number of cases

As an example of λ, consider the relationship between fathers' and mothers' party identification as reported by respondents in the 1976 CPS survey. Those data are presented in Table 6.7. It can be concluded that the knowledge of fathers' and mothers' party identification (as reported by survey respondents) reduces by 64 percent the amount of error in predicting one from the other.

Table 6.7
Father's Party Identification by Mother's Party Identification

Father's Party Identification	Mother's Party Identification			
	Democratic	Independent	Republican	Total
Democrat	798	36	77	911
Independent	23	89	10	122
Republican	63	25	432	520
Total	884	150	519	1553

$$\lambda = \frac{(798+89+432) + (798+89+432) - (911+884)}{2(1553) - (911+884)}$$

$$= \frac{2638-1795}{3106-1795}$$

$$= \frac{843}{1311}$$

$$= 0.643$$

Source: CPS, 1976 American National Election Study.

Other Nominal-Level Tests of Association

Although phi and lambda are probably the most widely used measures of association for nominal variables, others are available. Various statistical packages will generate these several tests. A brief synopsis of some of the more common of these tests of association is presented here; the reader is advised to consult a general text in statistics for more detailed discussion.

Goodman and Kruskal's Tau. Goodman and Kruskal's *tau* (τ) is similar to lambda in that it is a proportionate reduction of error statistic. The method of error calculation, however, is more restrictive than lambda and thus the coefficient of association is generally smaller than that produced by the lambda routine. Tau ranges from 0 to 1.0 and can be used regardless of the number of tabular rows or columns.

Yule's Q. Yule's Q is an easily computed statistic based on the products of the diagonals and used with dichotomous variables. Q can achieve a value of 1.0 when the number of cases in any cell is reduced to 0. Some question exists as to whether such a relationship is to be considered a perfect relationship (see the discussion of gamma below).

Pearson's C. Pearson's C (sometimes called the *contingency coefficient*) is a chi-square-based test of association (chi square will be discussed in Chapter 9). Having obtained the chi-square value, Pearson's C is easy to calculate; however, it has the disadvantage of never achieving the value of 1.0, even if a perfect relationship exists. In the case of a 2×2 (dichotomous) table, the upper value limit for C is 0.71.

Tschuprow's T. Tschuprow's T is a variant of Pearson's C designed to achieve a value of 1.0 in the case of a perfect relationship. However, a 1.0 is achievable only in the case of a perfectly symmetrical table (equal number of rows and columns).

Cramer's V. Cramer's V is a variation of phi designed for use with a table of any size. Like phi, V has no operational interpretation.

Ordinal Tests of Association

In the past few years, a number of tests of association appropriate for ordinal-level data have been developed. These range in value from -1.0 (*perfect negative relationship*) to $+1.0$ (*perfect positive relationship*) and most rely upon comparisons of paired relationships in the data. The greater the number of paired relationships for which one member of the pair has a higher ranking on both variables being considered than the other member, the

Table 6.8
Hypothetical Relationship between Two
Dichotomous Ordinal Variables

Dependent Variable, Y	Independent Variable, X		Total
	Low	High	
Low	A 1	B 1	2
High	C 1	D 1	2
Total	2	2	4

stronger is the relationship in a positive direction. Similarly, the greater the number of paired relationships for which one member of the pair has a lower ranking on one variable and a higher ranking on the second than the other member of the pair, the stronger is the relationship in a negative direction.

The possible combinations of paired relationships generated by four observations (people, states, nations, etc.) is made clearer by reference to a dichotomous table such as that shown in Table 6.8. In any table, the total possible number of paired observations may be found by application of the following formula:

$$\text{total number of pairs} = N(N - 1)/2$$

where N is the total number of observations. In this hypothetical table, the total number of possible pairs of observations is six. This can be derived by application of the formula $4(4 - 1)/2 = 6$, or simply by pairing off all possible combinations of cases as is accomplished with the dashed lines in the table, (each of which represents one possible pair).

As before, the table cells in Table 6.8 are labeled A through D. In this manner it can be seen that the pair of cases in cells A and D are related so that one member of the pair (the one in cell D) is higher on both variables than the other member of the pair (the one in cell A). The pair of cases in cells B and C are related so that one member (the one in cell C) is higher on the Y variable but lower on the X variable than the other member of the pair (the one in cell B). The pairs of cases in cells A and C and in cells B and D are related in that they have tied values on the X variable (the pair in cells A and C each have the value of "low," the pair in cells B and D each have the value of "high"). The pairs of cases in cells A and B and in cells C and D are related in that they have tied values on the Y variable (the pair in cells A and B each have the value of "low," the pair in cells C and D each have the value of "high"). All this may seem somewhat confusing at first, but it is important to grasp these

Table 6.9
Hypothetical Relationship Between Two
Dichotomous Ordinal Variables

	Independent Variable, X		
Dependent Variable, Y	Low	High	Total
Low	A 4	1 B	5
High	C 2	3 D	5
Total	6	4	10

total numbers of pairs $= 10(9)/2$

$= 45$

concepts, since all the ordinal tests of associations to be discussed in this chapter are based on such paired relationships.

Another example and an elaboration on the foregoing discussion will further clarify these points. Table 6.9 presents a different relationship for a similar hypothetical example. Applying the formula, it can be seen that there are 45 possible pairs among these 10 observations. To calculate the various ordinal statistics, we must determine how these 45 pairs relate to each other. There are several symbols conventionally used to represent all possible combinations of pairings discussed above.

Pairing Symbols

P Pairs. It is conventional to label all pairs in the table for which one member of the pair is ranked higher on both variables than the other member as *P pairs*. These are also called *concordant pairs*. In the example above, these are the pairs formed by the observations falling in cells *A* and *D*. The product of the two (4 × 3) yields a total of 12 concordant pairs. The greater the proportionate number of concordant pairs in any table, the stronger will be the relationship in a *positive* direction. If all observations fell on this (the main) diagonal, the correlation would be $+1.0$.

Q Pairs. It is convenient to label all pairs in the table for which one member of the pair is ranked higher on one variable and lower on the other than the other member of the pair as *Q pairs.* These also are called *discordant pairs*. In the example above, these are the pairs formed by the observations falling in cells *B* and *C*. The product of the two (1 × 2) reveals a total of two discordant pairs. The greater the proportionate number of discordant pairs in any table, the stronger will be the relationship in a *negative* direction. If all observations fell on this (the off) diagonal, the correlation would be -1.0.

123

X Pairs. Those pairs of observations in a table tied on the *X* (independent) variable may be symbolized as the *X pairs.* These are those pairs having the same value on the *X* variable but different values on the *Y* variable. In the example above, these are the pairs formed by the observations falling in cells *A* and *C* and those falling in cells *B* and *D.* The product of cells *A* and *C* (4 × 2) added to the product of cells *B* and *D* (1 × 3) yields a total of 11 pairs tied on the *X* variable.

Y Pairs. Those pairs of observations in a table tied on the *Y* (dependent) variable may be symbolized as the *Y pairs.* These are those pairs having the same value on the *Y* variable but different values on the *X* variable. In the example above, these are the pairs formed by the observations falling in cells *A* and *B* and those falling in cells *C* and *D.* The product of cells *A* and *B* (4 × 1) added to the product of cells *C* and *D* (2 × 3) renders a total of 10 pairs tied on the *Y* variable.

Z Pairs. Finally, there are those pairs of observations tied on both the *X* and *Y* variable. These pairs, not used in the calculation of the statistics discussed below but logically exhaustive of the number of paired relationships, are those pairs of observations falling in the same cells and for Table 6.9 can be calculated according to the formula

$$Z = \tfrac{1}{2}\left[A(A-1) + B(B-1) + (C-1) + D(D-1)\right]$$

$$= \tfrac{1}{2}\left[4(3) + 1(0) + 2(1) + 3(2)\right]$$

$$= \tfrac{1}{2}(20)$$

$$= 10$$

Thus the total number of possible paired relationships in Table 6.9 is

P (concordant) pairs	= 12
Q (discordant) pairs	= 2
X pairs	= 11
Y pairs	= 10
Z pairs	= 10
Total pairs	= 45

This is, of course, the same number of pairs (45) as was derived from the general formula presented in Table 6.9.

Prediction and Shape of the Relationship

Having determined the possible pairings of observations, the actual calculation of the ordinal tests of association is a very simple task. However, before applying such tests, the researcher should be certain of the nature of the model (or hypothesis) being examined. A number of factors are related to

124

the type of model being examined,[5] but two are particularly important. The first relates to the predictive nature of the relationship, the second to the shape of the distribution.

Considering *prediction*, the same issue arises as that discussed in our consideration of the lambda coefficient. Here, the question is whether the hypothesis being tested is symmetric or asymmetric. An asymmetrical relationship, it will be recalled, posits one variable as the independent variable and the second as the dependent variable. It is assumed that variation in the independent variable is at least one possible "cause" of variation in the dependent variable. A symmetrical relationship makes no assumption about the direction of causation between two variables; there simply is the assumption of association.

The *shape of the relationship*, as the term is used here, refers to the nature of the model being tested, or the conditions under which a perfect association between the independent and dependent variables is said to exist. A strong monotonic model requires an increase in the values of one variable as values of the other increase. A weak monotonic model is satisfied when the values of one variable increase or remain at the same level as the values of the second variable increase.

Tests

Having calculated the possible categories of paired relationships in the table and determined the appropriate model to be tested, the various ordinal-level tests can be calculated and applied. These various tests, their formulas, and the conditions under which they are appropriately used are discussed below.

Gamma. Gamma (γ) is used as a symmetrical (nondirectional) weak mono-tonic test for a table of any size. Referring to the symbols for paired relationships presented above, gamma is calculated as

$$\gamma = \frac{P - Q}{P + Q}$$

Like lambda, gamma is a proportionate reduction-in-error statistic.[6] For the example presented in Table 6.9, the gamma value would be

$$\gamma = \frac{12 - 2}{12 + 2}$$

$$= 0.714$$

[5] For a thorough discussion of all these factors, see Herbert F. Weisberg, "Models of Statistical Relationship," *American Political Science Review*, 68 (December, 1974), 1638–1655.

[6] This interpretation of gamma refers to the predictability of ordered pairs, not individual cases.

125

Table 6.10
Attitudes Toward Government Aid to Minorities by
Liberalism-Conservatism Measure[a]

Attitudes Toward Government Aid to Minorities	Liberalism–Conservatism		
	Liberal	Moderate	Conservative
Government should help minority groups	185	169	115
In between	61	148	122
Minority groups should help themselves	88	206	317

Source: CPS, 1976 American National Election Study.

[a]The original seven-point scales recorded by the Center for Political Studies for both of these items were collapsed to three values for the purpose of illustrating the calculation of gamma, thus resulting in a nine-cell table. However, reducing the number of values and thus reducing the number of tabular rows and columns is likely to result in an increase in the number of tied pairs and (since gamma is calculated on untied pairs) a reduction in the amount of information used to calculate gamma. It is usually desirable when calculating gamma to have as many values per variable as possible.

The calculation of gamma is somewhat more tedious in a nondichotomous situation. Consider Table 6.10, which has nine cells relating attitudes toward government aid to minority groups with a measure of liberalism-conservatism as these were measured and reported in the 1976 CPS American National Election Study. In such a situation, the value for P in the gamma formula can be obtained by (1) multiplying each cell frequency by the sum of all cell frequencies occurring below and to the right of it and, (2) summing the product of these calculations. For Table 6.10, this becomes:

$$P = 185(148 + 122 + 206 + 317) + 61(206 + 317)$$
$$+ \ 169(122 + 317) + 148(317)$$
$$= 146{,}705 + 31{,}903 + 74{,}191 + 46{,}916$$
$$= 299{,}715$$

The value of Q can be obtained by (1) multiplying each cell frequency by the sum of all cell frequencies occurring below and to the left of it, and (2) summing the product of these calculations. For Table 6.10, this becomes

$$Q = 115(148 + 61 + 206 + 88) + 122(206 + 88)$$
$$+ \ 169(61 + 88) + 148(88)$$
$$= 57{,}845 + 35{,}868 + 25{,}181 + 13{,}024$$
$$= 131{,}918$$

Gamma for this table, then, is calculated as

$$\gamma = \frac{299{,}715 - 131{,}918}{299{,}715 + 131{,}918}$$

$$= \frac{167{,}797}{431{,}633}$$

$$= 0.39$$

As another example of the use of gamma, consider Joel Aberbach's work dealing with feelings of political powerlessness and education.[7] Specifically, Aberbach was interested in the impact of education on stated reasons for power dissatisfaction. Examining groups of white and black Americans who felt dissatisfied with their power position, Aberbach found the information listed in Table 6.11. The reader will note that two separate tables (and two separate gamma coefficients) are presented in this table. One represents the responses of 129 black Americans; the other, responses of 193 white Americans. The gamma coefficients indicate that for both races some relationship between education and perceived reasons for power dissatisfaction exists. The college-educated appear more likely to blame system inadequacies (and less likely to blame personal inadequacies) for personal powerlessness. Concerning blacks, Aberbach concluded: "My data... indicate that college educated blacks have

Table 6.11
Power Dissatisfaction Reasons by Education and By Race
(percent)

Stated Reason for Power Dissatisfaction	Blacks: Education			Whites: Education		
	Grade School	High School	College	Grade School	High School	College
Personal inadequacies	29	39	14	30	20	12
Isolation or group weakness	46	35	27	39	28	19
Political system problems	25	27	59	30	52	68
Total %	100	101	100	99	100	99
Total N:	24	83	22	33	103	57
		$\gamma = 0.26$			$\gamma = 0.36$	

Source: Joel D. Aberbach, "Power Consciousness: A Comparative Analysis," American Political Science Review, 71 (December, 1977), 1554.

[7]Joel D. Aberbach, "Power Consciousness: A Comparative analysis," *American Political Science Review*, 71 (December, 1977), 1544–1560.

127

broken the chains of self-blame which may once have gripped them, but that high school educated blacks are still more likely than comparable whites to blame an unsatisfactory power situation on themselves and not on problems with the political system."[8]

Gamma is an especially easy coefficient to calculate in the case of a 2×2 table when its simplified formula is equivalent to Yule's Q (mentioned above):

$$\gamma \text{ (or Yule's } Q) = \frac{AD \times BC}{AD + BC}$$

where A, B, C, and D refer to cell placements as labeled in Tables 6.8 and 6.9.

Gamma is a very useful statistic in that its proportionate reduction of error characteristic renders it intuitively understandable. Gamma's weakness, however, is that in stressing discordant (Q) and concordant (P) pairs, it ignores pairs that are tied (X, Y, and Z). As a result, the gamma coefficient may be calculated on a comparatively few number of paired observations, and also will yield the highest value of any of the ordinal coefficients (except, of course, in those instances when all the coefficients result in a value of 1.0 or 0). This can become especially troublesome in the case of a 2×2 table where any vacant cell will result in a gamma of 1.0. Thus other ordinal tests of association may be considered.

Kendall's τ_b *and* τ_c. Tau-b and tau-c (τ_b and τ_c) are used as symmetrical (nondirectional) strong monotonic tests. Referring to the symbols for paired relationships presented above, τ_b is calculated as

$$\tau_b = \frac{P - Q}{\sqrt{(P + Q + Y)(P + Q + X)}}$$

For the example presented in Table 6.9, τ_b would be

$$\tau_b = \frac{12 - 2}{\sqrt{(12 + 2 + 10)(12 + 2 + 11)}}$$

$$= 0.408$$

Tau-b will achieve a maximum value of ± 1.0 only in the case of perfectly symmetrical tabular dimensions (equal number of rows and columns). If the table being examined is 2×2 (two rows and two columns), 3×3, 4×4, 5×5, and so on, τ_b will achieve a ± 1.0 if a perfect relationship exists. However, τ_b

[8] *Ibid.*, p. 1555.

128

will not reach 1.0 when calculated with any other shape of table. Tau-c corrects for this and its formula is as follows:

$$\tau_c = \frac{P - Q}{\frac{1}{2}N^2\,[(m-1)/m]}$$

where

$N = $ total number of cases

$m = $ smaller of rows or columns (in a 5×3 table, $m = 3$)

Tau-c, then, should be used as a substitute for τ_b when considering rectangularly shaped tables; however, in practice the actual magnitude of the differences between the values of τ_b and τ_c is typically very slight.[9]

An interesting use of the tau statistic is provided by Benjamin Page and Richard Brody in their examination of the relationship between the public's 1968 attitudes toward Vietnam policy alternatives and voter choice in that year.[10] Their results from a nationwide sample are given in Table 6.12. Page

Table 6.12
Vietnam Policy Preference and the Major Party Vote, 1968

1968 Vote	Opinion on Vietnam		
	Pull Out Entirely	Keep Soldiers, Try to End Fighting	Take Stronger Stand, Even if It Means Invading North Vietnam
Nixon	88 (51%)	174 (47%)	180 (62%)
Humphrey	86 (49%)	194 (53%)	109 (38%)
Total N:	174	368	289
Total %:	100%	100%	100%

$$\tau_b = -0.10$$
$$\tau_c = -0.06$$

Source: Benjamin I. Page and Richard A. Brody, "Policy Voting and the Electoral Process: The Vietnam War Issue," American Political Science Review, 66 (September, 1972), 983. Page and Brody report τ_b; the present author calculated τ_c.

[9]The argument here follows the distinction usually made between τ_b and τ_c. See Robert H. Somers, "A New Asymmetric Measure of Association for Ordinal Variables," American Sociological Review, 27 (1962), 799–811. Weisberg, however, points out that the choice between τ_b and τ_c involves substantive as well as technical issues. See the discussion that follows in this chapter and especially Herbert F. Weisberg, "Models of Statistical Relationship."

[10]Benjamin I. Page and Richard A. Brody, "Policy Voting and the Electoral Process: The Vietnam War Issue," American Political Science Review, 66 (September, 1972), 979–995.

and Brody report the τ_b for this table to be -0.10. The τ_c calculated for this same table is found to be -0.06. Both are very low values and Page and Brody are justified in concluding: "It is apparent that Vietnam policy preferences did not have a great effect on voting for the major party candidates in 1968."[11]

Somers' d_{yx}. Gamma and the tau coefficients are symmetric in their treatment of the variables. That is, no distinction is made between independent and dependent variables. Somers suggests a refinement of these coefficients which is asymmetric in interpretation.[12] d_{yx} (as it is symbolized) is considered appropriate for the test of an asymmetric relationship. (Somers also argues that d_{yx} is the ordinal analog of the ordinary regression coefficient, a topic that will be discussed in Chapter 7.) Thus, when distinguishing between the independent and dependent variables, or specifying one variable as the cause of another, Somers' d_{yx} would appropriately be used. Referring again to the symbols for paired relationships presented above, the formula for d_{yx} becomes

$$d_{yx} = \frac{P - Q}{P + Q + Y}$$

For the hypothetical relationship presented in Table 6.9, d_{yx} would be calculated as follows:

$$d_{yx} = \frac{12 - 2}{12 + 2 + 10}$$

$$= 0.417$$

An example of the actual use of d_{yx} is provided by John Sullivan and Robert O'Connor in their examination of the relationship between preelection attitudes of candidates to the U.S. House of Representatives and postelection roll-call voting patterns of those successfully elected.[13] Their findings for nonincumbents in the area of open housing are presented in Table 6.13. On the basis of these data (and the d_{yx} value of 0.58), Sullivan and O'Connor conclude that a relationship between preelection attitudes and postelection behavior (roll-call voting) does exist. They state: "Generally the winners voted as our preelection [attitudinal] scores indicated they would."[14]

[11] *Ibid.*, p. 982.

[12] Somers, "A New Asymmetric Measure of Association for Ordinal Variables."

[13] John L. Sullivan and Robert E. O'Connor, "Electoral Choice and Popular Control of Public Policy: The Case of the 1966 House Elections," *American Political Science Review*, 66 (December, 1972), 1256–1268.

[14] *Ibid.*, p. 1263.

Table 6.13

Relationship Between Scale Scores on Preelection Open-Housing Attitudes and Postelection Roll-Call Behavior: Nonincumbents

Postelection Roll-Call Scale Score	Preelection Attitude Scale Scores			
	Liberal	Moderate	Conservative	Total
1	15	7	7	29
2	0	0	1	1
3	4	6	39	49
Total	19	13	47	79
	$d_{yx} = 0.58$			

Source: John L. Sullivan and Robert E. O'Connor, "Electoral Choice and Popular Control of Public Policy: The Case of the 1966 House Elections," *American Political Science Review*, 66 (December, 1972), 1263. Data reported by Sullivan and O'Connor are based on a survey conducted in 1966. The dependent-variable, roll-call scale scores, range from liberal voting (1) to conservative voting (3) patterns.

Summary: Selecting the Most Appropriate Statistic

We now have presented what may seem to be a bewildering array of nominal- and ordinal-level measures of association. The student may well ask whether consideration of all these statistics is really necessary. In answering this question, let us consider once again the hypothetical distribution presented in Table 6.9. That table is reproduced in Table 6.14, together with the values of the ordinal tests of association calculated for this table. The information presented in Table 6.14 illustrates a very important point about

Table 6.14

Various Ordinal Tests of Association for Hypothetical Relationship Between Two Dichotomous Ordinal Variables

Dependent Variable, Y	Independent Variable, X		
	Low	High	Total
Low	A 4	1 B	5
High	C 2	3 D	5
Total	6	4	10

$$\gamma \text{ (or } Q) = 0.714$$
$$\tau_b = 0.408$$
$$d_{yx} = 0.417$$

131

the nature of the various correlation coefficients. As can be seen, the coefficients may vary considerably in magnitude. Gamma, as always, is the largest of the ordinal coefficients. Had cell B contained no cases (and all four cases with high values on variable X had fallen in cell D), γ would have been 1.0 Tau-b in this instance would have been calculated as 0.617, and d_{yx} would have been 0.667.

Thus the researcher must be very cautious in using and interpreting correlation coefficients, which can vary greatly in magnitude. The beginning researcher (as well as, sometimes, the more experienced) may be tempted to select the coefficient that best demonstrates his or her own preassessment of the relationship being examined. Those seeking a large relationship, for whatever reason, might report gamma to the neglect of the other coefficients, and those expecting to find a slight relationship might report only the smallest coefficient generated. By careful selection and reporting of coefficients, the researcher may attempt to maximize his or her own expectations.

This, of course, would be an inappropriate and ill-advised use of correlation analysis. The researcher has an obligation to report the appropriate statistic for the relationship being examined, regardless of whether that statistic supports the researcher's own theories and hypotheses.

How, then, does one determine the appropriate statistic to be applied in a particular research situation? This is not always an easy question to answer. Often scholars will say that the all-around superior test of association for nominal data is lambda, and that the all-around superior test of association for ordinal data is τ_b. While the student would not go far wrong in generally applying these two coefficients, additional issues may be considered in selecting the appropriate statistic for the research at hand.

The choice of the correct statistic is in part a technical issue and in part an issue that concerns the substantive nature of the theory being tested. The technical issues — those dealing with nature of the data, shape of the table, and so forth — are easy to resolve. Nominal data require tests designed for that level (phi, lambda, etc.). Tests designed for ordinal data (gamma, tau, d_{yx}) are appropriately used at that level. Some tests are appropriately used only for 2×2 tables, some for perfectly symmetrical tables, and some for tables of any size. These issues can generally be resolved simply by inspecting the data, and, in fact, many of the packaged statistical programs make some of these decisions automatically.[15]

The substantive nature of the theory being tested is much more difficult to assess. Here, the question becomes: Just what does the theory we are testing say about the expected relationship between the variables? What, in other words, is the precise nature of the model being examined? Does the model specify a one-way causal influence? If so, only an asymmetrical test such as λ_a or d_{yx} would be appropriate. Does the model specify that each and every

---

[15]SPSS, for example, generates phi only for 2×2 tables, and Cramer's V for tables of any other size.

change in the level of one variable should be associated with a corresponding change in the level of the second (in which case a strong monotonic statistic such as τ_b or d_{yx} would be appropriate), or does the model allow for the values of one variable to remain stable as values of the other change (in which case a weak monotonic statistic such as gamma would be appropriate)? These questions can only be answered by careful consideration of the theory being examined. The student should seek answers to these questions and precisely specify his or her model *before* applying the tests of association. In some instances, gamma may be the appropriate statistic for the model being tested. In other instances, other coefficients may be appropriate. Answers to the question of model specification will dictate the appropriate test to be used.[16]

Exercises

1. Consider the following hypothetical relationship between education (measured as low, medium, and high) and levels of political information:

Level of Political Information	Education		
	Low	Medium	High
Very low	80 (40%)	50 (20%)	0 (0%)
Fairly low	60 (30%)	50 (20%)	35 (10%)
Average	30 (15%)	50 (20%)	70 (20%)
Fairly high	20 (10%)	50 (20%)	35 (10%)
Very high	10 (5%)	50 (20%)	210 (60%)
Total *N:*	200	250	350
Total %:	100%	100%	100%

a. In the above table, the independent variable most probably is _____.
   The dependent variable in the above table most probably is _____.
b. Explain the 210 and the 60% values found in the lower right cell and the 80 and 40% values found in the upper left cell. What (if anything) do these values tell you about those having high and low levels of education? What (if anything) do these values tell you about those having very high and very low levels of political information?
c. What is the apparent overall relationship between education and levels of political information as revealed by this table? What evidence supports this conclusion?

[16]This argument has been presented most forcefully by Weisberg, "Models of Statistical Relationship."

133

    d. What statistical measure of association do you believe would be most appropriate to apply to this table? Why is this so?

2. Based on data supplied by the 1972 and 1976 CPS American National Election Studies the following relationships between sex and strength of partisan identification were found in those years:

Strength of Party ID	1972		Strength of Party ID	1976	
	Male	Female		Male	Female
Strong	291 (42%)	384 (38%)	Strong	209 (39%)	337 (39%)
Not Very Strong	403 (58%)	636 (62%)	Not Very Strong	321 (61%)	532 (61%)
Total N:	694	1020	Total N:	530	869
Total %:	100%	100%	Total %:	100%	100%

    a. By inspecting the frequency and percent cell entries in the above tables, what can be said about the relationship between sex and strength of partisan attachment in these two election years?

    b. Calculate the phi (ϕ) value for each table.

    c. How does the phi value assist in understanding these relationships? How "strong" is the relationship in each year and does what ever difference which may result between the phi values for the two election years appear to you to be important? Why or why not?

3. The following table presents the relationship between a measure of respondents' liberalism-conservatism (measured here as a three-point scale) and opinion as to whether or not civil rights leaders are pushing too fast as revealed in the CPS 1976 American National Election Study:

Civil Rights Leaders are Pushing	Liberal	Moderate	Conservative
Too Fast	89 (26%)	232 (43%)	254 (45%)
About Right	188 (55%)	263 (49%)	288 (51%)
Too Slowly	67 (19%)	42 (8%)	19 (3%)
Total N:	344	537	561
Total %:	(100%)	(100%)	(99%)

    a. By inspection, alone, what can be said about the general relationship between liberalism-conservatism and opinion as to whether civil rights leaders are pushing too fast as those variables are measured and presented in the above table?

134

b. Calculate the gamma coefficient for this table.
c. How does the gamma coefficient assist in understanding this relationship? What does the "sign" of the gamma value reveal about this relationship?
d. What other statistical measures of association might be computed for this table and how do you believe they would compare in magnitude with the gamma coefficient? Why? Under what circumstances might those other measures be more appropriate than gamma?

7

EXAMINING RELATIONSHIPS: BIVARIATE TESTS FOR INTERVAL DATA

Interval-level data permit a degree of precision in stating relationships that is not possible with nominal or ordinal data. Statistical techniques designed for use with interval data indicate the magnitude and the direction (positive or negative) of the relationship between two variables. These techniques also permit the mathematical expression of one variable (the dependent variable) as a function of the other (the independent variable). Using these techniques, we are able to predict with a certain degree of accuracy (to be measured by the correlation coefficient) the effect of unit changes in the independent variable on changes in the dependent variable. Let us briefly introduce some of the terms and concepts that will be examined in this chapter.

In a *linear* model (discussed below), the relationship between two interval variables is defined by the *regression equation*, $Y = a + bX$ where X is a given value of the independent variable and Y the predicted value of the dependent variable. The values of a (*intercept*) and b (*slope*) are constants to be calculated. The *correlation coefficient* is a measure of the extent to which the regression equation accurately predicts all values of Y.

By permitting the expression of one variable as a function of another and thereby enhancing our ability to *predict* the values of one variable given the values of another, interval-level tests are considered to be much more "powerful" than those previously discussed. Additionally, interval-level techniques greatly facilitate examination of the relationship between two variables *controlling for* the influence of one or more additional variables.

Because of the attractive features of interval-level techniques, researchers are often tempted to apply these techniques in situations where the criteria for interval-level data are not fully met. In reading political science journals and papers presented at political science conferences, one often finds examples of the use of interval-level statistical techniques with ordinal data and sometimes even with dichotomous nominal data. Currently, there is some debate among social scientists as to just how great a distortion results from the application of interval-level tests with non interval data. Some believe that, with caution, the tests may be applied to lower-level data;[1] others believe that the risk is too severe.[2] The position taken here is that at least at the beginning research stage, the student should make every effort to apply the most appropriate statistic to the level of data being examined. This rule may be relaxed as the student becomes more familiar with data analytic techniques, the assumptions that are being made, and the strengths and weaknesses of the various routines.

The Regression Equation

Regression analysis is used to improve our ability to predict the values of a particular variable. When examining nominal data and the lambda statistic, it was seen that given the distribution of a single variable, the best prediction for any value of that variable is the mode. If most of our respondents in a sample of 1000 are Democrats, the best guess of the values of that distribution would be Democrat.

Similarly, with interval data the best guess of the values of a single distribution is the mean of that distribution. In a statistical sense the mean score of a distribution of interval data minimizes the variance of error in estimating all values of that distribution.

An example will clarify these points. Suppose that we are interested in examining percent of voting turnout in a group of 10 American states and, for purposes of analysis, have collected from those states the percent of the voting age population casting votes in the 1976 election for U.S. Representatives. This information is presented in Table 7.1.

We saw in Chapter 5 that the variance of a distribution may be defined as

$$\sigma^2 = \frac{\Sigma(Y_i - \bar{Y})^2}{N}$$

READER NOTE: Y's have been substituted for the X's used in Chapter 5 to facilitate consistency with the use of X and Y symbols in the remainder of this chapter.

We can calculate the variance for our voting-turnout data (Table 7.1) according to the formula above as shown in Table 7.2.

---

[1] See Sanford Labovitz, "The Assignment of Numbers to Rank Order Categories, "*American Sociological Review*, 35 (1970), 515–524.

[2] David M. Grether, "Correlations with Ordinal Data," *Journal of Econometrics*, 2 (1974), 241–246.

Table 7.1
Percent of Voting Age Population Voting: U.S. House of Representatives, 1976[a]

State	Percent Voting Turnout[b]
Massachusetts	56
New York	46
Wisconsin	61
Missouri	57
Arkansas	22
Mississippi	41
Utah	70
Idaho	60
Louisiana	40
Florida	33

Mean percent of Voting turnout = 48.6

Source: Statistical Abstract of the United States, 1977.

[a] For simplicity of illustration, only 10 states are included in this and subsequent examples. In an actual research situation, the researcher would wish to include all 50 states in the analysis.

[b] All voting percents rounded to nearest whole percent.

Table 7.2
Calculation of the Variance

State	Percent Voting Turnout, Y	$Y - \bar{Y}$	$(Y - \bar{Y})^2$
Massachusetts	56	7.4	54.8
New York	46	-2.6	6.8
Wisconsin	61	12.4	153.8
Missouri	57	8.4	70.6
Arkansas	22	-26.6	707.6
Mississippi	41	-7.6	57.8
Utah	70	21.4	458.0
Idaho	60	11.4	130.0
Louisiana	40	-8.6	74.0
Florida	33	-15.6	243.4
Total			1956.8

$$\sigma^2 = \frac{\Sigma(Y - \bar{Y})^2}{N}$$

$$= \frac{1956.8}{10}$$

$$= 195.68$$

Table 7.3
Substitution of 40 for the Mean Value in Calculating the Variance

State	Percent Voting Turnout, Y	Y − 40	(Y − 40)²
Massachusetts	56	16	256
New York	46	6	36
Wisconsin	61	21	441
Missouri	57	17	289
Arkansas	22	−18	324
Mississippi	41	1	1
Utah	70	30	900
Idaho	60	20	400
Louisiana	40	0	0
Florida	33	−7	49
Total			2696

$$\sigma^2_{40} = \frac{\Sigma(Y-40)^2}{N}$$

$$= \frac{2696}{10}$$

$$= 269.6$$

Here σ^2_{40} implies the substitution of 40 for the mean value in calculating the variance.

The variance for this particular distribution is found to be 195.68. As it turns out, the mean of the squared deviations of all observations from the mean of a particular distribution is less than the mean of the squared deviations of all the observations from any other value. Arbitrarily selecting 40 (rather than the mean of 48.6), the variance for this array of data would be calculated as shown in Table 7.3.

If the value of 50 had been selected for our voting-turnout distribution, the variance around this value would have been calculated as 198. By substituting other values for the mean, the student should satisfy himself or herself that *no other value yields as low a variance score for a particular distribution as the mean of that distribution.* Stated another way, the mean yields the smallest average squared deviation (error) from all the scores of a particular distribution. Put simply, having no other information, the mean of a distribution is the most efficient predictor of all the values of that distribution. The extent of error in guessing values based on the mean is represented by the variance, but no other *single* predicted value will result in as small an error factor. The mean, then, becomes the standard by which we gauge the predictive ability of other variables. To be useful, predictive variables must be at least as efficient in estimating values of the dependent variable as is the dependent variable's own mean. Regression analysis is a technique that seeks to minimize the error factor by reference to knowledge of another variable.[3]

The mean percent voting turnout in our group of 10 states, then, is 48.6, and the variance is found to be 195.68. Can we reduce this variance (error) factor by reference to another variable? Assume that we also have collected information on percent of the population having completed 12 grades or more of education in each of the 10 states. We might, in fact, be testing the hypothesis that voting turnout at the state level is, in part at least, a function of state educational levels.[4] We might expect states with higher proportions of more educated citizens to experience higher levels of voter turnout. The question we are asking is whether educational status (measured here as percent completing 12 or more grades of school) is a better predictor of voter turnout (here measured as percent voting in the 1976 congressional elections) at the state level than is simply the mean percent voting turnout of these 10 states. Adding this information to our distribution of states, the result might appear as in Table 7.4.

The Scattergram

Relationships such as that presented in Table 7.4 are often displayed graphically in the form of a scattergram. A *scattergram* depicts the relationship between the two variables by plotting on intersecting axes the

Table 7.4
Percent of State Completing 12 Years of School and Percent Voting Turnout

State	Percent Completing 12 Years of School, X	Percent Voting Turnout, Y
Massachusetts	59[a]	56
New York	53	46
Wisconsin	55	61
Missouri	49	57
Arkansas	40	22
Mississippi	41	41
Utah	67	70
Idaho	60	60
Louisiana	42	40
Florida	53	33

Source: Statistical Abstract of the United States, 1977.
[a]All percents rounded to nearest whole percent.

[3]An excellent discussion of regression analysis is provided in Linton C. Freeman, *Elementary Applied Statistics* (New York: John Wiley & Sons, Inc., 1965), pp. 89–107.

[4]For a thorough discussion of those factors associated with voting turnout in the American states, see Jae-On Kim, John R. Petrocik, and Stephen N. Enokson, "Voter Turnout Among the American States: Systemic and Individual Components," *American Political Science Review*, 69 (March, 1975), 107–123.

points representing the X and Y observations for each case (here states). Utah, for example, has an X (educational status) coordinate of 67 and a Y (percent voting turnout) coordinate of 70. Moving out along the horizontal (X) axis to 67 and up the vertical (Y) axis to 70, we locate the point representing these coordinates. This point for Utah may be written as $X = 67$, $Y = 70$, or, more simply, as (67, 70). Similarly, points representing the X and Y values for all states could be plotted and the resulting scattergram would appear as shown in Figure 7.1. The plotted positions of all 10 states for these two variables are shown in the figure.

It always is a good idea to examine the scattergram of any relationship before proceeding with the techniques of analysis discussed in this chapter. The scattergram itself will provide a rough indication of the *nature* of the relationship. If the general flow of the plotted points is upward and to the right, the relationship is "positive" — as one variable increases in value, so does the other. If the plotted points appear to be randomly spread, there is little or no relationship between the variables. Also, the scattergram indicates the *shape* of the relationship. If the plotted points are distributed so that the values of the dependent variable appear to increase or decrease in relation to the independent variable at a more-or-less consistent and constant rate, a *linear relationship* is said to exist. If a nonlinear relationship is discovered, the techniques discussed in this chapter would be inappropriate.

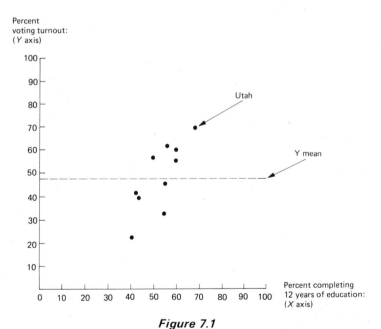

Figure 7.1

Scattergram of relationship between percent of voting turnout and percent completing 12 years of education. The Y mean is shown by the horizontal broken line.

141

When constructing scattergrams, it is customary, as illustrated in Figure 7.1, for the vertical axis to represent the dependent (or Y) variable and for the horizontal axis to represent the independent (or X) variable. Examining Figure 7.1, it can be seen that for this scattergram the mean percent voting turnout for all 10 states (48.6) is represented by a single horizontal line. As discussed above, this mean score provides the "best guess" for all values of Y (the dependent variable) when no other information is provided. Although there is considerable variation about this mean score (i.e., the line comes close to the scores of some states but is far from the scores of some others), no *horizontal* line would result in as small a variance score (which was calculated above as 195.68).

Now, however, we have additional information regarding each state: percent of population completing 12 grades of education. The question that regression seeks to answer is: Can this new information be used to construct a new line that will be closer to all the points plotted in Figure 7.1 than is the line representing the mean? Put another way, can knowledge of educational status help construct a line that will reduce the variation in percent of voter turnout for these 10 states?

As it turns out, the formula defining such a line (in the case of linear relationship) is as follows:

$$Y_p = a + bX$$

In this equation, X refers to values of the independent variable and Y_p to predicted values of the dependent variable. In this sample, the X values are those *actual* values of the independent variable (educational status) for each state. The Y_p values will be those *predicted* values of the dependent variable (percent voting turnout) for each state for each value of X. The constants a and b will have to be determined. The constant a is called the Y *intercept* because it defines the location where the new line should intercept with the Y axis. The symbol b is called the *slope* (or regression coefficient) and is interpreted as the average change in the dependent variable associated with a 1-unit change in the independent variable. A b value of 2, for example, would mean that every unit increase in the independent variable corresponds to an average increase of 2 units in the dependent variable. If our dependent variable were annual income and our independent variable years of education, a b value of 1500 would imply that each additional year of education results in a higher average yearly salary of $1500.

Having calculated a and b, we can insert in our scattergram the new *least-squares line* — the straight line that will minimize the variation in the dependent variable. One formula for calculating b is as follows:

$$b = \frac{N(\Sigma\,XY) - (\Sigma\,X)(\Sigma\,Y)}{N(\Sigma\,X^2) - (\Sigma\,X)^2}$$

The value of a may be calculated by application of either

$$a = \frac{\Sigma Y - b \Sigma X}{N}$$

or

$$a = \bar{Y} - b\bar{X}$$

For the data on state educational status and percent voting turnout presented in Table 7.4, b and a would be calculated as presented in Table 7.5.

Table 7.5
Calculating the Simple Regression Equation

State	Percent Completing 12 Years of School, X	Percent Voting Turnout, Y	X·Y	X²
Massachusetts	59	56	3,304	3,481
New York	53	46	2,438	2,809
Wisconsin	55	61	3,355	3,025
Missouri	49	57	2,793	2,401
Arkansas	40	22	880	1,600
Mississippi	41	41	1,681	1,681
Utah	67	70	4,690	4,489
Idaho	60	60	3,600	3,600
Louisiana	42	40	1,680	1,764
Florida	53	33	1,749	2,809
	$\Sigma X = 519$	$\Sigma Y = 486$	$\Sigma XY = 26,170$	$\Sigma X^2 = 27,659$

$$b = \frac{10(26,170) - 519(486)}{10(27,659) - 269,361} \qquad a = \frac{486 - 1.31(519)}{10}$$

$$= \frac{9466}{7229} \qquad\qquad = \frac{-193.89}{10}$$

$$= 1.31 \quad \text{(rounded)} \qquad\qquad = -19.39$$

or

$$a = 48.6 - 1.31(51.9)$$

$$= -19.39$$

Thus, $\quad Y_p = -19.39 + 1.31(X)$

Table 7.6
Application of the Regression Equation

State	Percent Completing 12 Years of School, X	Predicted Percent Voting Turnout, Y_p
Massachusetts	59	57.9
New York	53	50.0
Wisconsin	55	52.7
Missouri	49	44.8
Arkansas	40	33.0
Mississippi	41	34.3
Utah	67	68.4
Idaho	60	59.2
Louisiana	42	35.6
Florida	53	50.0

$$Y_p = a + bX$$
$$= -19.39 + 1.31\,(X)$$

We now have determined the constants (a and b) which are to be utilized in the regression equation. For linear relationships, these constants provide our "best guess" of values of the dependent variable (here percent voting turnout) given values of the independent variable (state educational status). For each value of the independent variable, the predicted value of the dependent variable would appear as shown in Table 7.6.

The regression routine, it should be obvious, provides a powerful predictive tool. We are using information on one variable (percent of population completing 12 or more grades of education) to predict expected scores on another variable (percent voting turnout). We know, of course, the precise turnout in our group of 10 states; but this information allows us now to state the effect on voting turnout associated with changing levels of educational status. It can be said for this group of states that an increase of 1 percent of the population of a state having completed 12 years of education was, on the average, associated with an increase of voting turnout in the 1976 congressional election of 1.3 percent. Further, if this sample of states were assumed to be representative of all states, this information can be used to predict the expected percent voting turnout in other states. Selecting another state and finding its percent of the population having completed 12 grades of school to be 45, we would predict that state's voting in the 1976 congressional election to be $Y_p = -19.4 + 1.3(45) = 39.1$ percent. But, remember, this is a predicted value; the actual percent turnout is likely to have been somewhat different.

The question that arises next is: Just how accurate is our prediction equation? That is, how good is our prediction of the percent voting turnout based on the percent of persons in the state who have completed 12 or more years of school? One gauge of accuracy can be provided simply by inserting into the scattergram the regression line generated by the regression formula.

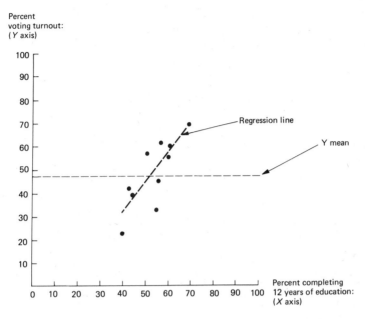

Figure 7.2

Plotting the regression line for the data in Figure 7.1. The regression line does not extend beyond the minimum and maximum values of the independent variable (X axis), illustrating one of the important points of regression analysis. The regression equation is to be used to summarize a relationship only within the given range of values. It would not be safe to attempt to predict percent voting turnout of some state having an educational status score higher or lower than the range of values included in the sample.

Plotting the data provided in Table 7.6 in the scattergram (Figure 7.1), the results obtained are given in Figure 7.2. The figure indicates that the regression line is a fairly close fit to the actual values. Certainly, the values represented by the regression line are closer to most of the actual values than is the mean line. We can conclude, then, that state educational status (as measured above) is a very accurate predictor of percent voting turnout in the 1976 congressional election for this group of states.

But, of course, we want to be more precise. We want to say just how much better able we are to predict voting turnout knowing educational status than knowing only the average percent voting turnout for all 10 states. The correlation coefficient provides this information. The correlation coefficient is essentially a measure of how closely our regression line "fits" the actual distribution of data. The closer the fit, the higher the correlation coefficient and the more confident we can be in predicting the values of the dependent variable based on the values of the independent variable.

145

The Correlation Coefficient

As is the case with most of the statistics discussed in this text, the actual calculation of the correlation coefficient is a relatively simple and straightforward (if sometimes tedious) task. However, prior to illustrating one of the typical ways to calculate the correlation coefficient, it will be helpful to consider for a moment what this statistic actually measures. This will assist in the proper use and interpretation of the correlation coefficient. In fact, a number of interpretations can be given to the value we call the correlation coefficient. One of these is the correlation coefficient as a reduction-of-variance ratio. As such, the coefficient to first be described below is known as the *coefficient of determination* and is symbolized as r^2. For positive relationships, the *simple correlation coefficient* (r) is obtained by taking the square root of r^2.

Returning to the notion of variance, it will be recalled that relying on the mean score, the total variance for the distribution of voting turnout in the 1976 congressional elections for our group of 10 states was found to be 195.68. It was also noted that no other *single value* would render a lower variance score than that given by the mean. Having now generated a predicted score for *each* value of Y (percent voting turnout), we can calculate the amount of variance in Y that remains unexplained after accounting for the independent variable (educational status) by substituting for $\bar{Y}$ in the variance formula the predicted values of Y (Y_p). The resulting sum is known as the *unexplained variance*, and this value, together with the total variance, can be used to calculate r^2. The procedure for obtaining the unexplained variance value is presented in Table 7.7.

For this group of 10 states, then, the total variance has been reduced considerably (from 195.68 to 71.48). The difference between these two values is known as the *explained variance*, and the ratio of explained variance to the total original variance provides the measure for the coefficient of determination and can be expressed for this set of data as

$$r^2 = \frac{\sigma^2 - \sigma_p^2}{\sigma^2}$$

$$= \frac{195.68 - 71.48}{195.68}$$

$$= 0.635$$

$$= 0.64 \quad \text{(rounded)}$$

It can thus be concluded that for this group of 10 states, about 64 percent of the variance in percent voting turnout in the 1976 congressional election is accounted for by reference to educational status (measured as the percent of

Table 7.7
Calculation of the Variance Unexplained

State	Actual Percent Voting Turnout, Y	Predicted Percent Voting Turnout, Y_p	$Y - Y_p$	$(Y - Y_p)^2$
Massachusetts	56	57.9	−1.9	3.61
New York	46	50.0	−4.0	16.00
Wisconsin	61	52.7	8.3	68.89
Missouri	57	44.8	12.2	148.84
Arkansas	22	33.0	−11.0	121.00
Mississippi	41	34.3	6.7	44.89
Utah	70	68.4	1.6	2.56
Idaho	60	59.2	.8	.64
Louisiana	40	35.6	4.4	19.36
Florida	33	50.0	−17.0	289.00
Total				714.79

$$\sigma_p^2 = \frac{\Sigma(Y - Y_p)^2}{N}$$

$$= \frac{714.79}{10}$$

$$= 71.48$$

Here σ_p^2 is the unexplained variance, or the mean-squared deviations of all Y's around the regression line.

state population having completed 12 grades of school). Since r^2 ranges from 0 to 1.0, this is a considerable amount of variance explained (1.0 would imply 100 percent of explained variance) and suggests that educational status is a very good predictor of voting turnout for these states. Put another way, we can be quite confident in predicting state voting turnout (at least in this congressional election) based on state educational status. An r^2 of 1.0 implies perfect predictability, all coordinate points representing the X and Y observations would lie on the regression line; all the variance would have been explained. An r^2 of zero indicates that the unexplained variance is equivalent to the total variance (thus, the explained variance is zero) and that the independent variable is of no assistance in predicting values of the dependent variable (again, assuming a linear relationship).

To repeat, the coefficient that has just been described (r^2) is known as the coefficient of determination, and it measures the proportionate amount of variance in the dependent variable explained by the independent variable. The value represented by $1 - r^2$ is known as the *coefficient of nondetermination*, and is a measure of the amount of variance left unexplained by reference to the independent variable (i.e., the proportion of variance that must be accounted for by other variables).

147

A Computational Formula for r

For positive relationships, the simple correlation coefficient (r) can be obtained by taking the square root of r^2. In actual research situations, the simple correlation coefficient (alternatively known as the zero-order correlation coefficient, the product-moment correlation coefficient, the Pearson correlation coefficient, or simply as r) is often calculated prior to the calculation of r^2. The definitional formula for r can be presented as

$$r = \frac{\Sigma(X - \bar{X})(Y - \bar{Y})}{\sqrt{\Sigma(X - \bar{X})^2 \, \Sigma(Y - \bar{Y})^2}}$$

Expressed in this manner, the numerator of r provides a measure of the extent to which X and Y vary together — a term known as *covariation*. Since the range of values for the covariation will vary from one distribution to another, a means of standardization allowing for meaningful comparisons from one distribution to another is required. This is accomplished in the formula by dividing the numerator by the denominator, a value that would be achieved if all observations fell perfectly on a straight line (i.e., a perfect correlation). The ratio between these two terms is the simple correlation coefficient, and this measure will range in value from -1.0 to $+1.0$ for all distributions. A positive correlation coefficient indicates that as one variable increases (or decreases) in value, so does the other. A negative correlation coefficient indicates a decline in the values of one variable as the values of the other increase. A correlation of zero implies the absence of a linear relationship between the two variables.

As the definitional formula given above is somewhat tedious to apply to a real set of data, the computational formula may be used to calculate r.[5] This is expressed as

$$r = \frac{N \, \Sigma X Y - (\Sigma X)(\Sigma Y)}{\sqrt{[N \, \Sigma X^2 - (\Sigma X)^2][N \, \Sigma Y^2 - (\Sigma Y)^2]}}$$

For the data on state percent voting turnout and educational status, the calculation of r according to this formula is presented in Table 7.8.

The simple correlation coefficient (r), like phi and τ_b, has no intrinsic meaning of its own. It is simply a measure of strength. By squaring r, we obtain the coefficient of determination (r^2), which, as discussed above, is a measure of variance "explained." We have already seen that the variance explained in this example is 64 percent, and the square of r (0.80) does equal 0.64 (as shown in Table 7.8). It can be concluded, once again, that state educational status is highly correlated with percent voting turnout as those variables have been defined for this example.

[5] For an excellent discussion of simple regression and correlation, see Hubert M. Blalock, *Social Statistics*, 2nd ed. (New York: McGraw-Hill Book Company, 1972), pp. 361–395.

Table 7.8
Calculation of the Simple Correlation Coefficient

State	Percent Completing 12 Years of School, X	Percent Voting Turnout, Y	X²	Y²	X·Y
Massachusetts	59	56	3,481	3,136	3,304
New York	53	46	2,809	2,116	2,438
Wisconsin	55	61	3,025	3,721	3,355
Missouri	49	57	2,401	3,249	2,793
Arkansas	40	22	1,600	484	880
Mississippi	41	41	1,681	1,681	1,681
Utah	67	70	4,489	4,900	4,690
Idaho	60	60	3,600	3,600	3,600
Louisiana	42	40	1,764	1,600	1,680
Florida	53	33	2,809	1,089	1,749
	$\Sigma X = 519$	$\Sigma Y = 486$	$\Sigma X^2 = 27,659$	$\Sigma Y^2 = 25,576$	$\Sigma XY = 26,170$

$$r = \frac{10(26,170) - 519(486)}{\sqrt{[10(27,659) - (519)^2][10(25,576) - (486)^2]}}$$

$$= 0.80 \quad \text{(rounded)}$$

$$r^2 = 0.64$$

Using the SPSS packaged program and data coded and stored on punchcards (or some other storage medium), the simple correlation coefficient calculated above could have been obtained from the following command:

PEARSON CORR   TURNOUT WITH EDUC

where   TURNOUT and EDUC are variable names representing the variables of state percent voting turnout and educational status as defined in this exercise

Similarly, the following command would produce the regression equation discussed above:

REGRESSION   VARIABLES = TURNOUT, EDUC/
                      REGRESSION = TURNOUT WITH EDUC (2)

where   the variable names are interpreted as above and the 2 in parentheses specifies the mode of regression solution

If desired, the following SPSS command would produce the scattergram for these variables:

SCATTERGRAM   TURNOUT WITH EDUC

Prior to considering some substantive examples of correlation analysis, one final word of caution is in order. Correlations based on rates or averages and data collected at the aggregate level (such as that used in the example of state-level voting turnout) are sometimes known as *ecological correlations* and must be used only with extreme caution. Obviously, states do not vote or attend classes, people do. Information collected at the aggregate level is not necessarily indicative of behavior at the individual level (i.e., voters) and should not be so interpreted. This point will be examined further in a later section of this chapter.

Some Substantive Examples

Use of the Pearson correlation coefficient is so common that a review of almost any issue of the leading political or social science journals will reveal at least one example of the technique. An interesting use of the statistic is provided by Terry S. Weiner's examination of the correlation between husbands' and wives' political party preferences.[6] Based on an initial and a follow-up survey of a sample of adults, Weiner found the correlations between spouse party identifications at age 21, spouse party identifications at age 31, and spouses' parents' party identifications (as reported by respondents) to be as shown in Table 7.9.

Based on these correlations, Weiner finds a tendency of husbands and wives to marry those with similar party IDs (r of 0.40) and finds also that wives are somewhat more likely over time to change their party preference to their husbands' (0.47) than vice versa (0.34). Most important, Weiner concludes that the difference between the initial husband and wife party choice correlation of 0.40 and the current correlation of 0.64 indicates that "homogeneity continues to increase over time implying that one or both partners is indeed socializing the other. . . . the high degree of homogeneity of party preferences between spouses is not only a function of 'assortative mating' but is also a function . . . of a more complicated process of 'political resocialization' that occurs after marriage."[7]

Another example of the use of the correlation coefficient is provided by Edward Carmines' study of the relationship between party competition and

---

[6] Terry S. Weiner, "Homogeneity of Political Party Preferences Between Spouses," *Journal of Politics*, 40 (February, 1978), 208–211.

[7] *Ibid.*, p. 211.

Table 7.9
Correlations Between Spouses' Initial and Current Party Identifications, In-laws and Spouses and In-laws[a]

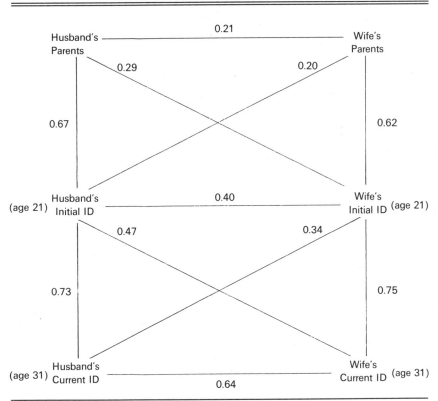

Source: Terry S. Weiner, "Homogeneity of Political Party Preferences Between Spouses," *Journal of Politics*, 40 (February, 1978), 208–211. Coefficients presented are the Pearson correlation coefficients.
[a]The values presented in this diagram are the sample correlation coefficients; each pair of variables is referenced by a solid line. For example, the simple correlation between husband's and wife's current party identification is 0.64.

welfare expenditures in the American states.[8] Carmines was testing the hypothesis that a stronger relationship between party competition (the extent to which parties actually compete for elected positions) and welfare expenditures would exist in those states with more "professional" legislatures. Legislative professionalism refers to such items as legislature compensation, expenditures for staff, length of time in sessions, and so forth. States scoring higher on measures such as these are assigned higher scores on the index of professionalism. Based on his analysis, Carmines reports the data given in Table 7.10. On the basis of these data, Carmines concludes that the

[8]Edward G. Carmines, "The Mediating Influence of State Legislatures on the Linkage Between Interparty Competition and Welfare Policies, *American Political Science Review*, 68 (September, 1974), 1118–1124.

Table 7.10
Zero-Order Correlation Coefficients Between Interparty Competition and Welfare Expenditures by Level of Legislative Professionalism

Welfare Expenditures	Among States High in Legislative Professionalism	Among States Low in Legislative Professionalism
Educational Expenditures	0.62	0.41
Total welfare expenditures	0.30	−0.15
Old-age assistance	0.51	0.23
Aid to dependent children	0.79	0.45
Aid to disabled	0.79	0.32
Aid to blind	0.61	0.35
Percent of public assistance supplied by state and local governments	0.86	0.68
Mean correlation	0.64	0.33

Source: Edward G. Carmines, "The Mediating Influence of State Legislatures on the Linkage Between Interparty Competition and Welfare Policies," *American Political Science Review*, 68 (September, 1974), 1120.

relationship between party competition and welfare expenditures is indeed stronger in states higher on the index of legislative professionalism. He concludes: "Overall the results support the ... proposition ... that the linkage between party competition and welfare policy is greater for those states with effective legislatures than for those states with ineffective legislative systems."[9]

A final example of the use of the correlation coefficient is provided by Maynard Erickson and Jack Gibbs' analysis of the association between crime rates and certainty of punishment.[10] Table 7.11 shows the data collected from the American states by Erickson and Gibbs. Interpreting the data presented in the table, it can be seen that in most cases the direction of the sign of the correlation coefficient is negative. This means that, as measures of certainity of imprisonment and severity of imprisonment increase, the rate of crime in the various categories of crime activities decreases. Erickson and Gibbs also point out that the magnitude of the correlation coefficients of columns (2) and (4) are generally larger than those in columns (1) and (3). They interpret this to mean that *general* perceptions of certainty and severity of imprisonment are often more directly related to lower crime rates than are perceptions of certainty and severity for *specific* crimes.

[9] *Ibid.*, p. 1120.

[10] Maynard Erickson and Jack Gibbs, "Specific Versus General Properties of Legal Punishments and Deterrence," *Social Science Quarterly*, 56 (December, 1975), 390–397.

Table 7.11
Zero-Order Correlations Among 48-States Between Crime Rates and Four Measures Pertaining to the Certainty–Severity of Imprisonment, Circa 1960

Type of Crime[a]	r's Between Crime Rates and Measures of Certainty of Imprisonment[b]		r's Between Crime Rates and Measures of Severity of Imprisonment[c]	
	(1) Crime-Specific[d]	(2) General[d]	(3) Crime-Specific[d]	(4) General[d]
Homicide	−0.21	−0.34	−0.37	−0.16
Rape	−0.53	−0.41	0.26	−0.31
Robbery	−0.51	−0.33	−0.06	−0.12
Assault	−0.23	−0.37	0.14	−0.20
Burglary	−0.46	−0.36	0.07	−0.21
Auto theft	−0.29	−0.32	0.19	−0.08
Larceny	−0.28	−0.37	0.12	−0.13

Source: Maynard Erickson and Jack Gibbs, "Specific Versus General Properties of Legal Punishments and Deterrence," *Social Science Quarterly*, 56 (December, 1975), 395.
[a] Crime rates were calculated from incidence of offenses reported by police.
[b] The measure of certainty of imprisonment was an index of the proportion of reported crime in each jurisdiction resulting in conviction and imprisonment.
[c] The measure of severity of imprisonment was an index of the median months served in state prison.
[d] "Crime-specific" and "General" refer to measures of certainty of imprisonment and severity of imprisonment for each listed crime (specific) and for all types of crime (general).

Using Correlation Analysis with Mixed Levels of Data

A question that has probably occurred to the reader concerns the use of correlation analysis in conjunction with "mixed" levels of data. To this point, all the examples presented and all the correlation tests examined have been appropriate for like-levels of data. That is, these chapters have been considering situations in which both the independent and dependent variables are nominal, ordinal, or interval. However, situations obviously arise in which the researcher is interested in assessing the relationship between mixed levels of data. A student of American voting behavior might be interested in the relationship between percentage of voting turnout (expressed as an interval measure) and region of the country (expressed as nominal data). A student of comparative politics might be interested in country-by-country (expressed as nominal data) variations in attitudes towards politics and politicians (expressed as ordinal data). What is the researcher to do, in cases such as these, when levels of data are incongruent?

In the first place, one always can apply "lower-level" statistics to "higher-level" data. Thus, nominal-level tests of association could be used to measure the relationship between nominal and ordinal data; ordinal-level tests of association could be used to measure the relationship between ordinal and interval data; and so on. A student examining the relationship between religion (measured as a nominal variable) and a seven-point scale of liberalism (assumed to be ordinal) could use lambda (or some other nominal measure) as the test of association. The drawback to applying a lower-level statistic to higher-level data is that the process results in a less-than-maximal utilization of all available information. Lower-level statistics are simply not as sensitive to variations in the data as are higher-level tests.

Second, *and this is a far more controversial option*, the researcher may in certain circumstances consider applying higher-level techniques to lower-level data. For example, one often will see the Pearson correlation coefficient used in conjunction with ordinal data. Another often-used procedure is to dichotomize nominal data for use in conjunction with ordinal- or interval-level statistics. Examining regions of the country, for example, one might collapse all possible values into two: South and non-South. This is assumed to be equivalent to an interval continuum having only two possible scores: all or nothing. Individuals are coded as either living in the South or not, and this variable might be used with higher-level statistics. The lesson to be remembered, however, is that *higher-level techniques may be used with lower-level data only with extreme caution*. The student must be thoroughly familiar with the data and with the assumptions of each technique before proceeding.

Additionally, some techniques have been specifically designed for use with mixed levels of data. Since the logic of most of these closely parallel that already discussed in conjunction with the other tests of association, these statistics are only briefly summarized here. For a more complete explanation, the reader should consult the sources cited or any introductory statistic text.

As a test of association between *one nominal and one ordinal variable*, Freeman has presented a statistic called *theta* (θ), which is based on pairs of rankings in a distribution.[11] In calculating theta, negative values can be generated, but since one scale is nominal, these should be ignored.

For examining the relationship between *one nominal and one interval (or ratio) variable*, a commonly used test is *eta* (sometimes called the correlation ratio when squared), symbolized as η.[12] Eta essentially is a measure of the difference of the magnitude of means within various categories of the independent variable. Eta (or eta^2) also should be reported as ranging in value from 0.0 to +1.0, since negative values have no meaning in conjunction with nominal data.

Special cases of the Pearson correlation coefficient have been developed for use when *one variable is ordinal and the other interval*. When the ordinal scale is composed of only two categories, the test is called the *point-biserial correlation;* when the ordinal scale is composed of more than two categories,

---

[11] See Freeman, *Elementary Applied Statistics*, pp. 108–119, for a thorough discussion of theta.

[12] A brief but useful illustration of the calculation of eta can be found in Gene V. Glass and J. C. Stanley, *Statistical Methods in Education and Psychology* (Englewood Cliffs, NJ: Prentice-Hall, 1970), pp. 150–152, and in Freeman, *Elementary Applied Statistics*, pp. 120–130.

the test is called the *point-multiserial correlation*. Each of these makes rather severe demands on the data and are rarely used in behavioral research except in psychological testing.[13]

Some Words of Advice and Caution in the Use of Correlation Analysis

Chapters 6 and 7 have discussed the calculation and application of the most commonly used tests of association between two variables currently in use in political science research. It is appropriate in concluding this discussion to summarize some of the major points raised in these chapters and to offer some advice in the application of the techniques.

In the first place, the student should not be "put off" by what may seem to be a large number of complex and tedious formulas. It is true that the hand calculation of many of these coefficients can be quite time-consuming. However, today, most of the packages of statistical programs generate these coefficients with only a minimum of human effort. Calculations that formerly might have taken days or even weeks for a single researcher to compute can now be generated within the time frame of only a few seconds of computer time. Thus political researchers do not today spend inordinate amounts of time with pencil and paper at the mundane tasks of calculating correlation coefficients. However, it is very important that the student understand the basis behind each measure and *it is critical that the student understand the conditions under which each measure is appropriately applied*. Nothing is so revealing of unsystematic research as is the inappropriate application and interpretation of statistical measures. In applying these techniques, the student may find helpful the following few words of advice and caution.

How to Interpret the Magnitude of the Correlation Coefficient

A common question is: "How do I interpret the magnitude of a correlation coefficient?" This is not so difficult for those reduction of error and variance tests (such as lambda, gamma, and r^2) which have intrinsic meanings of their own. This is difficult, however, when considering measures that lack such easily stated meanings. Just what is the verbal interpretation of a phi of 0.30, a τ_b of 0.68, or an r of -0.45? There is no easy answer to this question; however, James Davis has suggested some appropriate phrases to describe the various ranges of values for Yule's Q.[14] In general, these descriptions will fit measures

---

[13]See Kenneth D. Hopkins and Gene V. Glass, *Basic Statistics for the Behavioral Sciences* (Englewood Cliffs, NJ: Prentice-Hall, Inc., 1978), pp. 138, for a discussion of this point.

[14]James A. Davis, *Elementary Survey Analysis* (Englewood Cliffs, N.J.: Prentice-Hall, Inc., 1971), p. 49.

Table 7.12
Suggested Verbal Interpretations of Correlation
Coefficients

Correlation Values	Appropriate Phrases
+0.70 or higher	Very strong positive association
+0.50 to +0.69	Substantial positive association
+0.30 to +0.49	Moderate positive association
+0.10 to +0.29	Low positive association
+0.01 to +0.09	Negligible positive association
0.00	No association
−0.01 to 0.09	Negligible negative association
−0.10 to −0.29	Low negative association
−0.30 to −0.49	Moderate negative association
−0.50 to −0.69	Substantial negative association
−0.70 or lower	Very strong negative association

Source: Adapted from James A. Davis, Elementary Survey Analysis (Englewood Cliffs, N.J.: Prentice-Hall, Inc., 1971), p. 49.

lacking in operational interpretation used to relate social science data. Davis' scheme is shown in Table 7.12.

In applying these phrases to describe the level of correlation, one must still be cautious, however. Since the magnitude of the various correlation coefficients, even for the same set of data, may vary considerably, the researcher might justifiably conclude that a tau-*b* value of .48 represents a substantially stronger relationship than a gamma value of .48. Also, although it generally is true that a correlation of 0.70 represents a very strong relationship, if a researcher were attempting to select items to construct a scale (such as social class, or political trust, or racial tolerance), correlations of even higher value probably would be sought. Thus the interpretation of the values of correlation coefficients — like the application of the tests themselves — is dependent to some extent on the model and underlying assumptions being tested. In reaching appropriate conclusions, the researcher must be thoroughly familiar with his or her own data and modeling assumptions.

Try to Examine All the Data, Not
Just the Correlation Coefficient

Another issue in the use of correlation analysis revolves, paradoxically perhaps, around too heavy a reliance on the correlation coefficient alone. One of the tremendous advantages of correlation analysis is its ability to summarize with a single number great amounts of data. But this may become a disadvantage if we focus only on the correlation coefficient and overlook the actual data distribution. By ignoring the actual data, we run the risk of overlooking important deviations from the major trend (as represented by the correlation coefficient). Often, the deviations from the mainstream will be just as interesting to the researcher and to the broader academic community.

Care should always be taken to examine the data distribution and to consider as much information, along with the correlation coefficient, as possible.

Beware of False Precision

Another advantage of correlation techniques is their precision. A huge array of data may give a blurred impression of the underlying relationship; a single number (the correlation coefficient) seems clear, precise, and "definitive." The disadvantage is that the hasty student can be lulled into a *false* sense of precision. The correlation coefficient is a product of many factors. One of these, obviously, is the actual relationship between the variables being examined. However, other factors also influence the correlation coefficient that is produced. Included may be errors in the recording and reporting of information, errors in sampling, values that are missing from some cases, and so forth. All these extraneous factors tend to distort the "true" correlation. Of course, the systematic researcher will want to minimize as many of these distortions as possible by careful data collection and analysis. But rarely can all distorting factors be completely eliminated, and in social science research, especially, one should think of the correlation coefficient as an approximation of the actual relationship. The true relationship may deviate somewhat.

Beware of Ecological and Individualistic Fallacies

In examining voting turnouts of American cities, urban scholars have made a very interesting discovery. It has been found that cities with higher proportions of poorly educated and ethnic populations often experience higher voter turnouts than do cities with well-educated, middle-class populations.[15] This is true *in spite of the fact that higher-educated, higher-social-status individuals are known to be more likely to vote than are the less educated.* Here, we confront the complex issues of "ecological" and "individualistic" fallacies in the interpretation of data.[16]

Ecological fallacy refers to the possibility of incorrectly reaching conclusions about the behavior of individuals based on data collected in the aggregate. For example, data collected at the county level showing wealthy counties to be more likely to vote Republican cannot necessarily be interpreted to mean that data collected from individuals in each county would show that wealthier individuals would always be more likely to vote Republican. In our

[15] See Robert R. Alford and Eugene C. Lee, "Voting Turnout in American Cities," *American Political Science Review*, 62 (September, 1968), 796–813.

[16] For additional discussion of the very important topics of ecological and individualistic fallacies, see Claire Selltiz, Lawrence Wrightsman, and Stuart Cook, *Research Methods in Social Relations*, 3rd ed., (New York: Holt, Rinehart and Winston, Inc., 1976), pp. 439–440; W. Phillips Shively, " 'Ecological' Inference: The Use of Aggregate Data to Study Individuals," *American Political Science Review*, 63 (December, 1969), 1183–1196; and W. S. Robinson, "Ecological Correlations and the Behavior of Individuals," *American Sociological Review*, 15 (June, 1950), 351–357.

earlier example of the relationship between percent voting turnout in the 1976 congressional election and educational status, we were analyzing the patterns of state voting behavior, *not* individuals. Those findings could not be reported as necessarily demonstrating that the same relationship would be found for samples of individuals in any or all of the states. Individuals comprising a large unit of analysis (county, state, nation) do not necessarily reflect the behavior of the larger unit. To make inferences about individuals, one needs to collect information at the individual level.

Conversely, an *individualistic fallacy* is made when inferences of group behavior are made on the basis of information collected from individuals. It should not be concluded from the finding that less wealthy individuals are less politically active that voting turnouts will be less among counties with lower mean income levels. If we wish to make a statement about voting behavior of counties, we need data collected at the county level.

Of course, we may not always be in possession of precisely the data we need to analyze the relationship that interests us most. Often, for example, information on individuals is not available; we have to rely on data collected at the precinct, city, county, or state level. In such instances it is not recommended that the researcher abandon his or her "real" interest, but that in reporting conclusions the limitations of the data and the possible errors in interpretation must be made explicit. In this manner the researcher is saying: "Based on the best available evidence, I believe the following to be true." Future research, based on the more appropriate unit of analysis, may confirm or refute this finding.

Do Not Confuse Correlation with Causation

Perhaps the most critical error that can be made in the application of correlation techniques is the assumption that correlation is equivalent to causation. Having found a correlation between a variable that we are calling the independent variable and one we are calling the dependent variable, it is tempting to leap to the conclusion that the former is a cause of the latter. It is true that the ultimate phase in the scientific process is the establishment of causal relationships, and it also is true that an important first step in establishing causation is the identification of a correlation. However, this is only the *first* step: correlation does not necessarily imply causation. In the first place, correlation is not an indication of direction. Even the finding of a high correlation between political participation and trust in the political system does not tell us whether greater rates of participation "lead to" greater levels of system trust, or whether greater levels of system trust "produce" greater rates of participation (or, indeed, if mutual causation is involved). The time order of variables is not always obvious.

The problem of time orderness can sometimes be resolved. This is especially true when dealing with data having clearly established time relationships (such as parent and child political attitudes) or with time-series data (data collected at an earlier point in time correlated with data collected at a later point). Much more important is the problem of spurious or confounding influences. That is, even when time order can clearly be established, it is still possible that the observed correlation between two variables may actually be the result of the influence of one or several other variables. That is, the apparent correlation between variables X_1 and X_2 may actually be the result of X_3's influence on both X_1 and X_2. If the influence of X_3 could be removed from both X_1 and X_2, it might be found that the observed correlation between X_1 and X_2 would vanish. This is the problem of "control," and it, too, is critical to the conduct of systematic political science research. We turn to this issue in the following chapter.

Exercises

1. The following table presents, for the same ten states examined in Table 7.4, the percent of population living in metropolitan areas and the rate of major crime per 100,000 population for each state.

State	Percent of Population Living in Metropolitan Areas (X)	Rate of Major Crime Known to Police per 100,000 Population* (Y)
Massachusetts	88	5821
New York	89	6225
Wisconsin	61	3901
Missouri	65	5035
Arkansas	38	3406
Mississippi	25	2468
Utah	80	4978
Idaho	16	4271
Louisiana	62	4362
Florida	84	7017

*Includes murder and manslaughter, rape, robbery, assault, burglary, larceny, motor vehicle theft.
Source: Statistical Abstract of the United States, 1977. All data rounded to nearest percent on whole number.

   a. Construct a scattergram for the above set of data. (Hint: present the crime rate axis in units of 500.) On the basis of the scattergram alone, what can be said about the apparent relationship between percent of population living in metropolitan areas and crime rate for these states?

   b. Compute the simple regression coefficient, the simple correlation coefficient, and the coefficient of determination for this set of data What is the interpretation of each of these coefficients in relation to this set of data?

   c. Compute the regression equation for this set of data and calculate the *predicted* crime rates for states having 30%, 50%, 65%, and 85% of their population living in metropolitan areas.

   d. What are the advantages and disadvantages of applying correlation and regression analysis to data such as these? What do these coefficients tell you about this set of data and what precautions should be taken in reporting such results?

2. Select randomly any other ten states and gather for those states the same information presented in the above table. Calculate the simple regression coefficient, the simple correlation coefficient, and the coefficient of determination for this new set of information. Compare these results with those obtained in exercise #1. To what extent do the coefficients differ and what does this imply about analysis, such as this, based on sample data?

8

SORTING OUT RELATIONSHIPS: MULTIVARIATE ANALYSIS AND THE ISSUE OF CONTROL

Life for the political scientist would be simplified indeed if phenomena always could be explained by reference to only one other factor. Unfortunately, this is rarely the case. Social relationships are extremely complex; it is unusual for one variable to be so strongly associated with another as to provide a satisfactory and complete explanation of that variable. To thoroughly understand a particular variable of interest, we often must examine that variable in reference to *several* independent variables.

In so doing, we often find that an original bivariate relationship that appeared to be strong may be quite weak. Sometimes we find our original relationship strengthened; sometimes the original relationship is virtually unchanged. Accounting for the influence of two, three, or more variables can affect an original zero-order correlation in many ways.

It is also true that we sometimes are not even sure of the precise nature of the relationship between a series of variables. We may know which variable we want to explain (the dependent variable) and which we believe to influence that variable (the independent variables), but the precise structure of the relationship between these variables may be obscure.

In situations such as these, reference to more than two variables becomes of interest to the political researcher. Because several variables are being examined at one time, the category of methods used in such analysis is called *multivariate analysis*. We also confront directly here the issue of *control*.

On the Nature of Control

Control is a concept basic to the scientist and layman alike. When we say that "This is a very nice day for August," or "This is an interesting class for political science," or "She is quite liberal for a Republican," we are employing (even if very imprecisely) the concept of control. We are saying that accounting (or controlling) for one factor (season, type of course, or party identification) helps explain our feelings toward another (pleasant day, interesting class, political views). In a different context, none of these statements may be true (an 85-degree day in October might be considered very unpleasant), but in the context of which they are spoken, these statements amplify and embellish our thoughts.

In a similar manner, the scientist uses the concept of control to amplify and focus his or her research interest. In the scientific process, control is the next logical stage beyond establishing a relationship. Properly used, controlling techniques assist in clarifying the critical issue of causation.

The adage that "correlation is not equivalent to causation" is firmly entrenched in the minds of beginning students of statistics (and, hopefully, political researchers as well). But, just what does this mean? If we have demonstrated that X_2 occurs before X_1 and that X_2 and X_1 are correlated, why not conclude that variations in X_2 cause (or at least are among the causes of) variations in X_1?

A moment's reflection will indicate why additional analysis is needed before finally concluding that a causal relationship exists between two apparently correlated variables. Assume that a college registrar has maintained for one year the final course averages of a group of students enrolled that year in both beginning biology and political science classes. Correlating the two course grade averages for this group of students, the registrar might find a fairly high positive correlation. Students who do well in freshman biology might also do well in their first political science course.

Now, it might be that some transference of knowledge between these two subjects exists which enables those who are more knowledgeable in one area to perform better in the other. Some might conclude on the basis of this correlation that dissecting frogs assists in the understanding of government and politics. Some might even say that an understanding of government and politics assists in the dissecting of frogs. However, these are quite disparate disciplines, and the careful observer would probably conclude that a third factor is influencing performance in each subject.

Perhaps the registrar also collected information on number of hours per week studied for each student. Examining this additional body of data, it might be found that those spending more time per week studying performed better in biology and those spending more time per week studying also performed better in political science. On the basis of this, the registrar might appropriately conclude that there is no causal relationship between performance in biology class and performance in political science. Even though the two appear to be correlated, it is really the influence of a third factor (time studying) that is important in each instance. It is concluded that performance in political science is affected by amount of time spent in studying, not by knowledge of biology.

When a third factor is really the cause of the apparent association between two variables, and when the original correlation vanishes or is significantly reduced when accounting for this third factor, the original relationship is said to be *spurious*. Much of political (and indeed all) scientific research deals with the attempt to rule out alternative explanations for the apparent relationship between two variables. This is the heart of the issue of control.

The example given above of the relationship between biology and political science grades obviously is fanciful; however, there are many occasions in social science research when it is not so apparent whether otherwise plausible associations between two variables are really spurious. Yet the systematic researcher must make every reasonable attempt to test and discard all possible confounding influences before concluding that a causal relationship apparently does exist.

This is probably the most difficult phase of scientific research. In the first place, it is impossible to examine *every* possible confounding influence. Since every phenomenon is potentially related to every other, this would literally mean reexamining the original relationship, controlling for all other phenomena. This is impossible, of course, but it is expected that the researcher will examine and control for all third factors that it might *reasonably* be expected would affect the original relationship.

This also means that the researcher must apply a considerable measure of foresight before setting out to collect his or her data. When collecting information to test the relationship of principal interest, the researcher must also obtain information pertaining to the relevant possible extraneous influences. If the data have not been collected, appropriate control is impossible.

The issue of control in the three-variable case can be thought of more formally by reference to Figure 8.1. In the example illustrated, we are hypothesizing that an observed relationship between X_1 and X_2 is actually spurious (indicated by the dashed line). We are saying that some third variable (X_3) may be the actual cause of variation in both X_1 and X_2. This is analogous to the situation discussed above when we were saying that hours spent studying (X_3) is the actual cause of the variance in biology (X_2) and political science (X_1) term averages. In testing for this possibility we reexamine the relationship between X_2 and X_1, *controlling for* the influence of X_3. If, in fact, the relationship between X_2 and X_1 is then substantially reduced, we conclude that a spurious relationship exists. If, however, the

Figure 8.1
Illustration of possible three-variable model.

Figure 8.2
Illustration of possible three-variable model.

relationship between X_2 and X_1 is not substantially reduced, we conclude that at least X_3 is not a confounding influence. We may want to test and possibly eliminate other potentially confounding influences as well (such as quality of instruction and precollege preparation).

Another possible type of relationship between three variables is illustrated in Figure 8.2. In this instance, we are testing for the possibility that the observed relationship between X_3 and X_1 is really a product of X_3's influence on X_2, which, in turn, influences X_1. Here, X_3 is said to be related to X_1 only through the mediating or intervening influence of X_2. We may, for example, be examining the relationships among grandparents' (X_3), parents' (X_2), and childrens' (X_1) party identification. We may be postulating a causal sequence of the nature that the apparent correlation between grandparents' and childrens' partisan choice is actually a function of grandparents' influence on parents and, in turn, parents' influence on children. If such a model does describe the relationship, the appropriate control for X_2 should significantly reduce the relationship between X_3 and X_1.

Comparing Models

There are, in fact, a number of possible models which may relate three variables. Sometimes the researcher may not be sure of which model most appropriately describes the relationship of interest. If this is the case, can the concept of control be used to assist in determining which model appears to "best fit" the data? The answer is, at least partially, yes.

In the three-variable case, if the researcher is able to specify one variable as the dependent variable, rule out the possibility of dual (or reciprocal) causation, assume that at least one relationship (or "path") should not exist, and make certain other statistical assumptions not discussed here,[1] the possible models specifying the relationships among these three variables can be presented as shown in Figure 8.3. Presenting models in this fashion, the researcher is predicting the results which should be produced if one (or possibly more than one) of these models fits the data after applying appropriate controls. In Model 2 (spurious model) the researcher is hypothesizing a zero (or close to zero) correlation between the variables X_2 and X_1 when controlling for the effects of X_3. Should the control for X_3 actually

---

[1] For a brief but illuminating discussion of these assumptions see Hayward R. Alker, *Mathematics and Politics* (New York: Macmillan Publishing Co., Inc., 1965), 112–129.

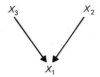

1. Double Cause Model

2. Spurious Model

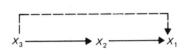

3. Developmental Model

4. Double Effect Model

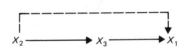

5. Intervening Model

Figure 8.3

Three-variable causal relationships between two independent variables and one dependent variable assuming one "path" to be zero. Solid arrow: non-zero correlation; broken arrow: predicted relationship approaching zero when controlling; no arrow: a predicted zero simple correlation. [Source: The models and terminology presented here follow that of Hayward R. Alker, *Mathematics and Politics* (New York: Macmillan Publishing Co., Inc., 1968), chapter 6.]

produce such a result then Model 2 might plausibly be considered as an accurate description of the relationship between the three variables. Similarly, Model 3 (developmental model) predicts a zero (or close to zero) correlation between variables X_3 and X_1 when controlling for X_2. Should the control for X_2 actually produce such a result, then Model 3 might plausibly be considered as an accurate description of these relationships.

In this manner then, the notion of control can be used not only to identify possible spurious relationships, but also may be of assistance in clarifying the relationship between a set of variables. This can be an important tool of systematic political research, but *note the limitations of such controlling procedures.* The researcher cannot *statistically* distinguish between Models 2 and 5 (the spurious and intervening models) or between Models 3 and 4 (the developmental and double-effect models). For both Models 2 and 5 the researcher is predicting that the relationship between X_2 and X_1 should be substantially reduced when controlling for the influence of X_3. Likewise, in Models 3 and 4 the researcher is predicting that the relationship between X_3 and X_1 should be substantially reduced when controlling for X_2. Should either of these predictions hold true, there is no statistical way to select between the appropriate alternate models. Additionally, it is obvious that comparison of some of these models makes little or no sense. Examining Model 2 and Model 4, for example, it can be seen that it would be impossible to postulate both as being valid at the same time. Model 2 asserts that X_3 has a direct influence on X_2 while Model 4 asserts just the opposite.[2]

All of this is to say that in formulating and testing models, the researcher must rely both on theory and common sense. If one model appears to be a more accurate representation than an alternative, then it is selected as at least the most *likely* candidate. Additional research and additional information may demonstrate still another model to be superior.

The "true," or classic experimental design situation deals with the issue of control through a process of random selection of subjects assigned to control and treatment groups and the actual manipulation by the researcher of the independent variable. Through careful pre-, post-, and follow-up testing procedures, precise measures of the impact of the independent variable are possible. The topic of experimental research design will be discussed later, but here it is noted that much of social and political research more typically relies on the *survey research design*.[3] Here, *one* sample is selected and statistical techniques are used to substitute for experimental control. In turn, two types of statistical control procedures are often employed in survey research. The first, often used in conjunction with nominal- or ordinal-level data, is known as tabular control (cross-tabulation). The second, used in conjunction with interval-level data, is known as partial correlation. Each of these is discussed below.

Cross-tabulation

Cross-tabulation is a method of control useful when analyzing nominal or ordinal data.[4] Using cross-tabulation procedures, we reexamine the original relationship between the independent and dependent variables for each

[2]For an insightful discussion of this point see Michael S. Lewis-Beck, "The Relative Importance of Socioeconomic and Political Variables for Public Policy," *American Political Science Review*, 71 (June, 1977), 559–566.

[3]For a classic discussion of the issues involved in experimental and quasi-experimental research, see Donald T. Campbell and Julian C. Stanley, *Experimental and Quasi-Experimental Designs for Research* (Chicago: Rand McNally & Company, 1963).

[4]A number of coefficients have been developed for use with nominal and ordinal data which are similar in interpretation to the partial correlation coefficient used with interval-level data

category of the control factor. The original correlation (represented by gamma, lambda, or τ_b, or whatever) is then compared with the correlation for each category of control, and any changes are said to result from the confounding influence of the third variable.

Perhaps the best way to explain this technique of control is by way of illustration. Assume that we are interested in the relationship between the voting patterns of state legislators and their party identification. We might be testing the hypothesis that at the state level legislative voting behavior is at least partially a function of party identification; Democrats are expected to vote with other Democrats, Republicans are expected to vote with other Republicans. In testing this hypothesis, let us say that for all 250 legislators in a state of particular interest,[5] we have gathered information both on party identification and vote on a recent bill designed to increase state-wide welfare payments. The relationship between party identification and the vote for this bill might appear as shown in Table 8.1.

Table 8.1
Hypothetical Relationship Between Party Identification and Legislative Vote on Welfare Bill

Vote on Welfare Bill	Party Identification		
	Democrat	Republican	Total
Yes	70	50	120
No	50	80	130
Total	120	130	250

$$\gamma = 0.38$$

(discussed below). Included are the partial gamma, the partial tau-b, and the partial Somers' d_{yx}. Most of these are based on weighted-average coefficients for categories of data. These partial coefficients for lower-level data are being increasingly applied in political research, and the student may wish to consult some of the sources that follow for an explanation of their calculation and interpretation. Still, cross-tabular analysis has its own advantages, which the discussion in this chapter should make clear. Because of the additional information it renders, the student is advised to consider cross-tabulation analysis even when other techniques may be available. See James A. Davis, "A Partial Coefficient for Goodman and Kruskal's Gamma," *Journal of the American Statistical Association*, 62 (March, 1967), 189–93; Robert H. Somers, "A Partitioning of Ordinal Information in a Three-Way Cross-Classification," *Multivariate Behavior Research*, 5 (April, 1970), 217–239; Robert B. Smith, "Neighborhood Context and College Plans: An Ordinal Path Analysis," *Social Forces*, 51 (December, 1972), 199–217; and the entire December, 1974 issue of *Social Forces*, which is devoted largely to a discussion of this topic.

[5] This example is only for purposes of illustration. Actually, only Massachusetts, with 240, and New Hampshire, with 400 legislators, have legislative bodies that approach the size selected for this hypothetical example.

167

The correlation between party identification and legislative vote is found to be 0.38. As expected, Democrats were more likely to join in support of the welfare measure, and Republicans were more likely to join in opposition. There is, then, a moderate positive correlation between party identification and the vote for this hypothetical group of state legislators. The question is whether this correlation will change when applying appropriate controls.

Let us assume further that we also suspect urbanization to affect legislator vote on the welfare bill. It may be that legislators from urban areas (regardless of party identification) might support welfare legislation more frequently than those legislators from rural areas (regardless of party identification). In other words, perhaps it is urbanization of the legislators' districts, not party labels, that is the more important factor in predicting legislative vote on this welfare measure.

To test for this possibility, we may reexamine the original relationship between party identification and legislative vote on the welfare bill *controlling for* urbanization of legislative district (categorized here for purposes of illustration simply as urban or rural). This technique, it will be seen below, actually divides the original table into two tables, one representing voting patterns of legislators from the urban areas, the other representing voting patterns of legislators from the rural areas. In this manner, the researcher can assess the influence of partisanship on legislative vote under conditions in which urbanization of legislative district does not vary. Using the SPSS packaged program and data stored on punchcards or some other medium, this could be accomplished by the following command:

CROSSTABS   TABLES = VOTE BY PID BY URBAN

where VOTE, PID, and URBAN are designated as variable names for the variables legislative vote on this welfare measure, party affiliation, and urbanization of legislative districts.

When controlling in this manner, any number of possible results may be obtained. Table 8.2 illustrates one possibility.

Table 8.2
Legislative Vote by Party Identification Controlling for Urbanization of District: Original Relationship Remains Unchanged

| Vote on Welfare Bill | Urbanization of District | | | | | |
| | Urban | | | Rural | | |
	Democrat	Republican	Total	Democrat	Republican	Total
Yes	37	13	50	33	37	70
No	23	17	40	27	63	90
Total	60	30	90	60	100	160

$\gamma = 0.36$ $\gamma = 0.35$

It can be seen in Table 8.2 that regardless of urbanization of legislative district, Democrats were more likely to support and Republicans were more likely to oppose this bill. In each control situation, the correlation coefficient (gamma) remains about as strong as for the original relationship (Table 8.1). We conclude in this instance that controlling for urbanization has *not* affected the original relationship and that party identification remains a factor of at least moderate importance in legislative voting behavior on this issue. Of course, factors other than urbanization may affect this relationship, and they too would have to be examined before concluding that the relationship between vote on this measure and party choice is not spurious.

Another result is possible when applying the technique of control by cross-tabulation as is illustrated in Table 8.3.

Here, it can be seen that the original correlation of 0.38 is virtually eliminated when the control for urbanization of legislative district is applied. Controlling for urbanization, these results (Table 8.3) justify the conclusion that there is no relationship between legislative partisanship and vote for this particular welfare measure. The original relationship (shown in Table 8.1) is thus said to be spurious. This finding, by the way, does not automatically lead to the conclusion that it is urbanization of legislative district which *must* be the cause of legislative vote on this issue. Before such a conclusion can be reached, the researcher must examine the relationship between voting and urbanization *and* subject this relationship to the same testing procedures as outlined above.

The above two illustrations (one in which the original relationship remained virtually unchanged, the other in which it was largely eliminated) do not exhaust the possible results of cross-tabular controlling techniques. Other results are possible as illustrated in Tables 8.4 and 8.5.

Table 8.4 illustrates an instance in which the association for one category of the control has been greatly reduced, but for the other, has increased. How is this to be interpreted? Examining the data and the correlation coefficients,

Table 8.3
Legislative Vote by Party Identification Controlling for Urbanization of District: Original Relationship is Substantially Reduced

Vote on Welfare Bill	Urbanization of District					
	Urban			Rural		
	Democrat	Republican	Total	Democrat	Republican	Total
Yes	56	28	84	14	22	36
No	4	2	6	46	78	124
Total	60	30	90	60	100	160
		$\gamma = 0.00$			$\gamma = 0.04$	

Table 8.4
Legislative Vote by Party Identification Controlling for Urbanization of District: Original Relationship is Substantially Altered

| Vote on Welfare Bill | Urbanization of District | | | | | |
| | Urban | | | Rural | | |
	Democrat	Republican	Total	Democrat	Republican	Total
Yes	33	17	50	37	33	70
No	27	13	40	23	67	90
Total	60	30	90	60	100	160
	$\gamma = -0.03$			$\gamma = 0.53$		

Table 8.5
Legislative Vote by Party Identification Controlling for Urbanization of District: Original Relationship is Substantially Altered

| Vote on Welfare Bill | Urbanization of District | | | | | |
| | Urban | | | Rural | | |
	Democrat	Republican	Total	Democrat	Republican	Total
Yes	25	25	50	45	25	70
No	35	5	40	15	75	90
Total	60	30	90	60	100	160
	$\gamma = -0.75$			$\gamma = 0.80$		

it can be seen that for urban legislators, party identification is *not* a differentiating factor in voting on this bill. A majority of both urban Democrats and urban Republicans were likely to support the bill ($\gamma = -0.03$). For rural legislators, however, party identification is a very important factor. Here, Democrats are far more likely to support the measure than are Republicans. The correlation coefficient (0.53) indicates a substantial association between party identification and vote on this bill for rural legislators. We conclude, then, that party identification *is not* a factor helping to explain the vote on this particular bill in the urban areas, but it is a very important factor helping to explain support of this bill in the rural areas.

One additional possible effect of cross-tabular control is illustrated in Table 8.5. Here we see that the control has dramatically altered the picture of the relationship between legislator party affiliation and support of this particular welfare bill as presented in Table 8.1. Table 8.1 showed a moderate, but not very strong relationship. Controlling for urbanization, we see in

Table 8.5 that in the rural areas, a substantial positive relationship exists between party identification and support on this bill. Democratic rural legislators were much more likely to support the bill than were Republican rural legislators ($\gamma = 0.80$).

For the urban legislators, the control shown in Table 8.5 has completely reversed the original relationship. Now it can be seen that a very strong relationship exists for the urban legislators but that this relationship is in a *negative* direction. In this case, Republican urban legislators are found to be much more supportive of this particular bill than are Democratic urban legislators ($\gamma = -0.75$). Without a doubt, the control has altered our interpretation of the relationship between party identification and support of this bill as originally presented in Table 8.1.

It can be seen in these hypothetical examples that controlling for the influence of a third factor can have any number of possible effects on the original relationship. The original relationship may be unchanged or it may be altered in ways that substantially affect our interpretation of the results. It is for this reason that the proper application of controlling procedures is so essential to systematic research.

Some Substantive Examples of
Cross-tabulation Control

An interesting example of cross-tabulation control is provided by Joel Aberbach and Bert Rockman's study of top federal bureaucrats.[6] Based on interviews of senior officials conducted in the early Nixon years, Aberbach and Rockman were interested, among other things, in the relationship between the partisan affiliation of these senior bureaucrats and their beliefs about how equally all groups of Americans are represented in the political process. Their original findings are shown in Table 8.6.

The gamma coefficient (-0.28) indicates that some relationship between party affiliation of top bureaucrats and their beliefs about equality of representation existed. Independents and Democrats were more likely than Republicans to believe that some groups are not adequately represented.

Aberbach and Rockman then proceeded to reexamine the relationship, controlling for whether the bureaucrats were employed in a social service (HHS, HUD, OEO) or a non-social service (labor, agriculture, etc.) department or agency. The results of this control are shown in Table 8.7. Controlling for agency affiliation, it is seen that the original relationship is much stronger for those employed in social service agencies (-0.49) than for those employed in non-social service agencies (-0.20). For social service agencies, especially, the relationship between party identification and beliefs about equality of representation for this sample of top bureaucrats was found to be moderately strong.

[6]As reported in Joel D. Aberbach and Bert A. Rockman, "Clashing Beliefs Within the Executive Branch," *American Political Science Review*, 70 (June, 1976), 456–468.

Table 8.6
Bureaucratic Beliefs About Equality of Representation by Party Affiliation (percent)

Beliefs About Equality of Representation	Party Identification		
	Republican	Independent	Democrat
Some groups inadequately represented	50	74	72
All groups considered with some reservations	29	4	14
All groups considered with no reservations	21	22	14
Total %:	100	100	100
Total N:	38	23	36

$$\gamma = -0.28$$

Source: Joel D. Aberbach and Bert A. Rockman, "Clashing Beliefs Within the Executive Branch," *The American Political Science Review*, 70 (June, 1976), 464.

Another example of the use of cross-tabulation as a control procedure is provided by Edward Carmines' study of the relationship between self-esteem and knowledge of political authorities for a sample of adolescents.[7] From his sample of 346 high school seniors, Carmines obtained measures of, among other items, respondents' self-esteem, knowledge of political authorities, and political interest. Principally interested in the relationship between self-esteem and cognitive orientations toward politics, Carmines examined the correlation between these factors, controlling for levels of political interest. The results are shown in Table 8.8. It can be seen that self-esteem was considerably related to the cognitive measure for those with high political interest ($\gamma = 0.51$) but not for those with low interest ($\gamma = 0.13$). Carmines concludes: "Among those for whom politics is salient [i.e., have high interest levels], a clear relationship emerges... between self-esteem and political knowledge. For the less interested [the relationship] falls..."[8]

An interesting sociological example of cross-tabulation control is provided by Leonard I. Pearlin and Clarice W. Radabaugh's study of the relationship between levels of anxiety and use of alcohol as a mechanism for distress control.[9] Table 8.9 shows the breakdowns based on a sample of 2300 people in the Chicago area. It can be seen that the correlation (gamma) between levels of anxiety and disposition to use alcohol for distress control decreases as levels of self-esteem increase. For those with high levels of self-esteem there

[7] Edward G. Carmines, "Psychological Origins of Adolescent Political Attitudes," *American Politics Quarterly*, 6 (April, 1978), 167–186.

[8] *Ibid.*, p. 178.

[9] Leonard I. Pearlin and Clarice W. Radabaugh, "Economic Strains and the Coping Functions of Alcohol," *American Journal of Sociology*, 82 (November, 1976), 652–663.

Table 8.7
Bureaucratic Beliefs About Equality of Representation by Party Affiliation Controlling for Agency Affiliation (percent)

Beliefs About Equality of Representation	Agency Affiliation					
	Social Service (HEW, HUD, OEO)			Non-Social Service (Labor, Agriculture, etc.)		
	Republican	Independent	Democrat	Republican	Independent	Democrat
Some groups inadequately represented	67	88	89	47	67	65
All groups considered with some reservations	22	22	11	30	—	15
All groups considered with no reservations	11	0	0	23	33	19
Total %:	100	100	100	100	100	99
Total N:	9	8	9	30	15	26
	$\gamma = -0.49$			$\gamma = -0.20$		

Source: Joel D. Aberbach and Bert A. Rockman, "Clashing Beliefs Within the Executive Branch," The American Political Science Review, 70 (June, 1976), 465.

Table 8.8
Self-esteem by the Knowledge of Political Authorities Index,
Controlling for Political Interest (percent)

Knowledge of Political Authorities	Political Interest					
	High Self-esteem			Low Self-esteem		
	Low	Medium	High	Low	Medium	High
Low	59	32	14	54	53	44
Medium	23	40	36	35	34	42
High	18	28	50	11	13	14
Total %:	100	100	100	100	100	100
Total N:	22	25	36	85	74	85

$$\gamma = 0.51 \qquad \gamma = 0.13$$

Source: Edward G. Carmines, "Psychological Origins of Adolescent Political Attitudes," *American Politics Quarterly*, 6 (April, 1978), 178. Reprinted by permission of the Publisher, Sage Publications, Inc.

was very little relationship between anxiety levels and disposition to use alcohol for distress control. Pearlin and Radabaugh conclude: "It is apparent that self-esteem enables one to bear a burden of anxiety without turning to practices that blunt awareness of the burden.... Intense anxiety, in sum, is especially likely to result in the use of alcohol as a tranquilizer of a sort if... self-esteem is low."[10]

Partial Correlation

Cross-tabulation control procedures are very useful in that they allow us to examine the correlation between two variables for each level of the control variable. Thus we are able to observe nuances in the relationships that would otherwise remain undetected. In addition, cross-tabulation procedures may be used with any level of data, although it is most common to see the procedure used with nominal and ordinal data.

Cross-tabulation procedures have two major disadvantages. First, cross-tabulation becomes very cumbersome when dealing with a control variable of several categories or especially when dealing with several control variables at the same time. In the illustrations presented above, we were always examining a single control variable having only two or three categories of control. Interpretation in such cases is relatively straightforward. But, imagine applying three or four control variables, each having several categories. A dozen or more tables might be generated, rendering the interpretation and reporting of such results quite complex and tedious.

[10] *Ibid.*, p. 661.

Table 8.9
Self-esteem, Anxiety, and Disposition to Use Alcohol for Distress Control (percent)

Disposition to Use Alcohol for Distress Control	Self-esteem								
	Low			Moderate			High		
	Intense Anxiety	Moderate Anxiety	Low Anxiety	Intense Anxiety	Moderate Anxiety	Low Anxiety	Intense Anxiety	Moderate Anxiety	Low Anxiety
Strong	37	29	17	20	20	17	13	7	10
Weak	18	14	26	22	18	15	15	16	14
Minimal	45	57	57	58	62	68	72	77	76
Total %:	100	100	100	100	100	100	100	100	100
Total N:	114	83	98	81	115	145	141	272	622
		$\gamma = 0.20$			$\gamma = 0.11$			$\gamma = 0.02$	

Source: Leonard I. Pearlin and Clarice W. Radabaugh, "Economic Strains and the Coping Functions of Alcohol," American Journal of Sociology, 82 (November, 1976), 662. By permission of University of Chicago Press.

More important, the application of cross-tabulation is limited by the size of the sample. Cross-tabulation divides the sample into smaller and smaller subsamples for each category of control. It does not take long, using this procedure, to exhaust all cases. Unless the number of cases is very large, it is difficult to apply more than two or three cross-tabulation controls at the same time.

A second method of control is the technique known as *partial correlation*. As is discussed in this chapter, the partial correlation technique is limited to interval-level data. However, it is not limited by sample size, and many controls can be applied even when the total number of observations is relatively small.

The partial correlation technique extends the logic of simple regression analysis discussed in Chapter 7. There, it will be recalled, we used knowledge of an independent variable to predict values of a linear dependent variable. In the example presented in Chapter 7, our regression equation was found to be a very accurate predictor of the values of the dependent variable, and the coefficient of determination (r^2) told us precisely the amount of variance reduction that was produced by this routine.

However, some error in prediction remained. In Chapter 7 we called the amount of variance remaining in the dependent variable after accounting for the independent variable the "unexplained variance." Another term often used to describe this value is that of *residual*. Residuals represent those deviations in the dependent variable left unaccounted for by variations in the independent variable. Residuals also help us to understand the concept of the partial correlation coefficient.

Assume that we are interested in the relationship between X_1 and X_2 but believe that a third factor, X_3, may also affect this relationship. It may be that we are testing a spurious model similar to that depicted in Figure 8.1, repeated in Figure 8.4. We suspect here that the association between X_1 and X_2 may really result from the fact that the two are related to X_3. The partial correlation routine tests for this by correlating the *residuals* of the regressions of X_1 on X_3 and X_2 on X_3. That is, two regression equations are generated: one predicting the values of X_1 based on X_3, the other predicting the values of X_2 based on X_3. The residual values that result represent the variation in both X_2 and X_1 that is *unexplained* by X_3. The correlation of these residuals, then, represents the correlation of X_2 and X_1, controlling for

Figure 8.4
Illustration of a spurious model

176

the effect of X_3 on each. The result is the partial correlation between X_1 and X_2, controlling for X_3.

A second way to think of the partial correlation coefficient is as an average of all the simple correlation coefficients between X_2 and X_1 that would result if the correlations were calculated for each value of X_3. For each value of X_3, a regression line could be plotted and a correlation coefficient calculated for the appropriate values of X_2 and X_1. The partial correlation coefficient is equivalent to the weighted average that would result from each of these separate simple correlations.[11]

Regardless of which interpretation is placed on the partial correlation coefficient, its computational formula may be presented as

$$r_{X_1 X_2 . X_3} = \frac{r_{X_1 X_2} - (r_{X_1 X_3})(r_{X_2 X_3})}{\sqrt{1 - r_{X_1 X_3}^2} \sqrt{1 - r_{X_2 X_3}^2}}$$

Or, the partial correlation may be defined more simply as

$$r_{12.3} = \frac{r_{12} - (r_{13})(r_{23})}{\sqrt{1 - r_{13}^2} \sqrt{1 - r_{23}^2}}$$

where 1 and 2 = dependent and independent variables
3 = control variable

In both of these formulas, the symbol to the right of the dot represents the control variable. Thus $r_{12.3}$ represents the partial correlation between X_1 and X_2, controlling for X_3.

By way of illustration, consider the following hypothetical example. Assume that we are interested in the relationship between income and attitudes of racial tolerance. From a sample of 2000 adults we may have found a simple correlation between the two of 0.40. Those with higher incomes were found to be more tolerant. But we suspect that some other factor may be responsible for this apparent correlation. Having also collected information on education, the *correlation matrix* for the three variables might appear as follows:

	X_1 (racial tolerance)	X_2 (income)	X_3 (education)
X_1 (racial tolerance)	1.0		
X_2 (income)	0.40	1.0	
X_3 (education)	0.50	0.60	1.0

[11] See Vanderlyn R. Pine, *Introduction to Social Statistics* (Englewood Cliffs, N.J.: Prentice-Hall, Inc., 1977), pp. 237–251; and Hubert M. Blalock, *Social Statistics* (New York: McGraw-Hill Book Company, 1972), pp. 433–440 for excellent brief discussions of the partial correlation coefficient.

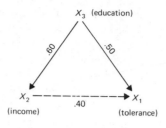

Where: dotted line represents a
possible spurious relationship

Figure 8.5
Proposed three-variable model.

We see that education is related to both variables, so, again, we may be dealing with a possible spurious situation. In this instance, the model we are testing might appear as shown in Figure 8.5. Applying the formula, we see that the partial correlation between income and racial tolerance, controlling for education, is

$$r_{12.3} = \frac{r_{12} - (r_{13})(r_{23})}{\sqrt{1 - r_{13}^2}\sqrt{1 - r_{23}^2}}$$

$$= \frac{0.4 - (0.5)(0.6)}{\sqrt{1 - 0.5^2}\sqrt{1 - 0.6^2}}$$

$$= 0.14$$

Here, the correlation between income and racial tolerance has been substantially reduced. In this hypothetical example, we would conclude that the relationship between income and racial tolerance is largely spurious. The important factor in each instance (at least until additional controls indicate otherwise) is education. Those with higher education levels have higher incomes and are more racially tolerant.

One additional fact should be observed from this example of the calculation of the partial correlation coefficient. Examining the formula, it can be seen that the numerator is a result of subtracting from the value of the simple correlation coefficient between the independent and dependent variables (r_{12}) the product of the simple correlation coefficients between the control variable and the independent variable (r_{23}) and the control variable and the dependent variable (r_{13}). From this it can be inferred that whenever the value of the product of the correlations between the control variable and the independent and dependent variables approximates the value of the correlation between the independent and dependent variables, the partial correlation between the independent and dependent variables will be reduced accordingly. If the two values are exactly the same, the partial correlation coefficient will be zero, since $r_{12} - (r_{13})(r_{23})$ would be equal to zero. These relationships can assist in gaining a rough estimation of the magnitude of the partial correlation coefficient before actually calculating its value.

It was mentioned above that control techniques can sometimes assist in our attempt to specify the nature of the relationship among variables. That is, the actual relationship among variables sometimes may not be obvious, and control techniques can provide a means of clarifying our model.

The distinctions between model types also were discussed above (Figure 8.3). Recall that it was noted there that several models may be used to describe the relationship between three variables and that if certain (rather restrictive) assumptions about the data are made, controlling techniques can help select the model which is said to "best fit" the data. As an example, assume that for a set of "democratic nations." the researcher has collected information pertaining to liberality of election laws, levels of political trust, and rates of citizen participation in national elections. The simple correlation matrix for this set of (hypothetical) data might appear as follows:

	Participation Rate (X_1)	Level of Political Trust (X_2)	Liberality of Election Laws (X_3)
Participation Rate (X_1)	1.0		
Level of Political Trust (X_2)	0.38	1.0	
Liberality of Election Laws (X_3)	0.48	0.64	1.0

Assume, further, that the researcher proposes two models which might plausibly depict these relationships. These are presented in Figure 8.6.

In Model 1 the researcher is hypothesizing a spurious relationship to exist. Here, it is suggested that liberality of election laws leads to increased trust in the political regime and also facilitates greater levels of participation in national elections. The correlation between political trust and level of participation is said in this instance to be spurious, dependent largely on the fact that both are correlated with liberality of election laws. If Model 1 is correct, the correlation between trust and participation should be substantially reduced when controlling for liberality of election laws.

In Model 2 the researcher is hypothesizing a developmental model to best represent the data. Here, it is said that increased liberality of election laws leads to increased political trust which, in turn, leads to greater levels of participation. The correlation between liberality of election laws and rates

179

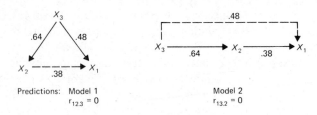

Predictions:　Model 1　　　　　　　　　　　Model 2
　　　　　　　$r_{12.3} = 0$　　　　　　　　　　　$r_{13.2} = 0$

Where:　X_1 = rate of participation in national elections
　　　　X_2 = levels of political trust
　　　　X_3 = liberality of election laws

Figure 8.6
Alternative models of relationship between liberality of election laws, levels of political trust, and rates of participation in national elections. Data are hypothetical.

of participation in this instance is said to be dependent on the mediating effects of political trust and, if this model is correct, should be substantially reduced when controlling for the trust variable.

As discussed above, the researcher can at least statistically determine which of these two alternative models more accurately represents this set of data by use of controlling techniques. If Model 1 best fits the data, it is predicted that $r_{12.3} = 0$ (the relationship between citizen participation and political trust, controlling for liberality of election laws, should be zero). If Model 2 best fits the data, it is predicted that $r_{13.2} = 0$ (the relationship between citizen participation and liberality of election laws, controlling for political trust, should be zero). It is a simple matter now to calculate the two partial correlation coefficients and compare the results. Whichever is closer to zero is said to represent the model that best fits the data.

Model 1　　　　　　　　　　　Model 2
(predicted $r_{12.3} = 0$)　　　　　　　(predicted $r_{13.2} = 0$)

$$r_{12.3} = \frac{0.38 - (0.48)(0.64)}{\sqrt{1-0.48^2}\ \sqrt{1-0.64^2}}$$
$$= 0.11$$

$$r_{13.2} = \frac{0.48 - (0.38)(0.64)}{\sqrt{1-0.38^2}\ \sqrt{1-0.64^2}}$$
$$= 0.33$$

Since the value of $r_{12.3}$ (0.11) is closer to the predicted value of zero, it is said that Model 1 best fits the data. The researcher would conclude, therefore, that the relationship as described in Model 1 is a better representation of the relationship among these three variables.[12]

We have been discussing to this point the partial correlation between an independent variable and a dependent variable controlling for one control

[12] For a more thorough discussion of the entire "causal modeling" issue, see Herbert B. Asher, *Causal Modeling* (Beverly Hills, Calif.: Sage Publications, 1976).

variable. This value is also called the *first-order partial correlation coefficient*, to indicate that only one variable is being controlled. Squaring the first-order partial correlation coefficient ($r^2_{12.3}$), we obtain a value analogous in interpretation to r^2. This value, known as the *partial coefficient of determination*, represents the variation in the dependent variable explained by the independent variable when controlling for the third factor.

As was the case with cross-tabulation, it is possible using partial correlation techniques to control for more than one variable at a time. When controlling for the effects of two variables, the formula for the partial correlation coefficient is

$$r_{12.34} = \frac{r_{12.3} - (r_{14.3})(r_{24.3})}{\sqrt{1 - r^2_{14.3}} \; \sqrt{1 - r^2_{24.3}}}$$

Using the SPSS packaged program and data stored on punchcards or some other medium, this partial correlation coefficient could be generated by the following command:

```
PARTIAL CORR    VAR001 WITH VAR002 BY VAR003,VAR004 (2)
```

where   VAR001 and VAR002 = dependent and independent variables
        VAR003 and VAR004 = control variables

By extension, it is possible to control for three, four, or more variables at the same time. It is important to remember, however, that no matter how many controls are attempted, the partial correlation routine will generate only *one value*. This differs from the cross-tabulation procedure, where a separate value is generated for each category of control.

Some Substantive Examples of Partial Correlation

One particularly poignant application of the partial correlation coefficient is illustrated by Thomas Dye's investigation of the relationships at the state level among competitiveness of political parties, welfare expenditures, and economic development. Testing for the expectation that state welfare expenditures would be strongly and positively correlated with two party competitiveness (the more competitive states were expected to spend more per capita on welfare services), Dye initially did find strong simple correlations between these variables in the direction predicted. But, when controlling for the effect of economic development (measures of urbanization, industrialization, income, and education) by use of partial correlation coefficients, these strong simple correlation coefficients were generally significantly weakened. According to Dye, "When the effects of economic development are controlled in the partial correlation coefficients ... almost all of the association between party competition and policy outcomes

181

Table 8.10
Relationship Between Party Competition and
Welfare Expenditures Among the States, Controlling
for the Effect of Economic Development

Welfare Expenditures	Party Competition[a]	
	Simple Correlation	Partial Correlation
Per capita welfare	0.12	−0.13
Per capita health	0.10	0.08
Unemployment benefits	0.72	0.05
Old-age benefits	0.64	0.01
Aid-to-dependent-children Benefits	0.77	0.04
Blind benefits	0.61	0.11
Kerr–Mills benefit	0.15	0.01
General assistance	0.70	0.16

Source: Thomas R. Dye, "The Independent Effect of Party Competition on Policy Outcomes in the American System," paper presented at the 1965 annual meeting of the *American Political Science Association*, Washington, D.C., and reprinted in Robert E. Crew, ed., *State Politics* (Belmont, Calif.: Wadsworth Publishing Company, Inc., 1968), p. 255.

[a] In this table, party competition is measured as 1 minus the percentage of seats in the lower house held by the majority party from 1954 to 1964. Dye also used measures of gubernatorial and upper house party competiveness as well as other measures of policy outcomes. In general, however, the results were similar to those reported here. The student should compare these results with those of Edward Carmines reported in Chapter 7.

[welfare expenditures] disappears. ... In short, party competition has *no apparent independent effect* on [the majority of the] policy outcomes investigated."[13] A portion of Dye's analysis is reproduced in Table 8.10.

Controlling techniques do not always dramatically alter the researcher's original findings, as is illustrated by Alan Monroe's study of voter turnout in Illinois.[14] Using counties as his unit of analysis and examining the relationship between voting turnout in the 1972 general election and several political and demographic variables, Monroe found the correlations listed in Table 8.11. Monroe notes the high *negative* simple correlation coefficients between most of these variables and voter turnout. Surprised at these findings, Monroe then reexamines each of these relationships, controlling in the first instance for percent urban and in the second for median age. While the magnitude of the correlations are then reduced, most of the signs are still negative and Monroe finds that while the controls altered the *magnitude*, they did not significantly

[13] Thomas R. Dye, "The Independent Effect of Party Competition on Policy Outcomes in the American System," paper presented at the 1965 annual meeting of the *American Political Science Association*, Washington, D.C., and reprinted in Robert E. Crew, ed., *State Politics* (Belmont, Calif.: Wadsworth Publishing Company, Inc., 1968), pp. 249–260 (emphasis in original).

[14] Alan D. Monroe, "Urbanism and Voter Turnout: A Note on Some Unexpected Findings," *American Journal of Political Science*, 21 (February, 1977), 71–78.

Table 8.11
Simple and Partial Correlations with 1972 Voting Turnout:
Illinois County Returns

Variables	Simple r	Partial r (controlling for percent urban)	Partial r (controlling for median age)
% Urban	−0.70	—	−0.55
Education	−0.32	−0.15	−0.12
Manufacturing	−0.37	−0.18	−0.18
Professional and managerial	−0.54	−0.18	−0.26
Income	−0.50	−0.21	−0.15
% Nonwhite	−0.32	0.17	−0.32
Age	0.62	0.41	—
Noncompetiveness[a]	−0.13	−0.18	0.00

Source: Alan D. Monroe, "Urbanism and Voter Turnout: A Note on Some Unexpected Findings," American Journal of Political Science, 21 (February, 1977), 74–75. For ease of presentation, I have combined two of Monroe's tables.
[a] Noncompetiveness is a measure of lack of interparty competition.

alter the *pattern* of the original relationships. Monroe says: "The conclusion is inescapable that it is the areas of Illinois most generally considered 'backward' or 'undeveloped,' characterized by rural isolation, lack of vigorous economic base, whether agriculture or industrial, and an aging and declining population, which demonstrate the highest degree of participation in the electoral process."[15]

Multivariate Analysis

To this point we have been discussing primarily the isolated impact of a single independent variable on a dependent variable. Control techniques (either cross-tabulation or partial correlation analysis) are used to help clarify this relationship.

In addition, we are often interested in assessing the relative and combined impacts of a number of independent variables on a dependent variable. We would like to know the relative and combined impacts of all those variables related to legislators' voting behavior, political activism among the electorate, state voting patterns, and so forth. The classification of techniques useful for such exploration is called *multivariate analysis.*

Multiple Regression

The general regression equation for multivariate analysis can be presented as an extension of the simple regression equation. The multiple regression

[15] *Ibid.,* p. 76.

equation is

$$Y = a + b_1 X_1 + b_2 X_2 + \ldots b_i X_i$$

where
$$\begin{aligned} a \quad &= Y \text{ intercept} \\ b_1 \cdots b_i \quad &= \text{partial slopes} \\ X_1 \cdots X_i \quad &= \text{independent variables} \end{aligned}$$

The b's generated by the multiple regression routine are known as *partial slopes*, since they represent the amount of change in the dependent variable associated with each independent variable, holding all other independent variables constant. Thus, in the case of two independent variables, the multiple regression equation can more appropriately be presented as

$$Y_p = a_{y.x_1 x_2} + b_{yx_1.x_2}(X_1) + b_{yx_2.x_1}(X_2)$$

where
$$\begin{aligned} Y_p \quad &= \text{predicted values of } Y \\ a_{y.x_1 x_2} \quad &= Y \text{ intercept value} \\ b_{yx_1.x_2} \quad &= \text{partial regression of } Y \text{ and } X_1, \text{ holding } X_2 \text{ constant} \\ b_{yx_2.x_1} \quad &= \text{partial regression of } Y \text{ and } X_2, \text{ holding } X_1 \text{ constant} \\ X_1 \text{ and } X_2 \quad &= \text{values of } X_1 \text{ and } X_2 \end{aligned}$$

The calculation of each constant is relatively straightforward.[16] Based on the simple regression coefficients, $b_{yx_1.x_2}$ would be equivalent to

$$b_{yx_1.x_2} = \frac{b_{yx_1} - (b_{yx_2})(b_{x_2 x_1})}{1 - (b_{x_1 x_2})(b_{x_2 x_1})}$$

Similarly, $b_{yx_2.x_1}$ may be calculated and the coefficient of the Y intercept can be thought of as

$$a_{y.x_1 x_2} = \bar{Y}_p - b_{yx_1.x_2}(\bar{X}_1) - b_{yx_2.x_1}(\bar{X}_2)$$

The partial slope of each independent variable generated through this routine is interpreted as the amount of expected change in the dependent variable (Y) associated with a 1-unit change in the independent variable, holding constant (controlling for) all other independent variables. The regression equation represents our best estimate of the values of the dependent variable for any combination of values of the independent variables.

[16]For a more thorough explanation, see Pine, *Introduction to Social Statistics*, pp. 214–217; and Dennis J. Palumbo, *Statistics in Political and Behavioral Science*, (New York: Appleton-Century-Crofts, 1969), pp. 210–214.

The partial slopes also allow us to compare the *importance* of the independent variables. If two subsamples of a population are being examined (let's say black and white Americans), the relative magnitudes of the partial slopes generated for each subpopulation indicate the relative strength of each independent variable. The higher in value the partial slope, the more important is that variable in explaining the dependent variable for the particular subpopulation.

If we wish to compare the relative impact of the various independent variables *with each other*, however, the partial slopes are of little use. This is because the variables in the equation may have been measured according to different scale values. One variable may be measured in terms of dollars, another years of education, and still another in terms of intelligence scores. With such disparate values, it makes little sense to compare the impact of a unit change of one variable with the impact of a unit change of another.

Therefore, if we wish to assess the relative importance of each predictive variable in a single regression equation, we make use of a statistic called the beta weight. The beta weight (symbolized as β) is simply the slope that would be obtained if all variables were standardized. The beta weight is thus known as the *standardized partial regression coefficient*, and its major advantage lies in allowing comparison of the *relative* impact of change in the independent variables on change in the dependent variable. The beta weight is calculated by multiplying the partial slope by the ratio of the standard deviation of the independent variable to that of the dependent variable. Thus $\beta_{yx_1.x_2}$ would be calculated as

$$\beta_{yx_1.x_2} = b_{yx_1.x_2} \frac{s_{x_1}}{s_y}$$

An example will help clarify these points. In the 1976 American National Election Study respondents were asked to indicate their opinion about medical coverage in the United States. This was accomplished by having respondents place themselves on a seven-point continuum ranging from those favoring a nationwide government insurance plan (1) to those favoring individual payment of medical expenses or private insurance (7). As variables assisting in explaining the distribution of response to this question, we might consider respondents' income and political views (measured on a liberal-to-conservative scale). We might hypothesize that those with higher incomes would favor private programs and that the more conservative would also favor private plans. In the 1976 survey, the Center for Political Studies coded income from 1 (less than $2000 annual income) to 20 ($35,000 and over). In this survey, respondents were also asked to place themselves on a seven-point political view continuum ranging from extremely liberal (1) to extremely conservative (7). Selecting opinions toward medical coverage as the dependent variable, the following equations present the partial regression and

185

standardized partial regression coefficients (beta weights) for income and political views[17]:

(1) $Y_p = 0.79 + 0.62(X_1) + 0.06(X_2)$ partial regression coefficients
(2) $Y_p = 0.79 + 0.37(X_1) + 0.15(X_2)$ beta weights

where X_1 = political views (extremely liberal to extremely conservative)
       X_2 = income
       Y_p = predicted opinion toward medical insurance

The first equation shows the actual partial regression coefficients for this equation. For any combination of X_1 (political views) and X_2 (income) values, we can predict (again, assuming a linear relationship) the expected Y (opinion toward medical insurance) values. Assume that an individual has an income of \$35,000 per year or more and considers himself extremely conservative. This person would receive a code of 20 on the income measure and a code of 7 on the political views scale. Placing these values in the first equation presented above, we find this person's expected score on the medical insurance scale to be

$$Y_p = 0.79 + 0.62(7) + 0.06(20)$$
$$= 6.33 \quad \text{(rounded to 6)}$$

Thus this individual would be expected to fall near the end of the medical insurance opinion scale stressing private insurance programs. A person with an income score of 1 (less than \$2000 annual income) and a political view score of 1 (extremely liberal) would have an expected score on the medical insurance opinion scale of 1.47 — or very near the end of the scale stressing government-provided insurance coverage. All other combinations of income and political view scores would produce predicted medical insurance opinion scores falling between these two extremes.

The second equation expresses the regression equation for these variables in terms of beta weights. Since the beta weight for political views (0.37) is stronger than that for income (0.15), it is concluded that the political view continuum (measured as extremely liberal to extremely conservative) is a more potent force in explaining opinions to the medical insurance question than is income.

The Multiple Correlation Coefficient

As was the case when considering simple correlation, the *coefficient of multiple determination* (R^2) represents the proportion of the variance in the dependent variable explained by all the independent variables.

[17] The reader will note that in this example I have used interval-level techniques with ordinal-level data. The pros and cons of this were discussed in Chapter 7. Among other problems, interval techniques will generate fractional predictions (such as 6.33) which have no meaning with ordinal data. In cases such as these, fractions should be rounded to the nearest whole number.

It will be helpful to understand R^2 if we first think of it in terms of a unique situation. We recall from Chapter 7 that the coefficient of determination (r^2) in the bivariate situation represents the amount of variance in the dependent variable explained by the independent variable. In the multivariate sense, the total variance explained by all independent variables is equivalent to the sum of the r^2 of each independent variable with the dependent variable *when the independent variables are totally uncorrelated.* But it is almost never the case that the independent variables are totally uncorrelated. Simply summing the r^2 of the dependent variable with several *correlated* independent variables would soon result in a sum of explained variance larger than 100 percent.

In most cases, then, R^2 is more appropriately defined as the sum of the *remaining* variance in the dependent variable explained by each independent variable after the influence of every other independent variable has been accounted for. In the case of two independent variables, the first variable (X_1) explains all the variance it can in the dependent variable, and the second variable (X_2) then explains all the remaining variance in Y which it can. The amount of variance in the dependent variable explained by X_1 is, as we have seen before, $r^2_{yx_1}$. The amount of remaining variance explained by X_2 will be expressed as the product of the variance in Y explained by X_2, controlling for $X_1(r^2_{yx_2.x_1})$, multiplied by the proportion of variance in Y left unexplained by X_1.

In the case of two independent variables, these relationships can be expressed as

$$R^2_{y.x_1x_2} \quad = \quad r^2_{yx_1} \quad + \quad r^2_{yx_2.x_1} \quad (1-r^2_{yx_1})$$

$$\begin{pmatrix} \text{total variance} \\ \text{in } Y \text{ explained} \\ \text{by } X_1 \text{ and } X_2 \end{pmatrix} = \begin{pmatrix} \text{proportion of} \\ \text{variance in } Y \\ \text{explained by} \\ X_1 \end{pmatrix} + \begin{pmatrix} \text{proportion of} \\ \text{variance in } Y \\ \text{explained by } X_2 \\ \text{in addition to} \\ \text{that explained} \\ \text{by } X_1 \end{pmatrix} \begin{pmatrix} \text{amount of} \\ \text{variance left} \\ \text{unexplained} \\ \text{by } X_1 \end{pmatrix}$$

It should be noted that the symbol for R^2 has only one character to the left of the dot. This is to signify that, in this case, the variable Y is the dependent variable and X_1 and X_2 are the independent variables. A more general symbol for R^2 is $R^2_{1.234...i}$, where variable 1 is the dependent variable and all those to the right are considered to be independent variables. R^2, as mentioned above, is called the coefficient of multiple determination. It ranges in value from 0 to $+1.0$. The *multiple correlation coefficient* (symbolized as R) is the positive square root of R^2. As was the case with r, R is a measure of how well actual values of Y fit with those predicted by the (in this case, multiple) regression equation.

For the example of opinions toward medical insurance presented above,

R^2 would be calculated as

$$R^2 = r^2_{yx_1} + r^2_{yx_2 \cdot x_1} (1 - r^2_{yx_1})$$
$$= 0.147 + 0.0246 (1 - 0.147)$$
$$= 0.168$$

Income and political views, it can be concluded, explain about 17 percent ($R^2 = .168$) of the variation in opinions toward medical insurance. Taking the square root of this, we achieve the R of 0.41.

Some Substantive Examples of Multivariate Analysis

An interesting example of the use of multiple regression is provided by Gary C. Jacobson's examination of the determinants of campaign spending by incumbent congressmen.[18] Using several variables as predictors of campaign spending by incumbents seeking reelection, Jacobson found the data given in Table 8.12.

Table 8.12
Determinants of Spending by Incumbents in the 1972 and 1974 House Elections

Variables	1972 Regression Coefficients	1972 Standardized Regression Coefficients	1974 Regression Coefficients	1974 Standardized Regression Coefficients
X_1	0.522	0.54	0.495	0.51
X_2	3.31	0.04	12.69	0.14
X_3	0.224	0.06	0.673	0.14
X_4	10.50	0.13	0.10	0.00
X_5	-0.789	-0.15	-0.035	-0.01
X_6	3.10	0.03	6.79	0.07
X_7	0.89	0.01	-12.50	-0.10
a (Y intercept)	$= 28.08$		$a = 14.11$	
	$R^2 = 0.39$		$R^2 = 0.47$	

where X_1 = campaign expenditure of challenger (in thousands of dollars)
X_2 = challenger's party
X_3 = strength of challenger's party in the district
X_4 = measure of whether the incumbent had run in a primary election
X_5 = number of years incumbent had been in the House
X_6 = measure of whether challenger had held elective office
X_7 = measure of whether the incumbent held a House leadership position

Source: Gary C. Jacobson, "The Effects of Campaign Spending in Congressional Elections," The American Political Science Review, 72 (June, 1978), 473.

[18] Gary C. Jacobson, "The Effects of Campaign Spending in Congressional Elections," The American Political Science Review, 72 (June, 1978), 469–491.

Examining the multiple coefficients of determination, it can be seen that in both years the combined impact of all these variables explained a considerable amount of the variation in incumbent campaign spending (39 percent in 1972 and 47 percent in 1974).

Jacobson's most important finding in this instance is revealed when examining the standardized regression coefficients (beta weights). Here, it is seen that for both years the most influential predictor variable by far is the amount of money spent by the incumbents' challengers. As the challenger spent more money in the campaign, so did the incumbent. According to Jacobson: "The evidence that incumbents are able to adjust their spending to the gravity of the challenge is convincing. ... the challenger's spending is the most important explanatory variable in these equations."[19]

Another example of the use of multivariate analysis is provided by Eugene Declercq, Thomas Hurley, and Norman Luttbeg's analysis of presidential voting from 1956 to 1972.[20] Using data provided by the CPS, the authors found the correlations shown in Table 8.13.

First, it is found that all these variables explain substantial proportions of voting for each of the five elections. The R^2 values range from 49 percent

Table 8.13
Determinants of Voting, 1956–1972
(Non-Southern Respondents Only)

	Determinants				
	Party Identification	Issue Orientation	Candidate Image	Party Image	R^2
1956 Vote					
β	0.41	0.11	0.18	0.23	0.59
b	0.09	0.05	0.04	0.03	
1960 Vote					
β	0.40	0.10	0.26	0.20	0.61
b	0.09	0.04	0.05	0.03	
1964 Vote					
β	0.35	0.21	0.23	0.17	0.55
b	0.07	0.05	0.05	0.03	
1968 Vote					
β	0.40	0.20	0.24	0.13	0.58
b	0.09	0.09	0.05	0.02	
1972 Vote					
β	0.27	0.29	0.29	0.10	0.49
b	0.06	0.07	0.09	0.02	

Source Eugene R. Declercq, Thomas L. Hurley, and Norman R. Luttbeg, "Presidential Voting Change in the South: 1956–1972," *The Journal of Politics*, 39 (May, 1977), 485.

[19] *Ibid.*, p. 472.

[20] Eugene R. Declercq, Thomas L. Hurley, and Norman R. Luttbeg, "Presidential Voting Change in the South: 1956–1972," *The Journal of Politics*, 39 (May, 1977), 480–492.

explained in 1972 to 61 percent explained in 1960. Second, it can be seen that throughout this period, with the exception of 1972, party identification is the most important predictor of the vote. Summarizing their findings, the authors conclude: "Party identification remains preeminent as an influence on the vote until 1972. After a loss of influence in 1964 and 1968, Candidate Image rebounds sharply in 1972 closely rivaling, if not tying, Issue Orientation in influence. Party Image lacks any substantial impact. And Issue Orientation follows a sawtooth pattern...."[21]

Some Concluding Comments on the Issue of Control

The student of political research should thoroughly consider the differences between "true" experimental and survey research and the implications of these differences for systematic scientific research. Earlier, we briefly noted these distinctions and observed that often political research is not amenable to the true experimental design.

Sometimes, however, the political researcher *will* be able to utilize a true experimental design situation. For example, the policy researcher interested in the impact of drug education programs on drug use, knowledge, and attitudes among secondary students might very well be able to apply an experimental design. With the permission of school authorities, parents, and students, the researcher could randomly assign some students to participate in the drug education program (or several varieties of drug education programs), and some could be assigned to a group of control students recieving no drug education program. Following exposure to the drug education program, all groups could be tested on measures of drug use, knowledge, and attitudes and these scores could be compared with pretest scores for each group. Any differences would be said to be at least partially attributable to the influence of the drug education program. Similarly, one interested in decision making at the level of the municipal council could, perhaps, persuade a group of council members to conduct, under a controlled setting, a council meeting at which all decision issues and parameters would be manipulated by the researcher.[22]

---

[21] *Ibid.*, 489.

[22] Perhaps the most ambitous policy research evaluation employing a design closely paralleling a true experiment is the New Jersey Graduated Work Incentive Experiment begun in 1969 and originally funded by the Office of Economic Opportunity. In this experiment a number of poor families were selected in an attempt to determine the social and economic impacts of differing levels of guaranteed income. A control sample of poor families receiving no payments was also included in the experiment. For evaluations of this effort, see David Kershaw and Jerilyn Fair, *The New Jersey Income Maintenance Experiment*, Vol. I (New York: Academic Press, Inc., 1977); Harold Watts and Albert Rees, eds., *The New Jersey Income Maintenance Experiment*, Vols II and III (New York: Academic Press, Inc., 1977); Peter Rossi and Katharine

The true experiment greatly clarifies the issue of causation. Differences between pre- and post-tests for control and treatment groups are said to result at least partially from the effect of the treatment. The independent variable (drug education programs, for example) is said to have been the cause of these differences if, indeed, meaningful change takes place.[23] The true experiment is superior to other research designs in ascertaining the direction of causation, and since this is the ultimate goal of all science, the true experimental research situation, when it can be applied, is clearly superior to quasi-experimental or nonexperimental research situations.

Why, then, do we not always use true experimental designs in political research? The answer to this question surely is obvious. In political (and, indeed, almost all social research), it is rarely the case that the researcher can actually manipulate the independent variable. People must be studied *as they are*. We cannot (nor would we want to) assign one group to the ranks of the rich, another to the poor; or one to the educated, another to the uneducated; or one to the Republican Party, another to the Democrats; or one to a politically active group, another to a politically inactive group. In much of political and social research, we study people who have *already* been exposed to the treatment variable (income, education, party identification, political activism) and try to infer, with tools such as those discussed in this chapter, the effects of this variable. But since many other intervening and confounding variables may influence the dependent variable as well, the best we can do is infer *possible* causation.

Yet, survey research has advantages of its own.[24] Perhaps its greatest advantage is its facilitation of the selection of a *representative sample* to be studied. Whatever results may have been obtained from the hypothetical experimental study of drug education in a school system or decision making of a city council can apply only to that school system and that city council. These results are not necessarily generalizable to any other school system or any other city council. Only at the greatest expense and trouble could even one treatment and one control group randomly selected from some large population (such as all high school students or all city council members) be assembled in one location for the purpose of participating in a true

---

Lyall, *Reforming Public Welfare: A Critique of the Negative Income Tax Experiment* (New York: Russell Sage Foundation, 1976); Joseph Pechman and Michael Timpane, eds., *Work Incentive and Income Guarantees: The New Jersey Negative Income Tax Experiment* (Washington, D.C.: The Brookings Institution, 1975); and a review essay of all of these by Peggy Heilig, entitled "The New Jersey Income Maintenance Experiment: Lessons for Policy Research," appearing in *Urban Affairs Quarterly*, 14 (September, 1978), 123–131.

[23]Even here, the determination of causation is not assured. A host of external and internal validity issues may influence the outcome. See Campbell and Stanley, *Experimental and Quasi-Experimental Designs for Research*, 5–6, for a discussion of these factors.

[24]For an excellent discussion of the advantages and disadvantages of experimental and quasi-experimental research, see Julian L. Simon, *Basic Research Methods in Social Science* (New York: Random House, Inc., 1969), pp. 228–255.

experimental research situation. However, at a reasonable cost, we can interview a random sample of the population (high school students, city council members, or even the American electorate) and can generalize from the results of that sample to the entire population. So, survey research facilitates the selection of a representative sample and our ability to generalize from that sample to a whole population.

The second advantage flowing from this is expense. Surveys may be less costly than a true experiment would be. This is especially true if interviews are solicited by phone or mail.[25]

Finally, as pointed out by Julian Simon, in survey research "... you can get closer to the 'real'... variables than with a laboratory experiment."[26] By this is meant that survey research, unlike the laboratory, does not construct an artificial situation — people are not asked to play "roles." In survey research we deal with people as they are — poor, rich; black, white; Democrat, Republican; alienated, trusting; politically active, politically inactive; and so on. Taking people as they really are provides insights that are impossible in a simulated laboratory situation.

Thus the methods of control used in survey research are clearly inferior to those used in the true experimental situation when it comes to assessing extent and direction of causation. Yet the methods used in survey research have advantages of their own. We are, at a reasonable cost, able to reach reasonable inferences of causality, and through proper sampling techniques to generalize these conclusions to the larger population. These, too, are very desirable objectives of systematic political research.

Exercises

1. A researcher is interested in the relationship between the public's attitude toward marijuana use and age. From a sample of 245 people interviewed in a particular community, the following results were obtained (all data hypothetical):

Attitudes Toward Marijuana Use	Age		
	35 or Less	Over 35	Totals
More Tolerant	80	50	130
Less Tolerant	40	75	115
Totals	120	125	245

[25] Of course, this may also mean that our standard of representation may have to be relaxed, since mail and phone interviews usually do not result in as high a rate of completed response as do personal interviews.

[26] Simon, *Basic Research Methods in Social Science*, p. 242.

a. Examining the cell entries in this table, what would the researcher conclude about the relationship between age and attitudes toward marijuana use for this sample?

b. Calculate the gamma, tau-b, and Somers' d_{yx} coefficients for this table. How do these coefficients assist in understanding this relationship?

Additionally, the researcher included in the survey questions pertaining to education (for simplicity dividing the sample into those attending and those not attending college). Reexamining the original relationship controlling for the education variable, the following results were obtained:

Attitudes Toward Marijuana Use	Not Attending College			Attending College		
	35 or Less	Over 35	Totals	35 or Less	Over 35	Totals
More Tolerant	3	7	10	77	43	120
Less Tolerant	22	58	80	18	17	35
Totals	25	65	90	95	60	155

c. How is the original relationship between attitudes toward marijuana use and age affected by the control for education as revealed by the cell entries in the above tables?

d. Calculate for the control tables the gamma, tau-b, and Somers' d_{yx} coefficients. How do these compare with the original coefficients calculated above and what do these comparisons reveal about the controlled relationship?

e. Summarize the relationships between age, education, and attitudes toward marijuana use as revealed by these tables. What is the likely explanation (or explanations) for these findings?

2. Assume that a pollster working for a gubernatorial candidate were interested in the relationship between socioeconomic status and voter support for the candidate. From a sample of 500 voters in this particular state the following results might have been obtained, dividing the sample into urban and non-urban residents:

Candidate Support	Urban			Nonurban		
	Low SES	High SES	Totals	Low SES	High SES	Totals
Low	5	115	120	175	5	180
High	55	25	80	65	55	120
Totals	60	140	200	240	60	300

a. On the basis of the cell entries in these tables, what can be said concerning the relationship between socioeconomic status and voter support of the candidate in this particular state?

193

b. From the above tables, reconstruct the original bivariate relationship between socioeconomic status and candidate support. How does the control for urbanization affect this original relationship and assist in a more thorough understanding of this relationship?

c. Calculate the gamma coefficient for the original bivariate relationship between socioeconomic status and candidate support and the gamma coefficients for this relationship controlling for urbanization. How do these coefficients assist in more precisely defining the relationship between socioeconomic status and candidate support in this instance?

3. Assume that a student of municipal politics is interested in the extent of *campaign participation* by the public in a particular local election and has operationalized this variable taking into account such factors as contributing money to a party or candidate, working for a particular candidate, and talking to friends or work associates about the election. Suppose, also, that the student is interested in those factors associated with such participation and has identified *interest in politics* and *exposure to campaign advertising* as possible contributing factors. It is believed that those more interested in politics and those receiving greater exposure to campaign advertising will be more inclined to participate at higher levels than others.

Assume further that the student is interested in testing two possible models relating these variables. These two models are presented below as:

Model 1   Model 2

Where dotted lines represent possible spurious paths.

Having collected data from a sample of 1000 voters in a particular locality, the following matrix of simple correlation coefficients was obtained:

	Interests In Politics	Advertising Exposure	Campaign Participation
Interest in Politics	1.0		
Advertising Exposure	.58	1.0	
Campaign Participation	.45	.25	1.0

a. Test both of the above models calculating the appropriate partial correlation coefficients.

b. What can be said based on these results of the relationships between interest in politics, exposure to campaign advertising, and campaign participation in this particular locality — which if these models appears to "best fit" this set of data?

194

9

HYPOTHESIS TESTING AND THE APPLICATION OF TESTS OF STATISTICAL SIGNIFICANCE

The previous several chapters have examined techniques useful for measuring the degree of association between a dependent variable and one or more independent variables. There, we were asking the question: To what extent does knowledge of the values of one variable (or several variables) assist in our ability to predict values of another variable?

When dealing with *sample data*, there is a second question that can also be asked. This is: How confident can we be that the association found in the sample data truly reflects an association in the population? This is an important question, since it is the population, not the sample, which is of central interest to the researcher. A sample has been selected because it may be impossible to examine all elements of the population. But the researcher is interested in the small number of cases which comprise the sample only to the extent that they allow meaningful projections to the total population. Sample values, as discussed in Chapter 3, may deviate from population values and, in fact, values of repeated samples drawn from the same population may deviate from each other. This deviation of values is known as *sample error*.[1] Because of the possibility of sampling error, there is a risk that the researcher may incorrectly infer, from the sample data, that a relationship exists in the population. Likewise, there is a risk that the researcher may incorrectly infer from the sample that no relationship exists in the population. The first of these are called *Type I*, or *alpha* (α), *errors*; the second are called *Type II*, or *beta* (β) *errors*. The researcher can never eliminate these risks. In fact, procedures that may be taken to reduce one type of risk increase the

[1] As used here, sampling error is contrasted with nonsampling error attributable to the various sources of error associated with collecting, coding, punching, and measuring information.

probability of making the other. It is possible, however, to state with some degree of precision the risks of making either error. In practice, researchers most often measure only the risk of making a Type I error, but it always should be kept in mind that in minimizing the risks of making a Type I error, the chance of making a Type II error increases. The researcher wants to minimize the risk of falsely reporting a relationship in the population that really does not exist (a Type I error). Thus the significance level reported in political research can be thought of as the probability of making a Type I error. There are many tests of significance; this chapter will examine some of those most often used in political research.[2]

Using Tests of Significance

The application of tests of significance involves a number of steps. Among those are:

1. Specifying a null and a research hypothesis.
2. Choosing the appropriate statistical test.
3. Specifying a significance level.
4. Computing the statistic.
5. Deciding whether to accept or reject the hypotheses.

The issues involved in these various steps will be examined in the following discussion.

Specifying Hypotheses

In Chapter 2, hypotheses were defined as "testable statements relating two or more concepts or variables." Here, we can be more precise and note that in the research situation *two* hypotheses are actually being tested. The first is called the research hypothesis (in fact, several research hypotheses may be tested); the second (implied but often not stated) is called the null hypothesis. The *research hypothesis*, symbolized as H_1 (and H_2, H_3, H_4, and so on if more than one alternative is tested) makes an assertion. A hypothesis expressed in Chapter 2 was that, "Alienated citizens are more likely than nonalienated citizens to support extremist political candidates." This is a research hypothesis; a relationship is asserted to exist between levels of alienation and candidate preference.

The *null hypothesis* (symbolized as H_0), on the other hand, assumes *no* relationship to exist. For the situation described above, the null hypothesis might be stated, "No difference exists between the candidate preferences of alienated and nonalienated citizens."

[2] An excellent brief overview of statistical tests of significance can be found in Ramon E. Henkel, *Tests of Significance*, Sage University Paper Series on Quantitative Applications in the Social Sciences, 07-004, (Beverly Hills, Calif.: Sage Publications, 1976).

What is the purpose of stating hypotheses in this fashion? Null hypotheses are necessary because it is never possible to prove an assertion to be true beyond any doubt. The researcher may find that alienated citizens are more likely to support extremist candidates, but this is not proof that it is alienation that leads to the support of extremist candidates. Support of extremist candidates may be explained by any number of other factors. However, hypotheses can be disproven if a hypothesis of no relationship can be shown to be false. By testing the null hypothesis it can be shown that it would be false to conclude that alienation is not possibly related to candidate preference. In so doing, support is lent to the research hypothesis.

Therefore, it can be observed that in the research situation it is actually the null hypothesis that is tested. Acceptance of the null hypothesis (of there being no relationship between two variables) is to conclude that whatever difference may have been evidenced in the sample could have occurred just by chance. The relationship in this case is said to be *not statistically significant*. Rejecting the null hypothesis (of there being no relationship between two variables) is to conclude that whatever difference may have been evidenced in the sample probably did not occur just by accident or by chance. The relationship in this case is said to be *statistically significant*.

The research hypothesis (or hypotheses), then, makes an assertion but is not directly tested. The null hypothesis is tested, and from the results substantive inferences about population characteristics are made.

The Sampling Distribution

The discussion returns at this point to the concept of the normal curve. It will be recalled from Chapter 5 that one property of the normal curve is that a constant proportion of cases can be expected to fall at given intervals lower and higher than the mean. These intervals, it was seen in Chapter 5, are defined in terms of standard deviation units. About 68 percent of all cases can be expected to fall within ± 1 standard deviation of the mean, about 95 percent can be expected to fall within plus or minus 2 standard deviations of the mean, and practically all of the cases can be expected to fall within ± 3 standard deviations of the mean.

As it turns out, these properties are very helpful in assessing the significance of a sample statistic. Consider for a moment the results of drawing repeated samples from a population and calculating for those samples the correlation between two variables when for the *population as a whole, the actual correlation between the two variables is zero*. That is, assume that in the population of all eligible voters, no relationship exists between alienation and candidate preference. Assume also that the researcher has the time and money to draw an infinite number of samples of 1500 or so individuals from that population (an obviously absurd assumption) and calculates for each sample the correlation between alienation and candidate preference. Some of these correlations, reflecting the true population relationship, will be zero;

some of the correlation values will be very close to zero; others will deviate somewhat from zero; and a very few might even be quite strong. In fact, the sampling distribution of these correlation coefficients will approximate a normal curve with a mean of zero. About 95 percent of all the sample correlation coefficients will cluster within 2 standard deviations of the mean (zero). However, a few (about 5 percent) will be expected to lie at a distance of more than ± 2 standard deviations from the mean. If, then, the actual (i.e., population) correlation between alienation and candidate preference is zero, it would be very unusual to achieve sample correlations deviating significantly from zero, although some may.

It is obvious that the researcher never actually draws an infinite number of samples from the population. Rather, one sample typically is drawn from the population and the researcher calculates and examines the correlations (or other statistics) between the variables of interest for that sample. These sample values (correlation coefficients, for example) are compared with an appropriate sampling distribution — a theoretical model representing all possible values that could be obtained and the probability of obtaining such values. There are many theoretical sampling distributions, corresponding to differing research situations and assumptions. Among those to be discussed in later sections of this chapter are the normal, t, chi-square, and F distributions.

Levels of Significance

It should be apparent from the foregoing discussion that the level of significance used to accept or reject a null hypothesis is based largely on the extent of actual variation between the hypothesized and sample values and that which could have occurred just by chance. If the difference between these two values (in the example above the difference between a hypothesized correlation of zero and a sample correlation of some nonzero value) is so great that the researcher is not willing to attribute this just to chance or sampling error, the relationship is said to be *statistically significant* and the null hypothesis is rejected.

But what level of significance must be reached for the researcher to confidently reject the null hypothesis? The more stringent the criteria set, the less the risk of making a Type I error (the incorrect rejection of a true null hypothesis). However, the precise magnitude of the difference to be sought is arbitrary. Although some research situations may require more stringency than others, conventions have developed. In the social sciences, it is typical to see the 0.05 level used as the level of significance. This means that the researcher in rejecting the null hypothesis knows that 5 percent of the time a sample difference as large as the one obtained would be expected to occur *just by chance.* More rigid standards may be set by selecting a significance level of 0.01, 0.001, or some more remote probability level. Having established the 0.001 level, for example, the researcher would not reject the null hypothesis unless the sample correlation were so large as to occur by chance in only 1 out of every 1000 samples. In reducing the risk of falsely reporting a population relationship to exist, however, it should be remembered that the risk of failing to reject a false null hypothesis increases.

One-tailed and Two-tailed Tests

An issue that arises in significance testing is whether to apply one-tailed or two-tailed tests. Actually, the question being asked is whether the hypothesis is directional or nondirectional. A *directional hypothesis* specifies direction of the relationship. The research hypothesis, "Alienated citizens will have a lower rate of voter turnout" is directional. A *nondirectional hypothesis* does not specify direction of the relationship. The research hypothesis, "The rate of voting turnout of alienated citizens will differ from the rate of voting turnout of nonalienated citizens," is nondirectional. In the latter example, the researcher is suggesting a relationship between alienation and voting turnout but is unsure of the direction of that relationship.

When hypothesizing a directional relationship, the *one-tailed test* is used. When hypothesizing a nondirectional relationship, the *two-tailed test* is used. The "tail" in these instances refers to the extremes of the theoretical sampling distribution. In a directional hypothesis, a sample value is said to be statistically significant if it falls in a region of the sampling distribution significantly greater (or lower if this had been the direction of the hypothesis) than the expected value (represented by the null hypothesis). In a nondirectional hypothesis, a sample value is said to be statistically significant if it falls in a region that deviates significantly in *either* direction from the expected relationship (it may, in other words, fall in regions at either end of the sampling distribution). Since the critical regions of acceptance are smaller for a two-tailed test (nondirectional hypothesis), the null hypothesis (of there being no relationship) is more likely to be rejected with the application of the one-tailed test. The two-tailed test, then, is somewhat more conservative; but the determination of which to use is based on the nature of the hypothesis. Directional hypotheses call for a one-tailed test; nondirectional hypotheses require a two-tailed test.

Summary Thus Far

Statistical tests of significance are applicable with sample data. The question to be answered is whether the relationships that may have been found in the sample actually reflect true population relationships. This question can never be answered with certainty, but the level of risk taken in generalizing from the sample to the population can be stated. In so doing, the researcher sets out a research and a null hypothesis. The research hypothesis that asserts a relationship to exist can never be proven, but the null hypothesis that assumes no relationship can be rejected (thus lending support to the research hypothesis). The null hypothesis is rejected (and the re-

199

lationship is said to be statistically significant) when it can be shown that the sample statistic probably did not occur by chance. This is accomplished by comparing the sample statistic with a theoretical sampling distribution, indicating the probability of obtaining such a sample value. The following sections examine some of the commonly used tests of significance.

Difference of Means Tests

A frequently encountered research situation deals with the testing of measures of central tendency (usually the mean). The researcher may have a *single sample*, in which case the question is whether the mean of the sample differs significantly from the mean of the population, or the researcher may have *two samples* (or *two subsamples* drawn from a single random sample), in which case the question is whether the samples have been drawn from populations having different mean values. When testing hypotheses about difference of means, either of two sampling distributions may be appropriate. One of these is known as Student's *t* (or the *t* distribution); the other is known as the normal (or standard) distribution. Since the two-sample test situation is generally more interesting, single-sample tests will be only very briefly considered.

Single-Sample Difference of Means Tests

For single-sample tests, when the population sampled is normally distributed[3] and the population standard deviation is known, the normal distribution is used. This formula becomes

$$Z = \frac{\bar{X} - \mu}{\sigma/\sqrt{n}}$$

where

$$\bar{X} = \text{mean score of the sample}$$
$$\mu = \text{population mean}$$
$$\sigma = \text{population standard deviation}$$
$$n = \text{sample size}$$

It can be seen in Table A, p. 261, that at the 0.05 level of statistical significance for a one-tailed test, a Z score of 1.65 or higher must be obtained to reject the null hypothesis of no difference between the sample mean and population mean. For a two-tailed test, a score of 1.96 or higher must be obtained at the 0.05 level.

[3] Actually, with large-sample sizes, the assumption of a normally distributed population can be relaxed.

200

Generally, of course, it is unrealistic to assume that the standard deviation of the population will be known. In such cases, the standard deviation of the sample can be used to estimate the standard deviation of the population and the appropriate formula becomes

$$t = \frac{\bar{X} - \mu}{s/\sqrt{n-1}}$$

where

$\bar{X}$ = sample mean
μ = population mean
s = standard deviation of the sample
n = sample size

An examination of the table of t values (Table B, p. 262) shows that there are several distributions for t corresponding to the size of the sample. These sample sizes are expressed in terms of degrees of freedom, which must be calculated before application of the table of t values. *Degrees of freedom* refer to the number of values in a distribution which are free to vary after imposing certain constraints.[4] In the case of the t distribution, the degrees of freedom needed to provide the most unbiased estimate of the population variance are calculated according to the formula $n-1$, where n = sample size. For a sample size of 25 (and thus 24 degrees of freedom) the t value needed to conclude statistical significance at the 0.05 level for the one-tailed test is shown in Appendix B to be 1.711. The two-tailed test at the 0.05 level requires a t value of 2.064 or higher for a sample size of 25. For larger samples (120 and over), the t values approximate the Z values.

The single-sample Z and t tests might occasionally be of use to the political researcher. One might be interested in knowing whether the most senior members of the House and Senate spend significantly less than all House and Senate members in their campaigns for reelection, whether the average ages of national party convention delegates selected to serve on important convention committees deviate significantly from the ages of all delegates, or whether the level of political information of political science students deviates significantly from the level of political information of all social science majors in a particular university. In each of these instances, it is assumed that the researcher has taken random samples from the groups being examined (senior House and Senate members, delegates selected to important committee positions, or political science students) and is comparing the characteristics of these samples with known values of each population (all House and Senate members, all convention delegates, or all social science majors).

---

[4] As discussed in Henkel, *Tests of Significance*, p. 89.

For the most part, however, the researcher will be interested in comparing the mean difference of two (or more) samples or subsamples. Here, two-sample difference of means tests are appropriately used.

Two-Sample Difference of Means Tests

A more complex situation arises when the researcher is interested in comparing the mean difference of two samples. Here, the concern is not with assessing the value of the population mean (as was the case with single-sample tests) but with comparing the magnitude of differences between them.[5] The null hypothesis in this situation is that there is no difference between the magnitude of the means of the populations sampled.

If the sample sizes are relatively large (and therefore the sampling distribution of the difference of means between the samples will be normally distributed), the Z test to be applied is expressed as

$$Z = \frac{(\bar{X}_1 - \bar{X}_2) - (\mu_1 - \mu_2)}{\sqrt{\sigma_1^2/n_1 + \sigma_2^2/n_2}}$$

where

$$
\begin{aligned}
\bar{X}_1, \bar{X}_2 &= \text{sample means} \\
\mu_1, \mu_2 &= \text{population means} \\
\sigma_1, \sigma_2 &= \text{standard deviation of populations} \\
n_1, n_2 &= \text{sample sizes}
\end{aligned}
$$

Compared with the Z formula discussed for single-sample tests, it can be seen that the numerator of $\bar{X} - \mu$ is replaced by $(\bar{X}_1 - \bar{X}_2) - (\mu_1 - \mu_2)$ (the mean difference of the two subgroups minus the mean difference of the two populations) and the denominator of $\sigma/\sqrt{n}$ is replaced by $\sqrt{\sigma_1^2/n_1 + \sigma_2^2/n_2}$ (an estimate of the standard deviation, or estimated standard error, of the difference of the sample mean scores). A brief discussion of this formula is in order.

In the discussion of single-sample tests of significance, it will be recalled that we were examining the extent to which a single mean score ($\bar{X}$) deviated from the population mean (μ). Now, we are interested in the extent to which the value of the *difference* between two sample means ($\bar{X}_1 - \bar{X}_2$) deviates from the value of the mean population differences ($\mu_1 - \mu_2$). Since our hypothesis is that $\mu_1 - \mu_2 = 0$, the $\mu_1 - \mu_2$ expression can be eliminated from the two-sample Z test and the numerator simply becomes ($\bar{X}_1 - \bar{X}_2$).

In the discussion of the single-sample test of significance, the denominator of $\sigma/\sqrt{n}$ provided an estimate of the standard deviation of the sampling

[5] As explained in Henkel, *Tests of Significance*, p. 61.

distribution. It can also be shown that an estimate of the standard error of the difference between sample means is equal to

$$\sigma(\bar{X}_1 - \bar{X}_2) = \frac{\sigma_1}{\sqrt{n_1}} + \frac{\sigma_2}{\sqrt{n_2}}$$

$$= \sqrt{\frac{\sigma_1^2}{n_1} + \frac{\sigma_2^2}{n_2}}$$

where $\sigma(\bar{X}_1 - \bar{X}_2)$ is the standard deviation of difference of sample means.[6]

Since σ_1 and σ_2 (standard deviations of population means) are presumed unknown, these must be estimated by reference to the standard deviations of the samples. In instances where sample sizes are relatively large, σ_1 and σ_2 may be replaced with s_1 and s_2 (standard deviations of each sample). Thus a simplified formula for the two-sample difference of means test becomes

$$Z = \frac{\bar{X}_1 - \bar{X}_2}{\sqrt{s_1^2/n_1 + s_2^2/n_2}}$$

where s_1 and s_2 are the standard deviations of each sample.

As an example of the use of the Z test in the two-sample case, assume that the researcher is interested in comparing the attitudes of various subsamples of women to the women's liberation movement. It might be expected that upper-educated women are more favorable to the women's liberation movement than are lower-educated women, and that women from the non-South are more favorable than those from the South. Since in this situation the researcher also believes that race may be a confounding factor (and since the real focus is to be on education and region), the researcher has decided only to examine white women.

Two hypotheses, then, are established for both situations. The research hypotheses assert that upper-educated women and those not from the South will be more favorable toward women's liberation than their counterparts ($H_1: \mu_1 > \mu_2$). The null hypotheses assume no population differences ($H_0: \mu_1 = \mu_2$). In order to test these hypotheses, the researcher might turn to the data provided in 1976 CPS American National Election Study. In that survey, respondents were asked to indicate on a "feeling thermometer" their attitude toward women's liberation. This feeling thermometer ranged from 0 degrees (very negative) to 100 degrees (very positive). Based on this survey, Table 9.1 shows the results obtained for white women in that sample (the assumption here, which some may question, is that this thermometer scale has interval properties).

[6]As demonstrated in Hubert M. Blalock, *Social Statistics* (New York: McGraw-Hill Book Company, 1972), pp. 224–226.

Table 9.1
Women's Attitude Toward Women's Liberation Movement by Education and Region

Education		Region	
Upper-Educated Women (some college)	Lower-Educated Women (high school or less)	Women from Non-South	Women from South
$n_1 = 289$	$n_2 = 605$	$n_1 = 720$	$n_2 = 174$
$\bar{X}_1 = 55.60$	$\bar{X}_2 = 51.44$	$\bar{X}_1 = 52.46$	$\bar{X}_2 = 54.12$
$s_1 = 21.86$	$s_2 = 20.88$	$s_1 = 20.73$	$s_2 = 23.41$
$H_1: \mu_1 > \mu_2$		$H_1: \mu_1 > \mu_2$	
$H_0: \mu_1 = \mu_2$		$H_0: \mu_1 = \mu_2$	

Source: CPS, 1976 American National Election Study (mean scores are shown only for white respondents).

Turning first to the expectation that women not from the South would be more favorable to women's liberation than those from the South, the data presented in Table 9.1 show that this research hypothesis can be rejected *without reference to the difference of means test.* It is found, in fact, that the mean score of women from the South was somewhat more *positive* than that for women not from the South (54.12 to 52.46).

Considering education, it is seen that the mean score of upper-educated women (those with some college) in this sample was found to be more pro-women's liberation than the mean score of those women having only a high school education or less (55.60 to 51.44). This is the sort of relationship anticipated by the research hypothesis, and the question now becomes: Is this difference statistically significant? Applying the Z test to this mean difference (and to that associated with regional distinctions as well), the results are found to be

$$Z = \frac{55.60 - 51.44}{\sqrt{\dfrac{21.86^2}{289} + \dfrac{20.88^2}{605}}} \qquad Z = \frac{52.46 - 54.12}{\sqrt{\dfrac{20.73^2}{720} + \dfrac{23.41^2}{174}}}$$

$$= 2.700 \qquad\qquad = -0.858$$

For the null hypothesis that education is not related to attitudes

For the null hypothesis that region is not related to attitudes

Since each original hypothesis was directional, the 1.65 Z score is used as the critical value of significance. In the first instance the Z score of 2.700 is greater than the critical value; therefore, the null hypothesis of there being no difference in the populations of upper and lower educated women is rejected and, instead, support, is lent to the research hypothesis. It appears that education is a factor significantly related to women's attitude to the women's liberation movement (for the white population).

The second research hypothesis, concerning regional differences, had already been rejected by an inspection of the *direction* of the mean differences alone. In that instance, the mean difference was opposite that expected. Having applied the Z test to this mean difference, moreover, it can be said that the observed mean difference was not statistically significant, and the most appropriate conclusion, it seems, is that region is not a significantly distinguishing factor between the attitudes of white women to the women's liberation movement.

The standard normal curve is inappropriate when the sizes of the samples are small (30 cases or less). In such instances, the t distribution is used. In the two-sample case, the formula for the t test (when it cannot be assumed that the two population variances are equal) becomes

$$t = \frac{\bar{X}_1 - \bar{X}_2}{\sqrt{s_1^2/(n_1 - 1) + s_2^2/(n_2 - 1)}}$$

When discussing the single-sample t test, it was mentioned that the researcher must calculate degrees of freedom before utilizing the table of t values (Table B, p. 262). This is also true in the two-sample case, where the degrees of freedom are calculated as $n_1 + n_2 - 2$.

As an illustration of the two-sample difference-of-means t test, consider the work of Susan B. Hansen dealing with the attitudes of local government officials and citizens.[7] In her research, Hansen was attempting to determine whether various political structures affect the extent to which attitudes of citizens would concur with the attitudes of community leaders. To this end, an index of congruency (the extent to which citizens and leaders agree on important community problems) was developed, and the specific research question addressed by Hansen was whether various political factors (such as type of election and method of selecting the chief executive) appear to affect this congruency index. A portion of her data is presented in Table 9.2.

In this instance, Hansen finds that the degree of congruency between citizens and heads of local government is greater in communities having partisan elections (i.e., candidates run on party labels) and in those communities where the chief executive is selected by popular vote rather than appointed by the city council. Further, the t test indicates each of these differences to be significant at the 0.05 level. In this manner, Hansen is able to conclude that the differences she found in her sample cities probably did not occur just by "accident" (or through sampling errors) but are reflective of true differences among all communities.

[7] Susan Blackall Hansen, "Participation, Political Structure, and Concurrence," *American Political Science Review*, 69 (December, 1975), 1181–1199.

Table 9.2
Mean Community Congruency Scores by Political Variables

	Number of Cities	Mean Congruency Scores	Difference	T-test
Type of election:				
Partisan	23	22.4		
Nonpartisan	32	16.2	6.2	>0.05
Method of selecting chief executive:				
Popular vote	47	19.6		
Council selection	8	11.4	8.2	>0.05

Source: Adapted from Susan Blackall Hansen, "Participation, Political Structure, and Concurrence," *American Political Science Review*, 69 (December, 1975), 1188.

Nominal Relationships:
The Chi-square Distribution

The *chi-square* (χ^2) is a very general test of statistical significance. While the test has many applications, it is often used in problems involving the cross-tabulation of two nominal variables. In general terms, the χ^2 test is used to determine the extent to which the actual (observed) values in a particular table deviate from the values that would have been expected *if the two variables are not related to one another*.

By way of example, suppose the researcher has a sample of 100 voters and is interested in the relationship between sex and party identification. For purposes of simplicity, assume the sample of 100 is comprised of 50 women and 50 men (although it is not necessary that the samples be of equal size) and that party identification is categorized only as Democratic or Republican (although any number of categories are possible). Assume, further, that the researcher knows that in the sample of 100 voters, 60 are Democrats. Based on this information, the number of men and women expected to be Democrats and Republicans, assuming that sex is *not* related to party identification, would be calculated as shown in Table 9.3. In this *expected* table, women are as likely to belong to the Democratic (or Republican) Party as are men, and men are as likely to belong to the Democratic (or Republican) Party as are women. Thus, in this expected table, party identification is said to be *independent* of sex.

If, however, it is found that the *actual* values are not those presented above, some degree of dependency between sex and party identification exists. Suppose, given the same data as discussed above, that the *actual* distribution appeared as shown in Table 9.4. In this example, it can be seen that the *actual* cell entries deviate to some extent from that which would be *expected* if no relationship between sex and party identification existed (see Table 9.3). While the *marginal values* have remained the same in each instance (marginal

Table 9.3
Illustration of Expected Cell Entries

	Sex		
Party Identification	Male	Female	Total
Democrat	30	30	60
Republican	20	20	40
Total	50	50	100

values, it will be recalled from Chapter 6, refer to column and row totals), the actual cell entries have deviated from the expected entries. Thus, sex and party identification cannot be said to be *independent* of each other; there is some degree of *dependency*. As is the case of all tests of significance, χ^2 tells us whether or not we could have expected our sample (in this instance, 100 voters) to display this degree of dependency if in the population as a whole sex and party identification are, in fact, *not related*. The general χ^2 formula is

$$\chi^2 = \sum \frac{(f_o - f_e)^2}{f_e}$$

where

f_o = observed frequency for each cell
f_e = expected frequency for each cell
(and where f_e is calculated as the product of the row and column marginals for each cell divided by the total number of cases in the table)

Table 9.4
Illustration of Actual Cell Entries[a]

	Sex		
Party Identification	Male	Female	Total
Democrat	40	20	60
Republican	10	30	40
Total	50	50	100

[a] It should be apparent that this table is used only for purposes of illustration and is not meant to be reflective of actual relationships. In reality, the partisan affiliations of men and women do not deviate to the extent depicted in this table.

Verbally, the formula states that the χ^2 value is obtained by first subtracting the expected value for each cell from the observed value and squaring the result (squaring eliminates negative differences, which would cancel the positive values in the summation process). This squared value is then divided by the expected value for each cell (a process that standardizes for different size cell entries), and each of these values is then summed. The total summed value is the χ^2.

As an illustration of the calculation of the χ^2 value, consider the regional distribution of party identification as measured by the 1976 CPS American National Election Study. Table 9.5 presents these data. By calculating a few percentages, it can be seen from the table that region is related to some extent to party identification. Approximately 56 percent of the sample living in the South identified with the Democratic Party (366/658), compared with only 36 percent of those from the Northeastern states. Likewise, almost 32 percent of the sample from the North Central states identified with the Republican Party (192/600), compared with only 21 percent of the sample from the South. The question is: Could differences such as these within the sample have occurred just by chance, or do they probably reflect true regional differences in the population of all American voters? In calculating the χ^2, it is helpful to follow the steps illustrated in Table 9.6.

In this manner, the χ^2 value for the data presented in Table 9.5 is found to be 83.38. In deciding whether this value of χ^2 is to be considered significant, we make use of the distribution of χ^2 values presented in Table C, p. 263. As was the case when examining the t distribution, we first need to calculate the degrees of freedom for the particular table being examined. In cases such as this, the degrees of freedom are calculated by the formula (number of columns -1) $\times$ (number of rows -1). For the example presented above, the degrees of freedom are calculated as $(4-1) \times (3-1) = 6$.

It will be noted from an examination of the chi-square table that several distributions of the chi-square value are presented. Having calculated the degrees of freedom, the researcher must select an acceptable level of risk. As

Table 9.5
Party Identification by Region

Party Identification	Region				
	Northeast	North Central	South	West	Total
Republican	103 (A)	192 (B)	135 (C)	105 (D)	535
Independent	189 (E)	184 (F)	157 (G)	107 (H)	637
Democratic	166 (I)	224 (J)	366 (K)	129 (L)	885
Total	458	600	658	341	2057

Source: CPS, 1976 American National Election Study.

Table 9.6
Calculation of the Chi-square Value

Cell	Observed Frequency	Expected Frequency[a]	$f_o - f_e$	$(f_o - f_e)^2$	$\dfrac{(f_o - f_e)^2}{f_e}$
A	103	119.12	−16.12	259.85	2.18
B	192	156.05	35.95	1292.40	8.28
C	135	171.14	−36.14	1306.10	7.63
D	105	88.69	16.31	266.02	3.00
E	189	141.83	47.17	2225.01	15.69
F	184	185.80	−1.8	3.24	0.02
G	157	203.77	−46.77	2187.43	10.73
H	107	105.60	1.4	1.96	0.02
I	166	197.05	−31.05	964.10	4.89
J	224	258.14	−34.14	1165.54	4.52
K	366	283.10	82.9	6872.41	24.28
L	129	146.71	−17.71	313.64	2.14
Totals	2057	2057.00			83.38

$$\chi^2 = 83.38$$

[a]The expected value for each cell is calculated as the product of the row and column marginals for that cell divided by the total number of cases. For cell A, this becomes $(458 \times 535)/2057 = 119.12$.

discussed previously, the 0.05 level means that only 5 out of a 100 times would we have selected a sample having the characteristics of those reported above if these characteristics are *not* truly reflective of the population. The 0.01 level means that such a sample would be expected to occur just by accident 1 out of 100 times, and so forth. Assuming that the 0.05 level has been selected, the chi-square distribution indicates that for 6 degrees of freedom, we need a value of 12.592 *or higher* to reject the null hypothesis of no significant relationship and to conclude, instead, that significant differences do exist. In this case, the chi-square value of 83.38 is considerably greater than that needed at the 0.05 level. In fact, it can be seen that this value is even greater than that needed for acceptance at the 0.001 level. We can conclude, then, that the regional differences found for this sample to exist for party affiliation *are* statistically significant; that is, they probably are reflective of "true" differences in the population. We can also say that less than 1 out of 1000 times would we have obtained a χ^2 of this magnitude if in the population there are no regional differences in party affiliation.

Before considering another example of the use of the χ^2 value, two modifications of the formula presented above should be mentioned. When the researcher has a 2×2 table (i.e., two rows and two columns), a special formula for the calculation of χ^2 may be applied. Consider Table 9.7, which examines the hypothetical relationship between sex and party identification. In the case of such a 2×2 table, the χ^2 value can be calculated by the following formula:

$$\chi^2 = \frac{n(AD - BC)^2}{(A+B)(C+D)(A+C)(B+D)}$$

209

Table 9.7
Hypothetical Cross-tabulation of
Party Identification by Sex

	Sex		
Party Identification	Male	Female	Total
Democratic	30 (A)	20 (B)	50
Republican	20 (C)	30 (D)	50
Total	50	50	100

where A, B, C, and D are the number of cases falling in each cell and n is the sample size. In the example presented in Table 9.7, the χ^2 value is calculated as

$$\chi^2 = \frac{100(900-400)^2}{(50)(50)(50)(50)}$$

$$= 4.00$$

Also, it is true that whenever some or all of the cell entries are small, the χ^2 value as calculated by either of the formulas presented above may provide a poor estimation of the actual χ^2 distribution. To correct for this, F. Yates, in 1934, suggested a modification which is widely used. Applying Yates' modification, the researcher simply reduces the distance between the observed and the expected frequencies by 0.5 prior to calculating χ^2. In a 2×2 table whenever any cell entry is less than 5, the correction developed by Yates should be used.

An interesting application of the use of the χ^2 statistic can be seen in Michael Suleiman's examination of the attitudes of Arab students and professionals in the United States (which he assumes to be fairly representative of all Arab elite) toward various aspects of the Middle East situation.[8] Among other items, Suleiman examined the relationships between various characteristics of this sample of Arab elites and their policy recommendations toward Israel. Table 9.8 reproduces a portion of his findings.

In each instance, it is seen that Suleiman found deviations in the attitudes of this sample of Arab elites toward Israel. Younger, less-educated, and single respondents were more likely to take a more militant stand; older, higher-educated, and married respondents were more compromising in their position. In each instance, the χ^2 value is greater than that needed at the 0.05 level (which, for 2 degrees of freedom, is 5.99), and it is therefore concluded

---

[8] Michael W. Suleiman, "Attitudes of the Arab Elite Toward Palestine and Israel," *American Political Science Review*, 67 (June, 1973), 482–489.

Table 9.8
Arab Elite Policy Suggestions for Israel by Age, Education, and Marital Status (percent)

Policy Suggestion	Age		Education			Marital Status	
	Up to 30	30+	B.A.	M.A.	Ph.D./M.D.	Married	Unmarried
Prepare for defeat of Israel	71.3	59.5	74.0	65.3	50.7	60.3	72.3
Continue economic boycott	8.5	8.3	8.1	8.4	9.9	7.4	9.2
Compromise and recognize	20.2	32.2	17.9	26.3	39.4	31.8	18.5
$n =$	223	121	173	95	71	148	195
$\chi^2 =$	6.3; $p > 0.04$		13.9; $p > 0.01$			8.1; $p > 0.01$	

Source: Adapted from Michael W. Suleiman, "Attitudes of the Arab Elite Toward Palestine and Israel," American Political Science Review, 67 (June, 1973), 486.

that these differences are significant — they probably are accurate reflections of the attitudes of Arab elite in general (at least as measured at that point in time).

Ordinal Relationships

For the ordinal measures of association (tau and gamma) discussed in Chapter 6, the normal distribution is used for the measure of significance. For both tau and gamma, the correlation coefficient is transferred to a Z score and the question being asked is whether a correlation coefficient of the magnitude obtained would be expected to occur just by chance, if in the population the two variables are not related. For tau, the formula is

$$Z = \frac{\tau}{\sqrt{\dfrac{4n+10}{9n(n-1)}}}$$

where

$$\tau = \text{tau value}$$
$$n = \text{sample size}$$

In Chapter 6, a τ_b correlation of 0.10 was reported between Vietnam policy preference and the 1968 party vote for a sample of 831 people.[9] The question that can now be answered is whether this is a statistically significant relationship. That is, if there really was no relationship in the total population between Vietnam policy preference and 1968 party vote when this sample was taken, what is the likelihood of obtaining a τ_b of 0.10 for the sample? Referring to the formula, the Z score is calculated as

$$Z = \frac{0.10}{\sqrt{\dfrac{4(831)+10}{9(831)(830)}}}$$

$$= 4.315$$

This score is above 1.65 (or 1.96 for the two-tailed test) and is therefore reported to be a statistically significant relationship. The tau value of 0.10 would have been expected to occur by chance much less than 5 out of 100 samples.

[9] As reported in Benjamin I. Page and Richard A. Brody, "Policy Voting and the Electoral Process: The Vietnam War Issue," *American Political Science Review*, 66 (September, 1972), 979–995.

This example can be used to demonstrate another important aspect of significance tests; this is their dependence on sample sizes. Had the size of the sample in this case been 100 (instead of 831) the Z score for a τ_b of 0.10 would have been 1.474. This value *would not* be considered statistically significant (even though the τ_b value was the same), and the researcher would have accepted the null hypothesis of there being no relationship in the population between Vietnam policy preference and candidate preference in 1968. Thus significance testing is directly related to sample size, a point that will be discussed in more detail later.

For gamma, the formula for calculating Z is[10]

$$Z = \frac{\gamma}{\sqrt{\dfrac{2n(1-\gamma^2)}{n^2 - ft}}}$$

where

$\gamma = $ gamma value
$n = $ sample size
$ft = \Sigma\, n_j^2 + \Sigma\, n_i^2 - \Sigma\Sigma\, f_{ij}^2$
  (where $n_j = $ column marginals,
  $n_i = $ row marginals,
  and $f_{ij} = $ cell frequencies)

As before, the obtained Z value is compared with the normal-curve table (see Table A). If the hypothesis is directional, any Z value of over 1.65 is considered statistically significant at the 0.05 level.

Metric-Level Relationships

The distribution often used to gauge the significance of the simple, partial, and multiple correlation coefficients is known as the *F distribution*. The *F* score represents a ratio of explained (r^2) to unexplained $(1 - r^2)$ variance, adjusting for degrees of freedom.[11] For the simple correlation coefficient, the *F* value is calculated as

$$F = \frac{r^2(n-2)}{1-r^2}$$

---

[10] See Leo A. Goodman and William H. Kruskal, "Measures of Association for Cross Classification III: Approximate Sampling Theory," *Journal of the American Statistical Association*, 58 (June, 1963), 310–364. For a simplified formula, see E. Terrence Jones, *Conducting Political Research* (New York, Harper & Row, Publishers, 1971), p. 171.

[11] As discussed in Blalock, *Social Statistics*, pp. 397–400.

where

$$r = \text{simple correlation coefficient}$$
$$n = \text{sample size}$$

In using the F score, two types of degrees of freedom are involved. The first is equivalent to the number of independent variables minus one (in the case of the simple correlation coefficient this always is equal to 1); the second is that associated with the unexplained sums of squares and is calculated as $n-2$ (where $n = $ sample size).

In Chapter 7, an r value of 0.40 was reported between husbands' and wives' initial party identification based on a sample of 2077 adults.[12] The F value for this correlation would be calculated as

$$F = \frac{0.40^2(2077-2)}{1-0.40^2}$$

$$= 395.24$$

Turning to the table of F values (Table D, pp. 264–266) notice that for 1 and 2075 (infinite) degrees of freedom, a value of 10.83 is required to conclude statistical significance at the 0.001 level. Obviously, this correlation (0.40) with an F value of 395.24 would be considered statistically significant — it probably represents true population values.

For the multiple-correlation coefficient, the F score is obtained by application of the formula

$$F = \left(\frac{R^2}{1-R^2}\right)\frac{n-k-1}{k}$$

where

$$R = \text{multiple correlation coefficient}$$
$$n = \text{sample size}$$
$$k = \text{number of independent variables}$$

For the multiple-correlation F test, the two sets of degrees of freedom are (1) the number of independent variables, and (2) the total number of cases minus the number of independent variables minus 1.

For the partial-correlation coefficient, the F value is calculated as[13]

---

[12] As reported in Terry S. Weiner, "Homogeneity of Political Party Preferences Between Spouses," *Journal of Politics*, 40 (February, 1978), 208–211.

[13] Discussed in Blalock, *Social Statistics*, p. 465.

$$F = \frac{(\text{partial } r)^2 \, (n-k-1)}{1-(\text{partial } r)^2}$$

where

partial r = the partial correlation coefficient
n = sample size
k = number of independent and
control variables

For the partial-correlation F test, the two sets of degrees of freedom are (1) the number of independent and control variables, and (2) the total number of cases minus the number of independent and control variables minus 1.

Tests of Statistical Significance: A Summary and a Warning

This chapter has introduced the concept of statistical significance and has examined some of the most often used tests of significance. Tests of significance, it should be made clear, are important tools in the conduct of systematic political research. The techniques allow the researcher to state with some degree of assurance (as measured by the level of risk) that relationships found in the sample actually do (or do not) represent population differences. When dealing with sample data, this obviously is an important consideration.

At the same time, the limitations of these tests should be clearly understood.[14] In the first place, tests of significance are appropriately applied only to *samples* of the population. That is, tests of significance have no meaning when applied to the total universe of cases, since, if the researcher is in possession of data for the total population, there is no possibility of making a sampling error when reporting observed differences. Thus, if one is using as the unit of analysis all 50 states, or all units of local government in the United States, or all nations in the world, and data have been drawn from each unit in the population, tests of significance would not be used.

A related question concerns the universe from which the sample is drawn. An obvious point, but one that is often overlooked, is that tests of significance are applicable only to the universe from which the sample is selected. For example, a researcher selecting a random sample of counties from the Southern states would be limited in generalizations only to all counties in the South. It would not be appropriate to generalize from such a sample to other counties in other regions or to all counties in the United States.

[14] For a thorough examination of the limitations of tests of statistical significance, see Denton E. Morrison and Ramon E. Henkel, eds., *The Significance Test Controversy* (Chicago: Aldine Publishing Company, 1970).

215

Also, tests of significance assume *random sampling*. Tests of significance are appropriately used only when all cases in the universe have an equal chance of being selected in the sample. Samples that are drawn by any other method should not be used with tests of significance.[15] As an example, consider the situation of a student wishing to conduct a survey of a sample of students at her college in order to make generalizations about the entire student body. Perhaps the student is interested in determining whether students who live on campus are more or less likely to participate in campus politics and activities than are students living off campus. In order to appropriately use tests of significance to make inferences such as this, the student must draw her sample so that every member of the student body has an equal chance of being selected in the sample. It would be inappropriate, for example, for the student to limit her surveying to one of her classes, to dorm friends, or to sorority members.

Finally, *and this is most important*, tests of statistical significance are not equivalent to measures of strength. That is, tests of significance are not designed to tell us how strong a relationship is, only whether or not the relationship (regardless of how strong or weak) probably reflects the true population relationship. As mentioned above, tests of significance are sensitive to the size of the sample. The larger the sample, the more likely are these tests to indicate significant relationships. This only makes sense because these tests are designed to determine whether characteristics of a sample are likely to deviate from the characteristics of the population. Intuitively, we are likely to have more faith in results obtained from large samples; but with large samples, even trivial differences often will be statistically significant. A simple example illustrates this.

Suppose that we have two samples, one whose size is 100, the other whose size is 10,000. Suppose further that the distributions of the two samples appear as shown in Table 9.9.

It can be seen in the table that the proportion of cases falling in each cell has not changed from sample to sample. The second sample has only 100 times more observations falling in each cell. However, the χ^2 value for the first sample is found to be not significant, whereas the χ^2 value in the second sample is found to be 100 times greater and is "very" significant. This is the case even though the correlation coefficient phi (ϕ) shows the strength of the association to be the same in both cases (0.08). Thus even though the strength of the relationship in each case has not altered, one is found to be statistically significant; the other is not.

Significance, then, is not equivalent to strength, and such tests should not be used or interpreted as measures of strength (such as those discussed in the previous several chapters). This is another way of saying that tests of significance and tests of association (strength) complement but do not replace

---

[15]In practice, this requirement is often relaxed, as in the case with samples drawn by use of multistage cluster techniques.

Table 9.9
Illustration of Chi-square With Differing *n*'s But with Proportionately Equivalent Cell Entries

	Sample A (n = 100) Characteristic A				Sample B (n = 10,000) Characteristic A		
Characteristic B	1	2	Total	Characteristic B	1	2	total
1	27	23	50	1	2,700	2,300	5,000
2	23	27	50	2	2,300	2,700	5,000
Total	50	50	100	Total	5,000	5,000	10,000

$\chi^2 = 0.64$ (not significant)
$\phi = 0.08$

$\chi^2 = 64.00$ (significant at 0.001 level)
$\phi = 0.08$

each other. In the particular research situation, the researcher should use whichever is most appropriate for the questions being asked and for the nature of the data being analyzed. Typically, tests of association are more revealing of relationships, but very often it is the case that *both* tests of significance and tests of association will be appropriate and will be reported.

Exercises

1. Assume a researcher is interested in examining the beginning salaries of those college graduates majoring in political science and in economics and in testing for the possibility that a statistically significant difference exists between the two. A random sample of 250 employed political science majors is drawn and the mean first year salary is found to be $14,500 with a standard deviation of $1000. A random sample of 150 employed economic majors is drawn and the mean first year salary is found to be $14,750 with a standard deviation of $2000.
   a. Present the likely null and research hypotheses for the testing of these mean differences.
   b. Apply the one-tailed Z test of statistical significance to test for the difference between these income levels.
   c. What conclusions can be drawn based on this test concerning the null and research hypotheses developed above?
   d. Assume the sample size for the sample of employed economic majors had been 300 (rather than 150). Recalculate the difference of means test and compare this result with that previously obtained. What does this indicate about the effect of sample size on the Z score?
2. Calculate the chi-square value for the table presented as exercise #3 of Chapter 6. Is the chi-square value large enough to be considered statistically significant? What does this indicate about this relationship?
3. From a random sample of 150 political science majors a tau-b of 0.42 has been found between a seven-point scale of ideology (measured as liberal to conservative) and a

217

five-point scale of attitudes toward marijuana laws (measured from more to less tolerant).

a. Would this be considered a statistically significant relationship?

b. What would be the risk of inferring from this sample that a similar relationship exists between ideology and attitudes toward marijuana laws for all 500 political science majors at this particular university?

c. To what extent could this finding (of a relationship between ideology and attitudes toward marijuana laws) be generalized to *all* students at this particular university? Why?

d. To what extent could this finding (of a relationship between ideology and attitudes toward marijuana laws) be generalized to all political science majors in *all* colleges and universities? Why is this so?

4. From a randomly drawn sample of 200 southern counties in the United States a researcher finds a Pearson correlation coefficient of 0.32 to exist between percent of the county living in urban areas and voting turnout in a recent election.

a. What is the F-score for this relationship and would it be considered statistically significant?

b. On the basis of the correlation coefficient and the test of significance, what can be said about the probable relationship between voter turnout and urbanization for all *southern* counties and for *all* counties in the United States? Why is this so?

10

PREPARING THE FINAL REPORT

It's late November. Many weeks have been spent selecting a research topic; reviewing the literature; developing hypotheses; collecting, coding, and punching information; measuring concepts; and analyzing the data. But these steps are finally complete. Now it is time to prepare the final report. When reaching this stage, the beginning researcher sometimes thinks that the "hard" work is over; that drafting the report is only a minor phase of the entire project. However, the report-writing phase is as central as any other to the successful completion of the research project. All that most readers are going to know about your research will be contained in the final report. A sloppy presentation can give the impression (sometimes correctly, sometimes falsely) of sloppy research. Not even the most brilliantly designed and carefully executed study will receive a very positive evaluation from its intended audience (whether that audience is a course instructor or the broader scientific community) unless that study is effectively presented.[1]

Thus the time for relaxation and celebration for a job well done has not yet arrived. It is important to the conduct of systematic research that the momentum which has carried the researcher through previous stages of the study not be lost, and that careful attention be given to this final phase of the research process as well.

At the same time, it is difficult to provide a set of instructions that will guarantee success in writing the final report. In this sense, the final stage of the research process is similar to the beginning, selecting a research topic: both are highly individualized; both largely reflect the personality and specialized skills of the researcher. But also like the topic selection stage, some pointers can be offered. These are discussed in this final chapter.

As a beginning, the student should pick up and review one of the several manuals dealing with the format and presentation of research papers. Among

---

[1] A point made similarly by Earl R. Babbie, *The Practice of Social Research* (Belmont, Calif.: Wadsworth Publishing Company, Inc., 1975), p. 453.

the most widely circulated of these are:

Kate L. Turabian, *A Manual for Writers of Term Papers, Theses, and Dissertations*, 4th ed. (Chicago: The University of Chicago Press, 1973).
A Manual of Style, 12th ed. (Chicago: The University of Chicago Press, 1969).
James D. Lester, *Writing Research Papers*, 2nd ed. (Glenview, Ill.: Scott, Foresman and Company, 1976).

These manuals will provide invaluable guidance in the important areas of proper footnoting; bibliographic preparation; the handling of quoted material; the proper preparation of tables, charts, captions, and figures; punctuation; and so forth. Beyond the numerous and helpful technical aids found in these publications, the student may consider the following suggestions in the areas of report length, format, and style.

Report Length

When discussing topic selection (Chapter 2), it was noted that one of the questions most often asked by students is: "What project does the instructor want me to pursue?" Undoubtedly, the second most often asked question is: "How long should the final report be?" Here it is especially difficult to provide an answer that will satisfy all possible research situations. Doctoral dissertations often are longer than 250 pages, master's theses often run in excess of 100 pages. At the other extreme, more narrowly focused topics may be handled nicely in a dozen pages or less. Some political science journals include a section entitled "research notes," where preliminary research articles of about a half dozen pages or so are published. Thus manuscript length can vary widely; perhaps the best that can be said is that the paper should achieve its purpose as briefly and as parsimoniously as possible. The purpose of the *research* paper, unlike the *literature review*, is not to detail exhaustively every book, article, and manuscript that might possibly relate to the area or to review all arguments that have been advanced on one side of the issue or the other. Some of this, of course, is necessary and desirable, but the primary purpose of the research paper is to convey to the reader the results of this particular analysis. This should be done as expeditiously as possible. The test is whether the reader is convinced that the argument has been made as forcefully and as efficiently as possible and whether the skeptical or curious reader can replicate from the data presented the author's own results.[2] If this has been accomplished, the paper is long enough. If not, the

[2]This parallels a suggestion made by Fred N. Kerlinger, *Foundations of Behavioral Research*, 2nd ed. (New York: Holt, Rinehart and Winston, Inc., 1973), p. 694.

paper should be strengthened (but not necessarily lengthened) in these critical areas.

But of course, this continues to beg the question of just how many pages the report should be. Recent years have witnessed an explosion of printed material in all areas of scientific and professional work. Along with this has come increasing demands for reports that are clear, concise, and *brief*. Most political science journals today attempt to limit published manuscripts to around 30 double-spaced typed pages. Although individual instructors certainly may have differing standards and expectations, this length of 30 pages would also appear to serve as an approximate *maximum* length for most graduate research papers. As an even rougher guide, undergraduate term papers, it would seem, could be prepared in about half this length. Certainly it would be a rare paper (especially at the undergraduate level) that would require more than 30 pages for adequate presentation. Other factors being equal, a premium is placed on papers that are brief, precise, and to the point. These objectives can almost always be advanced by carefully considering what is to be said and how it is to be presented *before* writing begins and by carefully editing and rewriting the paper *after* the first draft is complete. We will return to this point later.

Report Format

In very general terms the report itself should contain the following: (1) a statement of the problem and review of the related literature; (2) a discussion of the research design; (3) a presentation of analysis and results; and (4) a summary of interpretations and conclusions. Each of these is more-or-less self-explanatory and, as a whole, they follow the procedures outlined in earlier chapters of this book. The *statement of the problem* may be the most difficult and important aspect of the research report. Here, the researcher must state with precision and focus the problem to be addressed, present the particular hypotheses that the research is designed to test, and relate this problem to the larger body of literature in the area, all in very short order. The undergraduate may have spent weeks pursuing this topic; the senior researcher may have spent months (or more) in this area. But all of these issues must be presented to the reader in a very few introductory paragraphs of the report (unless, of course, a dissertation or book-length manuscript is proposed, in which case the writer can be more thorough and more circumspect). In relating this research to the broader context of the literature, it is important to convey a general idea of what has been attempted in the area before, the general areas of agreement and disagreement, and what incremental addition to this body of literature this project proposes to make. Remember, again, that we are not talking about an exhaustive and extensive review of all possible books, articles, and manuscripts that might relate to the

221

topic, but are concerned in particular with those key sources that relate most directly to the research being proposed. It is obvious that considerable care must be devoted to this early stage of the report. This section sets the tone for the entire report. Without promising more than can possibly be delivered, the writer must demonstrate the importance of this research effort and sufficiently stimulate the reader's interest to press on with the report.

The report should also discuss and justify the study's *research design and methodology*. The type of data collected and the method of data collection should be detailed. If the research involves sampling, the researcher must describe the population that was sampled, the techniques of sampling, the rate of completed surveys or interviews, and any biases that may have resulted. If questionnaires are used, the researcher should discuss the type of questionnaire and the procedures for coding the information. If other sources of information are used (i.e., data collected by someone else), the researcher should indicate who collected the data, by what techniques, and under what circumstances. Here, also, the researcher should indicate the methods adopted for testing the hypotheses. If this is to be an experimental research design, the researcher should indicate how the control and experimental samples were selected, how testing was conducted, and how representative were the samples of the total population. If a quasi-experimental research design is selected, the researcher should indicate which statistics will be used to test the hypotheses developed and why they were selected.

The body of the report, of course, is reserved for the *presentation of analysis and results*. This is the heart of the report; in the opinion of the reader the project will stand or fall largely on this section. Special care must be taken to ensure that the results of the analysis are presented as clearly and unambiguously as possible. This means that the report should be presented in a manner most convenient for the reader. Tables, charts, and figures should be presented in the body of the text near the point of discussion, not at the end.[3] Critical points should be presented in the text itself, not relegated to footnote status. All quotes should be properly cited, and the sources of all data and information should be clearly presented. At this stage, the reader should ask of himself or herself, "Have I made my case as convincingly as possible — have the data been presented in a manner so as to maximize and facilitate the reader's understanding of what I am saying and evaluation of the conclusions that I have made?" Note that this is *not* to suggest that the researcher include in the body of analysis only that information which seems to confirm the argument being made and discard all else. On the contrary, the researcher has an obligation to present *all* relevant evidence, and cannot selectively present some and dismiss others. The question being asked, however, is whether the information that is discussed is presented in a manner allowing clear interpretation by the reader. The reader should be able to reproduce from the

---

[3] A point made by Babbie, *The Practice of Social Research*, p. 459.

data presented the statistics that are reported. From the data the reader should also be able to evaluate the appropriateness of the statistics calculated. The key word here is *replication*; the data should be presented in a manner permitting the replication of results and the independent evaluation of conclusions drawn.

The report should contain a brief *summary and conclusion section*. Here the researcher summarizes the major points of the paper; discusses, once again, the implications for the hypotheses (and theory) being tested; and points the direction for needed future research. Also, in the conclusion it is typical to find a statement or two of the *limitations* of the study. Those interested in the topic will benefit not only from your *findings*, but also from the *problems* encountered in conducting your research. All scientific research has limitations. By candidly discussing the problems faced and how and why they were handled as they were, the researcher not only provides the reader with additional criteria for evaluating this particular research, but just as important (sometimes more so), provides valuable guidelines and directions to those contemplating future work in the field. In this sense, interested readers learn not only from your findings but also from the problems you faced along the way.

An Example

As has so often been suggested in this text, the student will find helpful in attempting to master these concepts a review of works of others published in the political science journals. There, one will find articles that illustrate, to varying degrees, the points raised above.

In the March, 1978, issue of the *American Political Science Review*, for example, an article appeared by Donley T. Studlar, entitled "Policy Voting in Britain: The Colored Immigration Issue in the 1964, 1966, and 1970 General Elections."[4] Studlar begins his article with a brief introductory section (two paragraphs), where he states, in part:

> Recent studies examining the question of mass issue voting in the United States have found that people vote more frequently on the basis of policy questions than has heretofore been thought. These findings have clashed with the conventional wisdom of American election studies, which maintains that issues are of little importance in determining electoral outcomes.....
>
> Few studies, however, have examined whether mass policy voting exists in countries other than the United States. Britain is a particularly appropriate setting for such an examination because of its "responsible parties," which supposedly translate mass preference into governmental policy through the

[4]Donley T. Studlar, "Policy Voting in Britain: The Colored Immigration Issue in the 1964, 1966, and 1970 General Elections," *American Political Science Review*, 72 (March, 1978), 46–64.

mechanism of presenting contending positions to the voters for their endorsement.[5]

In these few sentences, Studlar succeeds in immediately informing the reader of (1) the general topical issue of this paper, (2) the controversy involved, and (3) the particular research focus of his effort. The next section of the article is entitled "An Overview of Previous Research." Here, Studlar summarizes in five paragraphs the important literature in this area. Note that this is probably not an exhaustive and extensive review of all the literature in the area of mass issue voting, but is representative of the major works, especially those which bear particularly on his topic — policy voting in Britain with specific reference to the colored immigration issue. Studlar calls his next section, "Data and Methodology." He tells the reader here: "This study relies most heavily on a secondary analysis of the postelection surveys of [David] Butler and [Donald] Stokes in 1964, 1966, and 1970. The number of people interviewed after each election ranged from 1200 to 2000, a suitably large sample for multivariate analysis.... In addition, variables taken from the ten percent sample census of Britain in 1966 are employed as controls.... The major techniques employed to analyze the data are simple cross-tabulation, correlation, and path analysis through the use of multiple regression."[6] Following this, Studlar's findings are presented under a section entitled "The Findings," which consists of four major subheadings: (1) Opinions on Immigration Policy; (2) Perception of Party Differences; (3) Opinion on Immigration and Perception of Party Differences; and (4) Immigration Policy Voting. Studlar concludes his essay with a section entitled "Discussion." At this point he discusses some of the possible limitations of his study and succinctly concludes the paper with his major findings: "In summary, the argument that voters adjust their perceptions of party differences on immigration to their partisan choice has some validity.... Immigration opinion had no discernible effect on voting behavior in 1964 and 1966 because the connection between parties and positions on the issue was not generally made.... [But] [t]he three conditions for issue voting were met in 1970, and opinion on immigration significantly affected voting choice in that year."[7]

All together, Studlar's introduction and review of the literature comprise less than 10 percent of his total article, the data and methodology section comprises about 20 percent, the findings about 55 percent, and the discussion (conclusions) about 15 percent. Of course, the precise proportion of space allocated to each of these areas will vary from paper to paper, but these proportions would probably be close to the "average." Again, readers are strongly advised to review other articles appearing in the *American Political Science Review* and in other journals to develop for themselves a comfortable

[5] *Ibid.*, pp. 46–47. Studlar's references are deleted from this quotation.
[6] *Ibid.*, pp. 48–49.
[7] *Ibid.*, p. 64.

working knowledge of the format used by political scientists and policy researchers in presenting the results of their research.

Writing Style

It is easy to say that the report should be written "clearly," "crisply," "precisely," "unambiguously," and all of the other stylistic terms used in this chapter. Yet it is much more difficult to define just what all these terms mean and more difficult still to instruct someone in the art of "good" writing style. Even William Strunk and E. B. White (whose little book, *The Elements of Style*,[8] has become a classic in the field) admit that, "There is no satisfactory explanation of style, no infallible guide to good writing, no assurance that a person who thinks clearly will be able to write clearly, no key that unlocks the door, no inflexible rules by which the young writer may shape his course."[9]

With all that going against us, one might be tempted to dismiss as futile any attempt at developing or improving good writing style. But of course, the argument to be made is that the beginner can with practice develop a satisfactory writing style, and that the writing style of almost any author can be improved. As a start, the student is advised to read completely Strunk and White's *The Elements of Style*. It is a little book (85 pages), but almost everyone will find there numerous helpful suggestions. At the conclusion of the book, Strunk and White list 21 suggestions that would help improve anyone's writing style. One of these should be particularly stressed: revise and rewrite. The beginning writer sometimes thinks that the first draft is equivalent to the final product. This is almost never the case. Almost any written work, regardless of how brief or informal, can be improved by rewriting. Those writing for publication will have the benefit of comments and suggestions from trained editors and skilled reviewers. Of course, the beginning student is not likely to have professional assistance, and more than likely will have to serve as his or her own proofreader. In this case, it is suggested that after completing the first draft the student set aside the paper and move on to other projects or simply relax for a while. But the student should come back to the manuscript in a day or two, refreshed and prepared to assume unmercifully the role of self-critic. At this stage, the writer must step back from the intricacies and complexities of the research itself, and for every sentence and every paragraph ask herself or himself once again: "Have I made the points I want to make as clearly and as unambiguously as possible?" On reexamination, the writer almost invariably will discover areas of confusion and ambiguity that can be improved by rewriting. The secret to successful writing, most authors would agree, is rewriting.

[8] William Strunk, Jr., and E. B. White, *The Elements of Style*, 3rd ed. (New York: Macmillan Publishing Co., Inc., 1979).
[9] *Ibid.*, p. 66.

Some Final Thoughts

This text began with the themes that (1) political research can be an enjoyable, rewarding opportunity; and (2) for greatest satisfaction, political research should be conducted in an orderly, systematic fashion. The focus of this text has been on the second of these themes: the conduct of systematic political research. We have tried to explore each of the major stages of systematic research — from topic selection, to hypothesis formation, to literature review, to data collection, to data analysis, to report writing — and to review those techniques and methods most helpful at each stage. It is hoped that the focus on method has not obscured the rewards of political research, and that through the presentation in this text of portions of the works of a variety of political scientists, a glimpse of the more exciting aspects of political and policy research has been achieved. But, of course, no textbook can ever fully describe and relate the joys of political research; this will come from personal experience in a research situation.

In conducting your own research, or in serving as part of a research team, you will learn another very important lesson about scientific research. This is that even with the best of research guides, with the most advanced of computers, with the most sophisticated statistical programs, and with the highest quality of data, research success is not guaranteed. All these tools help maximize the probabilities of research success, but the ingredient missing from the list is the human intellect. No technique can guarantee scientific breakthroughs; no computer can guarantee a successful research effort. Above all else, it is the human imagination, unbridled as we argued in Chapter 1, that remains the key to creative research. This, as it turns out, is the truly exciting aspect of political research, the blending of the imagination with available technology to produce the highest quality of research product — that which is not only technically correct but which is also speculative, experimental, and innovative.

In conducting research, it is hoped that the student may benefit from the correct use of the tools discussed in this text, but it is hoped more fervently that the student will recognize and never lose sight of the difference between the techniques of research and the creativity of research. Creativity is a product of the human imagination — not the computer, not the technique, not the method. It is creativity in scientific research that is to be cherished and pursued above all. This is the final, and most important, lesson of this book: the imagination, uninhibited and unrestrained, stands without challenge as the greatest of all research tools.

Exercises

1. Select a recent issue of a political science journal in an area of particular interest to you. Examine each empirically-oriented article in that issue and for each of these articles *report* the following:
   a. The problem or issue addressed, and the hypotheses (if any) being tested.
   b. The design of the research, including the type of data examined and the method of collecting the data.
   c. The results of the study as they relate to the problem or hypotheses being examined.
   d. The study's conclusions.
2. *Critically analyze* each study reviewed above. Include in your analysis a discussion of the following:
   a. Were the author's hypotheses clearly stated at the outset? Could they have been stated more precisely? If so, how?
   b. Do you find the research design to have been adequate? If not, how might it have been improved? What alternative sources of data might you suggest?
   c. Were the statistics used appropriate for the nature of the data employed and hypotheses being tested? If not, which would have been more appropriate? Why is this so?
   d. Were the conclusions reached appropriate from the analysis presented? Why or why not?
   e. What *one* major weakness do you find in *each* study? What suggestions would you offer to future researchers to overcome this weakness?

_____Research Examples_____

Author's Note: I am fortunate to be able to conclude this book with example research papers prepared by two political science students at the George Washington University. I believe the reader will find these papers most instructive. In terms both of style and content, I believe they represent the quality of research effort students would want, and instructors would expect, given the time limitations of a one semester course.

The first essay, by Robin B. Steiner, examines those social background factors associated with levels of alienation in America in the 1972 to 1976 period. Robin relies for his data on the American election surveys conducted by the Center for Political Studies at the University of Michigan. The second essay, by Steven M. Schneider, analyzes the networks' coverage of President Sadat's 1977 visit to Israel. Steve's primary method of data collection is content analysis of network news presentations.

The reader should examine carefully both of these papers since they provide useful guidelines in the important areas of research methodology, format, and style. As when reviewing any research, the reader should evaluate these papers applying the following standards: has the author sufficiently reviewed and summarized the relevant literature?; have testable hypotheses been developed and clearly stated?; were the collected and analyzed data appropriate for the testing of the hypotheses?; were the appropriate analytic techniques applied to the data?; and, were the conclusions reached appropriate to the findings presented? Having so evaluated the works of others, the researcher should be no less demanding in applying these same standards to his or her own work.

ALIENATION IN AMERICA:

EXAMINATION OF SOCIAL BACKGROUND FACTORS, 1972-1976

by

Robin B. Steiner

INTRODUCTION

The concept of alienation has long occupied a central role in studies of the political and social order.[1] For classical theorists such as Locke, Hobbes, Rousseau, Hegel, and Marx, alienation was a key variable in their theories of the evolving polity, and the relationship of the citizen to the state.[2] Contemporary scholars also view alienation, or in modern terminology, lack of system support, as an important variable both in the maintenance of system stability (or instability) and in accounting for and understanding individual political behavior. For Gamson (1968), the term alienation has both input and output dimensions. On the input side, which he calls efficacy, Gamson finds that alienation "refers to people's perception of their ability to influence (the system)" (p. 42). On the output side, which he calls "trust," Gamson finds that alienation refers to "beliefs about the outputs of the political system" (p. 42). These two aspects of alienation are central to Gamson's predictions about how people will behave politically, given different responses from the political system. For Easton (1965), popular support is critical to system maintenance and stability. He finds that, "where . . . support falls below a minimum, the persistence of any kind of system will be endangered" (p. 220). According to Miller (1974, p. 951), "when such support wanes, underlying discontent is the necessary result, and the potential for revolutionary alteration of the political and social system is enhanced." Almond and Powell (1966) state that support classifications (including trust, obedience and allegiance) "provide the resources which enable a political system to extract, regulate and distribute--in other words to carry out its goals" (p. 96).

Alienation, then, truly is an important concept to the political analyst. It plays a significant role in our understanding both of individual behavior and systems survival. Furthermore, studies indicate that the proportion of alienated Americans has risen appreciably in recent years. Miller (1974) found that in 1964 22 percent of the electorate believed that they could trust the government in Washington only some of the time; by 1970 this had increased to over 44 percent. Similarly, Gilmour and Lamb (1975) note a significant increase in the proportion of those classified as "extremely alienated" in the 1960 to 1970 period.

This study examines the concept of political alienation of America in the 1972 to 1976 period, and is concerned especially with identifying and assessing those social background factors related to increased alienation. Available literature suggests many possible correlates of political alienation and is ripe with explanations of those conditions giving rise to increased alienation. Among those variables which have been examined are background and demographic factors (Finifter, 1970); personality factors (Bowen, et al., 1968); reactions to political issues and public policy directions (Miller, 1974); and political expectations (Aberbach and Walker, 1970; Gamson, 1968). Aberbach and Walker (1970) have covered much of this ground and summarized much of the existing literature when they note four broad explanations of causes of alienation. These are, they say, trust in people measures, social background factors, political expectation variables, and feelings of psychological deprivation.

Of all the studies of the causes of political alienation, Aberbach and Walker's is the most complete and in many ways the most relevant. Aberbach and Walker (1970) dismiss simple background theories as unimportant to an understanding of alienation, at least for their sample of Detroit residents. Rather they focus especially on measures of political expectations for, "a more satisfactory explanation" (p. 1205).

While Aberbach and Walker argue persuasively that social background factors are slightly or indirectly related to alienation, there are at least three reasons why this linkage deserves further scholarly inquiry. First, Aberbach and Walker's sample was limited to residents in and around Detroit. It is possible that studies based on a national sample would yield different conclusions. Secondly, their study was conducted in 1967. Given the rapidity of social, economic, and political change in the 1970's, it is possible that changes in the correlates of alienation may have occurred as well. Finally--and this is the major thesis of this paper--while demographic factors in general may not be strongly related to alienation, those social and demographic factors which are, themselves, measures of political experiences and expectations may be signifi-

231

cantly related to the alienation variable. That is, social variables which divide the populace into the political "haves" and "have-nots" may well be found to be related to political alienation. The underlying assumption here retains Aberbach and Walker's basic premise that alienation is, in part at least, the result of dissatisfaction with the decisions and actions of our government. The political have-not groups are, by definition, unable to influence politics and will, it is predicted, be more alienated than the political "haves."

Considerable evidence supports the contention that those demographic groups defined as the political have-nots will be the most alienated. Gilmour and Lamb (1975) found that in the 1960 to 1972 period women were more likely to be alienated than men, older Americans than younger Americans, and lower income groups more than higher income groups. Finifter (1970) found the measures of race, education, and occupation to be among the highest correlates of her dimensions of alienation. Other studies, using the University of Michigan Survey Research Center data, consistently show that efficacy and cynicism are related to such demographic variables as sex, education, income and occupational status--all measures which also reflect power divisions within our society.[3]

In this regard special attention should be paid to the variable of education. Education, some studies indicate, appears to have a mediating or intervening effect on the relationship between alienation and demographic measures of political powerlessness. Finifter (1970) found that a control for education greatly affected the association between race and alienation. In her words, "Given similar educational achievement, Negroes apparently feel hardly any more powerless than do whites" (p. 339). And Aberbach and Walker (1970) found that more highly educated Blacks are more satisfied than less educated Blacks, and are less likely to be very bitter about government when they fail to achieve personal goals.[4] Education, then, may serve as a sort of buffer between demographic measures of powerlessness and alienation. The highly educated, regardless of their group identities, may be highly trusting in the political system. This link is to be tested in this study as well.

The following hypotheses, then, are to be pursued in this study:

1. Demographic measures of political powerlessness will be

significantly related to political alienation.

2. Education will have a moderating effect on this relationship.

3. Over time, the alienation levels of those classified as
the political have-not groups in society will increase at a pace
greater than those classified as the politically powerful.

DATA AND METHODOLOGY

Any study of alienation first encounters the difficult problem of operationalizing the term. Finifter (1970) identified at
least four major ways in which the term alienation might be used.
She called these "political powerlessness," "political meaningless-
ness," "perceived political normlessness," and " political isolation."
Using the American component of the Almond and Verba five-nation
study, Finifter went on to empirically derive two distinct dimensions:
political powerlessness and perceived political normlessness. Most
students of alienation probably have relied on the trust and
efficacy questions as constructed and administered by the Survey
Research Center. Surely trust (or cynicism) and efficacy (or ineffi-
cacy) are important components of the overall concept of alienation
and seem to conform relatively well to Finifter's dimensions of normlessness and powerlessness.[5]

In constructing an overall measure of alienation, this study
combined into a single scale the measures of cynicism and efficacy
as asked by the Center for Political Studies in its American National
Election Studies.[6] While this deviates from the usual practice of
separately analyzing these two dimensions of alienation, it is hoped
that the combined measure will both facilitate the analysis and
result in a more succinct and perhaps more accurate picture of the
correlates of alienation as examined in this effort.

The measure of political haves and have-nots is difficult to
define in a manner so as to satisfy all scholars and all perspectives.
Powerlessness, Parenti (1978) says, "means the inability to get what
one needs or wants . . . and the inability to influence others
effectively in ways furthering one's own interests" (p. 64). Yet,
Parenti reminds us that power is situationally defined and that "few
people are powerless in all instances, under all conditions" (p. 64).
Given this caveat, Parenti goes on to identify various powerless

groups in America, and relying largely on his suggestions the following groupings will be used as measures of political haves and have-nots for the present study.

Demographic Group:	Have Group:	Have-not Group:
Age	31 - 65	18 - 30, Post 65
Sex	Male	Female
Race	White	Non-White
Social class	Upper class	Lower class
	Average middle	Lower
	Middle	Average working
	Upper middle	Working
	Upper	Upper Working

Each demographic variable is broken down into either powerful or powerless groups. A brief explanation of the scheme of classification is now called for.

AGE: The youth of America has not had time to establish economic and political strongholds. The aged, on the other hand, have passed their prime as revenue producing individuals. Furthermore, the elders of our society are often physically incapable of political expression. Thus the young and old are placed in the powerless category.

SEX: Our society is dominated by the male. "Fifty-eight percent of the stock shares are owned by institutions whose boards of directors and brokers are male: (L. Richard Wallum, 1979, p. 191) Thus the political and economic systems are effectively controlled by men.

RACE: Because of their smaller numbers, limited wealth, and poorer education, Non-Whites have been the victims of White domination nad, political and economic exploitation for many years. Therefore, Non-Whites are considered relatively powerless in comparison to the White population.

SOCIAL CLASS: According to Marx (Gilmour and Lamb, 1975) the worker is powerless in the capitalistic society. The state and its accompanying power structure is alien to the lower classes; it serves as the ruling class' tool for the continued suppression of the subordinate classes. Furthermore, the ruling class in the U.S. is composed of individuals from the upper classes.

Individuals do not merely define themselves as black, or rich, or lower class, or old. Rather, individuals see themselves as composites of different demographic groups. Therefore, a composite scale was designed. This scale, called the have/have-not scale, is based on the assumption that political power is additive. That is to say that a rich Black man has more political clout than a poor Black man; and a rich White man has more power than a rich Black man. Individuals who lie on the have-not end of the continuum would be expected to be more alienated and less allegiant than those who fall on the more powerful end. The have/have-not scale is composed of the following variables, coded in the following manner.

234

	Code:
Demographic Variables:	

Demographic Variables:	Code:
AGE	18 - 30 = 1 31 - 65 = 7 Post 65 = 1
SEX	Male = 7· Female = 1
SOCIAL CLASS	Lower Class = 0 Average Working Class = 1 Working Class = 2 Upper Working Class = 3 Average Middle Class = 4 Middle Class = 5 Upper Middle Class = 6 Upper Class = 7
INCOME PER ANNUM	$ 0 to 6999 = 1 7000 to 9999 = 2 10,000 to 13,999 = 4 14,000 to 22,999 = 6 23,000 and above = 7

The weighted responses were summed to determine a cumulative score for each respondent.[7] Originally, the have/have-not scale was weighted to facilitate a seven point scale. However, the seven-point scale proved too cumbersome for meaningful analysis. Thus by collapsing the scale in the following manner a three point scale was created.

$$0 - 3.49 = 1 \text{ (have-nots)}$$
$$3.50 - 4.49 = 2 \text{ (middle)}$$
$$4.50 - 7.00 = 3 \text{ (haves)}$$

FINDINGS

Gilmour and Lamb (1975) found that "Americans over sixty-five have consistently been the most alienated citizens . . . (while) those in the most youthful groups were typically less estranged from politics than their seniors" (p. 63). Table 1 shows each age group's level of alienation.

Table 1

Alienation By Age

	1972			1976		
	Youth (18-30)	Middle Age (31-65)	Senior Citizens (Post 65)	Youth (18-30)	Middle Age (31-65)	Senior Citizens (Post 65)
Allegiant 1:	30.9%	30.5%	19.8%	29.4%	31.2%	24.6%
2:	27.0%	25.2%	25.9%	20.2%	20.5%	17.4%
Alienated 3:	42.1%	44.4%	54.2%	50.4%	48.3%	58.0%
Chi-Square Significance:		.0002			.0266	
Gamma Correlation Coefficient:		.10			.05	
N:		2678			2212	

Source: CPS 1972 and 1976 American National Election Studies.

235

Although the table shows only weak gamma correlations, they are statistically significant, and show that by 1976 American youth were no longer the most allegiant group. From 1972 through 1976, there was an almost 8 percent increase in the proportion of alienated youth, compared to a slight increase in the percent of middle aged allegiant individuals. By 1976, the most allegiant category is the middle age group. In 1972, 54 percent of America's senior citizens were politically alienated, making this the most alienated age group in America. Between 1972 and 1976, this age group became about 4 percent _more_ alienated.

Table 2 examines the relationship between sex and alienation.

Table 2

Alienation By Sex

	1972			1976	
	Male	Female	:	Male	Female
Allegiant 1:	31.5%	27.2%	:	32.5%	27.5%
2:	26.9%	25.0%	:	20.9%	19.2%
Alienated 3:	41.6%	47.8%	:	46.6%	53.3%
Chi-Square Significance:	.0049		:	.0062	
Gamma Correlation Coefficient:	.10		:	.12	
N:	2678		:	2208	

Source: CPS 1972 and 1976 American National Election Studies.

In both years, it can be seen that, as hypothesized, women were more alienated than men. The differences in the levels of alienation between the sexes ·is statistically significant. However, the correlation coefficients for both 1972 and 1976 are low. It is of interest that the strength of the relationship between alienation and sex increases during the time frame of the analysis.

Table 3 examines the relationship between alienation and social class. The CPS eight-point measure of social class was split into two approximately equal groups: upper and lower social classes.

In 1972 a moderate correlation existed between social class and the level of alienation. However, by 1976, although the direction of the relationship remained the same, the strength had dropped. Thus, as hypothesized, alienation runs highest in the class with the least ability to exercise choice and influence in our society.

236

Table 3
Alienation By Class

	1972			1976	
	Lower Class	Upper Class	:	Lower Class	Upper Class
Allegiant 1:	21.9%	37.8%	:	25.0%	33.7%
2:	25.9%	25.5%	:	17.1%	23.3%
Alienated 3:	52.2%	36.7%	:	57.8%	43.1%
Chi-Square Significance:	.0000		:	.0000	
Gamma Correlation Coefficient:	-.30		:	-.23	
N:	2603		:	2132	

Source: CPS 1972 and 1976 American National Election Studies.

At the outset of this essay, it was argued that the political structure in the U.S. works in favor of the White majority. As Table 4 illustrates, alienation, is in fact, highest among Non-Whites.

Table 4
Alienation By Race

	1972			1976	
	Non-White	White	:	Non-White	White
Allegiant 1:	16.9%	30.6%	:	27.7%	30.3%
2:	22.3%	26.3%	:	15.4%	20.5%
Alienated 3:	60.8%	43.1%	:	56.9%	49.5%
Chi-Square Significance:	.0000		:	.0579	
Gamma Correlation Coefficient:	.32		:	.11	
N:	2678		:	2193	

Source: CPS 1972 and 1976 American National Election Studies.

There was a statistically significant difference in the levels of alienation between the races in 1972. However, by 1976, this difference was no longer significant. Not surprisingly, the gamma for 1972 was moderate (.32); but by 1976 the relationship had weakened appreciably (.11).

For all the variables examined thus far, the results have lent at least partial support to the hypotheses being tested. The powerful groups in America have been more allegiant and less alienated than the powerless groups. The relationship between the have/have-not composite scale and alienation, shown in Table 5, will illustrate the effects of cross-cutting peer pressure on alienation.

```
                              Table 5

                  Alienation By the Have/Have Not Scale

                      1972                          1976

          Have                       :  Have
          Not    Middle    Haves     :  Not    Middle    Haves
          (1)    (2)       (3)       :  (1)    (2)       (3)

Allegiant 1:  21.3%   29.8%    36.5%    :  25.4%   26.8%    34.5%

        2:    24.1%   26.1%    27.4%    :  15.7%   20.2%    23.0%

Alienated 3:  54.6%   44.1% ·  36.1%    :  58.9%   53.0%    42.5%

Chi-Square                              :
Significance:          .0000            :           .0000

Gamm                                    :
Correlation                             :
Coefficient:          -.23              :          -.19

N:                    2678             :           2212
```

Source: CPS 1972 and 1976 American National Election Studies.

For the have-not group, the proportions falling at the alienated and (surprisingly) allegiant ends of the continuum increased from 1972 to 1976. The have group became more alienated. As one might expect, the effects of the composite scale serve to magnify the relation between level of power and alienation. With the exception of race in 1972 and class in both 1972 and 1976, no other correlations have been as strong as those for the have/have-not scale when crosstabbed with alienation. Once again, it was found that as time progresses, the relationship between alienation and these measures of power groupings grows weaker.

Summarizing the analysis to this point, it was found in all cases that alienation levels were greatest in the powerless groups. With the exception of age in 1972, the powerful groups were consistently more allegiant. Excluding the sex variable, the strength of the correlations between the independent power variables and the dependent alienation scale dropped during the analysis. Since alienation is greatest among the powerless, and allegiance greatest among the powerful, credence is given to the original hypothesis: The least powerful group will report the most alienation, as it has the least say over which policies are proposed and finally adopted. Almost all the relationships were found to be statistically significant; however, the strengths of the relationships (gamma) were modest at best. This would indicate that other factors also influence the level of alienation in American society.

CONTROLLING FOR EDUCATION

Finifter (1970) finds that when controlling for education, the strength of the relationship between race and alienation is weakened. This would indicate that education may serve as a buffer between alienation and the power variable. Thus it is important to re-examine each of the above relationships controlling for education.

Table 6 presents the 1976 gamma correlation coefficients for the power variables when crossed with the alienation scale, while controlling for education. For purposes of this analysis, education was divided into the three following categories:

1. Low: Individuals who received no more than a ninth grade education.

2. Medium: Individuals who received no more than a high school diploma.

3. High: Individuals who have had at least some college.

The simple gamma correlations are presented first, followed by the gammas when controlling for education.

Table 6

Alienation and Power Variables
Controlling for Education

| | | Education Level: | | |
Ind. Var.	Original Gamma:	Low:	Medium:	High:
Race	.11	.01	.05	.30
Class	-.23	-.20	-.10	-.18
Sex	.12	.12	.15	.04
Age	.05	.02	.04	-.15
Have/ Have not scale	-.19	-.09	-.16	-.08

Source: CPS 1976 American National Election Study.

The assumption that education serves as a uniform and consistent buttress against alienation from the political system is simplistic. Such a statement covers only a few cases. The table presented above reflects a very complicated story. For the poorly educated, education does mask differences in the levels of alienation among different racial groups. However, relatively strong correlations are found between race, class and age, and alienation among highly educated individuals.

It can be seen that the control for education reduces the relationship between sex and alienation at the highest, but not the lowest, levels of education. A possible explanation may be that as a result of equal employment actions and the women's movement, well-educated women have begun to assert themselves, and as a result feel more powerful and more important in the system's decision making processes and thus less alienated.

Age and racial groups show similar tendencies. The well educated in both groups show the strongest relationship. But, the -.15 correlation between levels of alienation and age is con-trary to the basic hypothesis of this essay. This is to say that, as well educated individuals become older, alienation decreases. One might posit that as an educated individual ages, he or she earns a better living. Consequently, the individual is freer from system constraints, and therefore feels less alienated.

The earlier findings showed that the have/have-not scale magnified the relationship between alienation and political power. However, although the direction of the relation remained the same when controlling for education, the gammas became considerably weaker.

Thus, Finifter was only partially correct. Often education does serve to mask or buffer the effects of alienation but its impact overall is complicated. In some instances (such as race and age) the correlations are stronger in the upper educated categories; in others (such as sex) the correlations are stronger in the lower educated categories. Perhaps future research may resolve these contradictions.

CHANGES OVER TIME

This analysis now turns to the relative[8] and absolute[9] changes in alienation among the various subpopulations examined in this study. The question to be examined is, which groups--the powerful or the powerless--have experienced the greatest increases in alienation during this time period?

Because of space limitations, only three variables will be examined here: sex, race, and social class.[10] To clearly illustrate how each group has been affected, three tables will be presented. Each table will show the absolute and relative change in alienation over time (1972 - 1976).

Table 7

Changing Alienation Levels by Sex, 1972 - 1976

	Male		Female	
	Absolute %Point Change:	Relative Change:	Absolute % Point Change:	Relative Change:
Allegiant 1:	.1	3.2%	.3	1.1%
2:	-6	-22.3%	-5.8	-23.2%
Alienated 3:	5	12.0%	5.5	11.5%

Source: CPS 1972 and 1976 American National Election Studies.

Table 7 shows a 3.2 percent increase in male allegiance, compared to only a 1.1 percent increase in allegiance for women. Alienation among males increased 12 percent, while slightly less for women, at 11.5 percent. Although the differences are not striking, it seems that the male population is slightly more likely to exper- ience shifts in both alienation and allegiance.

Table 8

Changing Alienation Levels By Race, 1972 - 1976

	White		Non-White	
	Absolute % Point Change:	Relative Change:	Absolute % Point Change:	Relative Change:
Allegiant 1:	-.6	-2.0%	10.8	63.9%
2:	-5.8	-22.1%	6.9	30.9%
Alienated 3:	6.4	14.8%	-3.9	-6.4%

Source: CPS 1972 and 1976 American National Election Studies.

Table 8 shows that alienation rose 14.8 percent in the White population. In the Non-White population, alienation increased by 6.4 percent. Allegiance in each group was a source of change. Among Non-Whites, allegiance increased drastically, 63.9 percent; while allegiance dropped by 2 percent for the White category. It is evident that alienation among Whites is increasing more rapidly than among the Non-White population. Thus, again, the powerful group is quicker to become estranged from the American political system than the less powerful group.

Table 9

Changing Alienation Levels By Class, 1972 - 1976

	Lower Classes		Upper Classes	
	Absolute % Point Change:	Relative Change:	Absolute % Point Change:	Relative Change:
Allegiant 1:	3.1	14.2%	-4.1	-10.8%
2:	-8.8	-34.0%	-2.2	-8.6%
Alienated 3:	5.6	10.6%	6.4	17.4%

Source: CPS 1972 and 1976 American National Studies.

Table 9 shows that allegiance dropped in the upper classes by over 10 percent; while increasing by 14.2 percent in the lower classes. Alienation increased in the lower classes by 10.6 percent; however, the rate of increase in the upper classes was 17.4 percent. Once again, alienation among the powerful is increasing at a greater rate than alienation among the less powerful. It is interesting to note that allegiance among the lower classes is increasing. As time passes, the lower class receives more tokens from the government; minimum standards of living are being raised. Perhaps this is the reason why allegiance has increased in this group. The rise in allegiance must be balanced against a 10 percent increase in alienation in this same group.

SUMMARY AND CONCLUSIONS

It has been suggested throughout the paper that the powerful groups are accustomed to dealing with and in the power structures of American Society. The "haves" have learned to see past and circumvent the bureaucratic and structural smoke screens which have come to be considered givens in our government. As a result, political actions and decisions are more visible to the powerful groups. Thus this group, having a better understanding and a larger stake in the economic and political superstructure, has quickly become disenchanted with and frustrated by our government.

The disadvantaged groups, for a long time, have been alienated from our system of government. Thus a thick layer of politically estranged citizens make up large portions of the powerless groups. In essence the politically powerless groups are nearer the political alienation saturation point than the politically powerful. Thus similar to the notion of diminishing returns, the powerful are quicker to become alienated.

To summarize, four conclusions seem justified in this study. First, Alienation over all groups increased dramatically during the period from 1972 through 1976. This is seen, first, by the increase in the frequency of the alienation category on the allegiant/alienation scale; and second, by the decreases in the simple gamma correlations from 1972 to 1976. This indicates that as time passes alienation is tied less and less to positions of power, and more to a general sentiment that pervades our society. A second conclusion may be drawn, that disadvantaged groups are more alienated than the advantaged. Third, while education often serves to weaken the relationships between alienation and political power, it sometimes strengthens the correlation. Finally, contrary to one of the initial hypotheses, it is the advantaged groups, and not the disadvantaged groups, that are quickest to become disenchanted with our political system.

NOTES

1. The data utilized in this paper were made available by the Interdata University Consortium for Political and Social Research, The University of Michigan. Neither the original collectors of the data nor the Consortium bear any responsibility for the analysis or interpretation presented here.

2. For a thoughtful, historical treatment of the term "alienation," see: Richard Schact, Alienation (N.Y., Doubleday and Co., Inc., 1970).

3. See for example, Angus Campbell, et al., The American Voter (N.Y., John Wiley and Sons, Inc., 1964).

4. Although in a latter study Aberbach finds college educated Blacks to be the least satisfied with their amoung of political power. See: Joel Aberbach, "Power Consciousness: A Comparative Analysis," American Political Science Review, 71 (December, 1977), 1544 - 1560.

5. For a similar conclusion see: Arthur H. Miller, "Political Issues and Trust in Government: 1964-1970," American Political Science Review, 68 (September, 1974), 951 - 972.

6. Each respondent's responses were weighted and then summed for a cumulative score. Because it was possible for a respondent to refuse to answer a question, making the cumulative score inaccurate, a means of accounting for missing respondents had to be designed. Thus, the cumulative score was divided by the number of valid responses. However, if the respondent failed to answer at least six questions, the score was discarded.

7. Once again (see note 6) a respondent could refuse to answer a question making the Have/Have-not scale inaccurate. To rectify this, the cumulative score was divided by the number of valid responses. However, if an individual failed to anser at least three questions his or her score was discarded.

8. Relative change is determined by subtracting the 1972 level of sentiment from the 1976 level of sentiment. The difference is then divided by the 1972 level. The end result is a determination of the linear rate of sentiment level change relative to 1972.

9. Absolute precentage point change is determined by subtracting the 1972 level of sentiment from the 1976 level of sentiment.

10. Analysis of other variables revealed patterns similar to those reported here.

REFERENCES

Joel D. Aberbach and Jack L. Wlaker, "Political Trust and Racial Ideology," American Political Science Review, 64, (December 1970), 1199 - 1219.

Gabriel A. Almond and G. Bingham Powell, Comparative Politics: A Developmental Approach. Boston: Little, Brown and Company, 1966.

David Easton, A Systems Analysis of Political Life. New York: John Wiley & Sons, Inc., 1965.

Ada Finifter, "Dimensions of Political Alienation," American Political Science Review, 64 (June 1970), 389 - 410.

William A. Gamson, Power and Discontent. Homewood, Ill.: The Dorsey Press, 1968.

Robert S. Gilmour and Robert B. Lamb, Political Alienation in Contemporary America. New York: St. Martin's Press, 1975.

Arthur A. Miller, "Political Issues and Trust in Government: 1964 - 1970," American Political Science Review, 68 (Sempember 1974), 951 - 972.

Michael Parenti, Power and the Powerless. New York: Doubleday and Co., 1970.

L. Richard Wallum, The Dynamics of Sex and Gender: A Sociological Approach. Chicago: Rand McNally Publishers, 1970.

A CONTENT ANALYSIS OF NETWORK NEWS COVERAGE OF

SADAT'S 1977 VISIT TO ISRAEL

by

Steven M. Schneider

Since the establishment of Israel over thirty years ago as a separate and independent nation, events of the Middle East have captured the attention of the American public and consequently received prime coverage by the American press. The extent of the press' interest is obvious--even in the late sixties the Middle East ranked second only to Vietnam in television foreign affairs coverage (Warner, 1968; Almaney, 1970). Throughout this time, considerable scholarly effort has been expended in attempts to determine what, if any, biases exist in Middle East coverage. Nearly all studies claim to have found an anti-Arab slant.[1] Popular literature as well charges the media with a pro-Israeli interest.[2]

In a content analysis conducted for coverage of the early stages of the 1956 Arab-Israeli war, the New York Times was found to be favorable towards Israel and critical of the Arab efforts (Batrouka, 1961). The same study, however, found the Christian Science Monitor balanced in its news coverage. Suleiman (1965) found seven major American news magazines[3] to be generally pro-Israeli and anti-Arab during the last six months of 1956. He noted especially the "reluctance on the part of the American press to criticize the Israelis" (Suleiman, 1965, p. 11).

Press coverage of the 1967 Middle East War has been analyzed in a number of studies, most of which have concluded that the American media were pro-Israeli during the Six Day War (AIPC, 1967; Belkaoui, 1978; Farmer, 1968; Howard, 1967; Suleiman, 1970). The defense most frequently offered by the media was the easier access to the news in Israel, an explanation which Suleiman (1970) disputed. Replicating his study of 1956 coverage of the Middle East War (Suleiman, 1965), he argued that "the campaign to present the Israeli version, and only the Israeli version of what was happening in the Middle East in the summer of 1967 . . . . was perhaps without comparison in its extent and intensity" (Suleiman, 1970, p. 138). During May and June of 1967, Suleiman contends that 84 percent of the reporting on the Middle East was pro-Israeli or anti-Arab during the 1967 war (pp. 140-141). Furthermore, Israel was consistently portrayed as something of a miracle maker, in a "David-Goliath" scenerio. For example, reports frequently compared the large Arab with the small Israeli population, rather than Israel's 300,000 troops to the 285,000 Arab troops (Suleiman, 1970). Other studies (AIPC, Belkaoui, Farmer, Howard) generally supported Suleiman's conclusions.

Belkaoui (1978) argues that the "prestige press"[4] in America created a neutral image for the Israelis in 1967, "who were more likely to tell, say, or announce than to threaten or warn" (p. 736). The Arabs, on the other hand, "tended to deliver messages in an aggressive, angry, or threatening style" (p. 736). Moreover, in 1967, Israeli figures were cast as "heroes" while Arab leaders were likely to be viewed as "villains" (Belkaoui, 1978).[5]

In a study of coverage from the end of the 1967 war through 1969, Wagner (1973) found the New York Times, Los Angeles Times and Washington Post's editorials to show a "generally pro-Israel tone" and a "preoccupation with [the] achievement of a negotiated settlement" (Wagner, 1973, p. 317).

Media coverage of the 1973 war may have marked a significant change in the pro-Israeli tendency of the American press. Gordon (1975) found network television news coverage in the United States to be balanced, even though Zaremba (1977) concluded that the New York Times treated the Arabs as the aggressor, as it had in the 1967 war (Wagner, 1973). Gordon's study is particularly interesting because it is the only published content analysis of television news coverage of the Middle East.[6] Gordon found no significant difference in the number of reports originating from Israel or Arab lands. Though he did identify some differences between the different networks' presentation of the news, these did not indicate any bias in overall coverage of the war.

This shift in the reporting of the Middle East--from a staunch pro-Israeli approach to coverage more favorable to the Arabs, was discussed by Belkaoui (1978). In a study of the American "prestige press," she concluded that a shift toward a more favorable image of the Arabs was present in the American media during and after the 1973 war. "The Israelis were increasingly described as angry, upset, worried and gloomy" (Belkaoui, 1978, p. 737). The Arabs, on the other hand, were the beneficiaries of a more positive image-changing campaign. "Discernable shifts can be observed which portray one country's leaders as villains in 1967 and heroes in

1973" (Belkaoui, 1978, p. 737). The most prominent example of this hero-villain image shift is Egypt, where "Anwar Sadat, while not completely without a negative side . . . is portrayed in a much more sympathetic manner" in 1973 than was Nasser in 1967 (Belkaoui, 1978, p. 737).

To summarize existing literature, it has been found that media began covering the Middle East from a pro-Israeli stance in the 1950s, became more and more supportive of Israel until 1967, and then became more supportive of the Arabs following the 1973 war.

In the years following the 1973 Yom Kippur war, alleged to be the "turning point" in Middle East coverage, new complaints were heard that coverage was slanted against Israel (see, for example, "Are the Media Fair to Israel?," 1975; Kenen, 1976a and 1976b; Laquer, 1977). ABC Middle East correspondent Peter Jennings, in a 1976 interview with the Journal of Palestinian Studies said:

> Traditionally, I think, more coverage has been given to the
> Israeli side than to that of the Arabs. But I think that
> this situation began to change--not dramatically, perhaps,
> but substantially, after the October War in 1973 and particu-
> larly after the Arab oil embargo against the United States.
> The news media generally have now taken a much more pro-
> lific if not always incisive look at the Arab world (Ghareeb,
> 1976, pp. 127-28).

Thus, the stage was set for the American media to display their new "pro-Arab look" when, on November 19, 1977, Egyptian President Anwar el-Sadat announced his intention to visit Jerusalem, Israel, and meet with Israeli Prime Minister Menachim Begin. His dramatic journey to Israel, with a massive American press entourage, was a classic "media event" (O'Conner, 1977).

Because of the alleged twist in the slant of the American media and the short, compact period of time which it appeared in the news, coverage of Sadat's trip to Israel was especially appropriate to study in order to answers these questions:

(1) Has American television news significantly deviated from the pro-Israel coverage habits of the American media?

(2) Were the pre-visit news reports of Sadat's trip to Israel covered in a way favorable to either Israel or the Arabs?

(3) What, if any, differences were there between ABC and CBS in their coverage of the Sadat visit?

In answering these questions, the overall hypothesis to be pursued is that television coverage of the 1977 Sadat visit will be generally pro-Arab, reflecting the "trend" of Middle East coverage

in the American media. Several more specific research hypotheses
advanced and tested are the following:

> H1: The Sadat visit will receive the highest priority in the
> evening news during the period covered by this study.

> H2: There will be no significant difference in the amount of
> time given the Sadat visit between ABC and CBS.

> H3: Sadat will receive significantly more newstime than Begin.

> H4: Pro-Arab themes will receive significantly more attention
> than pro-Israeli themes.

> H5: Sadat will receive more favorable visual background in
> anchor (studio) stories than Begin.

METHODOLOGY

In attempting to answer the research questions and test the
hypotheses presented, this study will cover the ABC and CBS evening
news reports during the week of November 11-18, 1977. (The first
news story about a possible trip to Israel by Sadat was broadcast on
Monday, November 11. Sadat went to Israel on Saturday, November 19.)
NBC news coverage was not analyzed because of time constraints.
However, previous research has indicated that the findings would not
deviate significantly had NBC been included in this paper (Lemert,
1974).

Each of the ten stories was divided into segments; a segment
was defined as representing one speaker (each reporter/anchor was
considered a separate segment; if a reporter/anchor spoke at two or
more different times on the same day it was considered to be only
one segment). The time devoted to each segment was noted, as well
as a major theme and up to three minor themes which the segment
expressed, although each segment did not necessarily have either a
major theme or minor themes. Table I presents a list of themes
used for coding. The visual background for anchor segments, or
segments that occurred in the studio, was classified. Table II
presents the code sheet used for classification.

THE FINDINGS

Table III presents the position, length, and percentage of each
newscast analyzed in this study by day. The "position" of the news
report refers to the "slot" the story occupies, with 1 (one) desig-
nating the first story of the program, and 5 (five) the last. Each

Table I

Major and Minor Themes Coded*

A. Sadat is making this trip at his own initiative.

B. Sadat is making this trip at both his and Begin's initiative.

C. Sadat is making this trip at Begin's initiative.

D. If peace is accomplished, Sadat alone will be responsible.

E. If peace is accomplished, Sadat and Begin both will be responsible.

F. If peace is accomplished, Begin alone will be responsible.

G. Sadat should make the trip to Israel.

H. Sadat should not make the trip to Israel.

I. Arabs support Sadat's trip to Israel.

J. Israelis support Sadat's trip to Israel.

K. Americans support Sadat's trip to Israel.

L. Arabs do not support Sadat's trip to Israel.

M. Israelis do not support Sadat's trip to Israel.

N. Americans do not support Sadat's trip to Israel.

*Note: Each of these could be a major or a minor theme depending on the context of the newscast.

Table II

Sample Code Sheet

INDICATOR:

DATE	NETWORK	SEGMENT	POSITION

SPEAKER	TIME
MAJOR THEMES	MINOR THEMES
CONTEXT	LOCATION
CAMERA ANGLE	CAMERA SHOT

VISUAL BACKGROUND:

	TERMS
SADAT	BEGIN

COMMENTS:

Table III

An Analysis of News Reports of Sadat's Visit to Israel on ABC and CBS by Day,
Position, Time and Percentage of Total News Time Available

	ABC			CBS			ABC & CBS		
	Position	Time	Percentage	Position	Time	Percentage	Position	Time	Percentage
MONDAY	1	3.67	15.9	1	8.67	37.7	1	12.34	26.8
TUESDAY	2	7.00	30.4	2	4.83	21.0	2	11.83	25.7
WEDNESDAY	1	6.17	26.8	1	5.83	25.3	1	12.00	26.0
THURSDAY	1	9.17	39.8	1	14.17	61.6	1	23.34	50.7
FRIDAY	1	14.67	63.8	1	12.00	52.0	1	26.67	57.9
TOTALS		40.68	35.3		45.50	39.6		86.18	37.4

newscast was considered to consist of 23 minutes of actual news time (Mudd, 1979).

These results support Hypotheses 1 and 3. The Sadat visit received the highest priority in the evening news during the period covered by this study, and no significant difference in the amount of time given the Sadat visit between ABC and CBS was observed.

Table IV presents an analysis of the total newstime allotted to the Sadat story by speaker. As would be expected, the "anchor/ reporter" category had the most time, consuming a total of 74 percent of the total newstime available.

Because Begin and Sadat are the principal actors in this analysis, the amount of time they appear on the news reports is of special importance. The findings refute H3: Sadat will receive significantly more newstime than Begin. On CBS, Sadat received only 10 seconds more air time than Begin but on ABC over two and a half minutes fewer than Begin. The fact that Begin and Sadat received nearly equal amount of air time on CBS would seem to suggest "balanced" coverage, but actually it was to Begin's advantage, as the original story was Sadat, and he would be justified in getting more air time (according to the "newsworthy" interpretation of news; see Robinson, 1978, p. 199).

H5: Pro-Arab themes will receive significantly more attention than pro-Israeli themes is also rejected, based on Tables V and VI. The most frequently expressed major themes (L, J, and B; see Table I) are all pro-Israeli themes, and combined were expressed in 55.79 percent of all available newstime as the major theme. Pro-Arab themes (i.e. D, I, and M) were expressed less than .34 minutes of a total of 86.18 minutes examined.

A similar picture emerges when considering minor themes. The results presented in Table VI show Themes E and L, both pro-Israeli, among the most frequently expressed. Although some pro-Arab themes are also expressed as frequently (i.e. A, G, I, and K) there is not enough support for H5. Television news was definitely not presenting Sadat's visit in pro-Arab themes.

253

Table IV

An Analysis of News Reports of Sadat's Visit to Israel
on ABC and CBS by Speaker

SPEAKER	ABC			CBS			ABC & CBS		
	Time	Mean	Percent	Time	Mean	Percent	Time	Mean	Percent
Anchor/Reporter	30.67	1.18	75.44	32.21	1.61	73.17	62.88	1.40	74.25
Sadat	1.50	.75	3.69	3.83	1.91	8.70	5.33	1.33	6.29
Begin	4.17	1.04	10.25	3.51	.87	7.97	7.68	.96	9.07
Egyptian Official	.34	.34	.84	--	--	--	.34	.34	.40
Israeli Official	2.00	1.00	4.92	--	--	--	2.00	1.00	2.36
American Official	.83	.41	2.04	2.02	.40	4.59	2.84	.40	3.35
Arab Citizen	.50	.50	1.23	2.11	.36	4.79	2.61	.43	3.08
Israeli Citizen	.17	.17	.42	--	--	--	.17	.17	.20
American Citizen	.50	.50	1.23	.34	.34	.77	.84	.42	.99
TOTALS	40.68		100.00	44.02		100.00	84.69		100.00

Table V

An Analysis of News Reports of Sadat's Visit to Israel
on ABC and CBS by Major Theme

THEME	ABC			CBS			COMBINED		
	Time	Mean	Percentage	Time	Mean	Percentage	Time	Mean	Percentage
A	3.84	1.28	9.43	3.67	1.22	8.07	7.51	1.25	8.71
B	5.84	.83	14.36	2.84	1.42	6.24	8.68	.96	10.07
C	--	--	--	--	--	--	--	--	--
D	--	--	--	--	--	--	--	--	--
E	4.00	1.00	9.83	.34	.34	.75	4.34	.93	5.42
F	--	--	--	--	--	--	--	--	--
G	.17	.17	.42	2.68	.89	5.89	2.84	.71	3.30
H	--	--	--	1.00	.50	2.20	1.00	.50	1.16
I	.17	.17	.42	--	--	--	.17	.17	.39
J	3.34	.67	8.21	6.34	1.59	13.93	9.68	1.08	11.23
K	1.50	.75	3.69	5.02	.84	11.03	6.02	.75	6.98
L	16.90	1.30	41.54	13.01	1.45	28.59	29.91	1.75	34.49
M	--	--	--	--	--	--	--	--	--
N	1.17	1.17	2.88	--	--	--	1.17	1.17	1.36

Table VI

An Analysis of News Reports of Sadat's Visit to Israel
on ABC and CBS by Minor Theme

THEME	ABC			CBS			COMBINED		
	Time	Mean	Percentage	Time	Mean	Percentage	Time	Mean	Percentage
A	10.36	1.48	25.78	4.01	1.00	8.81	15.03	2.15	17.44
B	4.01	1.34	9.98	--	--	--	4.01	1.34	4.65
C	--	--	--	1.84	.92	4.04	1.84	.92	2.13
D	1.66	.83	4.31	2.83	2.83	6.22	4.49	1.50	5.21
E	4.34	1.09	10.80	5.01	1.25	11.01	10.01	1.25	11.61
F	--	--	--	--	--	--	--	--	--
G	13.50	1.13	33.60	5.67	1.89	12.46	19.17	1.47	22.24
H	6.85	1.37	17.04	.34	.34	7.47	7.02	1.17	8.15
I	5.83	.97	14.51	5.51	1.38	12.10	12.34	1.21	15.48
J	7.01	1.67	17.45	2.00	2.00	4.40	9.01	1.29	10.45
K	6.51	1.09	16.24	11.68	1.30	25.67	17.34	1.10	20.58
L	3.84	.96	8.42	9.52	1.36	19.92	13.36	1.21	14.39
M	--	--	--	--	--	--	--	--	--
N	7.18	1.80	17.87	--	--	--	7.18	1.8'	8.33

H6: Sadat will receive more favorable visual background in anchor (studio) stories than Begin on both ABC and CBS is accepted for ABC and rejected for CBS. On ABC, Sadat was pictured in the studio background, alone, with a symbolic "peace dove" behind him, four of the five days covered in this study, giving the impression that he, alone, symbolized peace. On the fifth day, there were neither pictures of Sadat nor Begin, but simply the words, "Israel/ Egypt/Mideast." CBS pictured both Begin and Sadat on three occasions, and Sadat alone once. At no time on CBS was Sadat (or Begin) shown with a peace symbol such as the dove.

Finally, overall coverage of the Sadat visit was found to be generally pro-Israeli. Coverage of the Sadat visit did not reflect any trends, if any exist, toward pro-Arab coverage in the American media.

SUMMARY AND CONCLUSIONS

What do these findings suggest? First, network news coverage of the Sadat visit was not pro-Arab. This leaves two possibilities: coverage was either balanced or pro-Israeli. It is my view that the news reports were not balanced, and in fact were decisively pro-Israeli. The "newsworthiness" of the story dictated that Sadat be given more coverage--not the same amount as Begin. Despite this, ABC gave Begin more time, and CBS gave both nearly equal time. In addition, the themes expressed in the news reports were not pro-Arab; instead they pictured the Arabs as "anti-peace," and unsupportive of Sadat's "peace mission."

In answer to the major question proposed in this study--Has American television significantly deviated from the pro-Israeli coverage tendencies of the American media?--the answer would have to be "no." If coverage of the Sadat trip is any indication, the American network television news programs continue to be pro-Israeli in their news reports, although they are neither as supportive of Israel nor as antagonistic to the Arabs as in the past.

There is no evidence of any trend toward a pro-Arab press, as suggested by Ghareeb (1976), Belkaoui (1978), and others, from this analysis of the Sadat trip coverage. Rather, there appears to be a "closing of the gap" between coverage of Israelis as "heroes" and

Arabs as "villains." However, this is likely true only in the case of Egypt, and only because of the extraordinary efforts of Anwar Sadat. Other Arab leaders and countries most likely continue to suffer from "bad" press, but as a result of their policies and views towards Western reporters, as well as the biases of the American press.

NOTES

1. See AIPC, 1967; Bartroukka, 1961; Belkaoui, 1978; Farmer, 1968; Howard, 1967; Suleiman, 1965 and 1970; Wagner, 1973; and Zaremba, 1977. Only Gordon, 1975 failed to find an anti-Arab slant.

2. See "Are The Media Fair To Israel?", 1975; "Bad News Is World News," 1976; Drummond and Zycher, 1976; "Disappointing Coverage," 1976; Kenen, 1976a and 1976b; and "Press Weighs The Blame," 1975.

3. Time, Newsweek, Life, U.S. News & World Report, The Nation, New Republic, and the New York Times "Week In Review."

4. See note 3.

5. See Robinson, 1978, p. 208, for a discussion of Heroes-Villains analysis.

6. Gordon, however, did not use tapes of the newscast, instead relying on the Vanderbilt Television News Index and Abstracts. Thus, he was unable to evaluate visual aspects of the news coverage, which are important in determining slant or bias in news (See Adams, 1978) or gain an exact count of the themes expressed in the reports. Vanderbilt advises against such use of its abstracts with a warning printed in the introduction of each edition of the abstract.

REFERENCES

General

Adams, William C. 1978. Visual Analysis of Newscasts: Issues in Social Science Research. In William Adams and Fay Schreibman, eds. Television Network News: Issues in Content Research. Washington, D.C.: School of Public and International Affairs, George Washington University, pp. 154-173.

Almaney, Adnan. 1970. International and Foreign Affairs on Network Television News. Journal of Broadcasting 14 (Fall 1970) pp. 499-509.

Frank, Robert S. 1974. The "Grammar of Film" in Television News. Journalism Quarterly 51 (Spring 1974) pp. 242-250.

Lemert, James B. 1974. Content Duplication by the Networks in Competing Evening Newscasts. Journalism Quarterly 51 (Summer 1974) pp. 238-244.

Mudd, Roger. 1979. Remarks at George Washington University, TV News: The Politics of Visibility, class session, January 31, 1979.

Robinson, Michael J. 1978. Future Television News Research: Beyond Edward J. Epstein. In William Adams and Fay Schreibman, eds. Television Network News: Issues in Content Research. Washington, D.C.: School of Public And International Affairs, George Washington University, pp. 197-212.

Tuchman, Gaye. 1973. The Technology of Objectivity: Doing "Objective" TV News Film. Urban Life and Culture 2 (April 1973) pp. 3-26.

Warner, Malcolm. 1968. TV Coverage of International Affairs. Television Quarterly 7 (Spring 1968) pp. 60-75.

Middle East

American Institute for Political Communication. 1967. Domestic Communications Aspects of the Middle East Crisis. Washington, D.C.: AIPC.

Are The Media Fair To Israel? 1975. Near East Report 19 (February 5, 1975) p. 22.

Bad News is World News. 1976. Jewish Observer and Middle East Review 25 (May 28, 1976) p. 7.

Batroukha, Mohammed Ezzedin. 1961. The Editorial Attitudes of the New York Times and the Christian Science Monitor Toward the Arab-Israeli Dispute (January 1, 1955-June 30, 1956): A Content Analysis Study. Ph.D. dissertation, Syracuse University, 1961.

Belkaoui, Janice Monti. 1978. Images of Arabs and Israelis in the Prestige Press, 1966-74. Journal of Communications 55 (Winter 1978) pp. 732-738, 799.

Disappointing Coverage. 1976. Near East Report 20 (June 2, 1976) p. 95.

Farmer, Leslie. 1968. All We Know is What We Read in the Papers. Middle East Newsletter (February 1968) pp. 1-5.

Ghareeb, Edmund. 1976. The American Media and the Palestinian Problem. Journal of Palestine Studies 5 (Fall-Winter 1976) pp. 127-149.

Gordon, Avishag H. 1975. The Middle East October 1973 War as Reported by the American Networks. International Problems 14 (Fall, 1975) pp. 76-85.

Howard, Harry N. 1967. The Instant Potboilers and the "Blitzkrieg" War. Issues 21 (Autumn 1967) pp. 48-52.

Kenen, I. L. 1976a. Monitor: Jerusalem Distorted. Near East Report 21 (June 15, 1976) p. 100.

Kenen, I. L. 1976b. Monitor: Petrodollars and the Media. Near East Report 20 (June 2, 1976) p. 102.

Laquer, Walter. 1967. Israel, the Arabs, and World Opinion. Commentary 44 (August 1967) pp. 49-59.

O'Conner, John J. 1977. TV: Symbolic Event is Highlighted by "Sheer Drama of Pictures." New York Times (November 22, 1977), p. 17:3.

Press Weights the Blame. 1975. Near East Report 19 (April 22, 1975) pp. 75-77.

Suleiman, Michael W. 1965. An Evaluation of Middle East News Coverage in Seven American News Magazines, July-December 1956. Middle East Forum 41 (Autumn 1965) pp. 9-30.

_____. 1970. American Mass Media and the June Conflict. In Ibrahim Abu-Lughod, ed. The Arab Israeli Confrontation of June 1967: An Arab Perspective. Evanston, Ill." Northwestern University Press, pp. 138-154.

Wagner, Charles H. 1973. Elite American Newspaper Opinion and the Middle East: Committment versus Isolation. In Willard A. Beling, Ed. The Middle East: Quest for an American Policy. Albany, N.Y.: SUNY Press, pp. 306-334.

Zaremba, Alan Jay. 1977. An Exploratory Analysis of National Perceptions of the Arab-Israeli Conflict as Represented Through World Newspapers: An International Communications Study. Ph.D. Dissertation at State University of New York-Buffalo, 1977.

Table A. Areas under the normal curve

Fractional parts of the total area (10,000) under the normal curve, corresponding to distances between the mean and ordinates which are Z standard-deviation units from the mean.

Z	.00	.01	.02	.03	.04	.05	.06	.07	.08	.09
0.0	0000	0040	0080	0120	0159	0199	0239	0279	0319	0359
0.1	0398	0438	0478	0517	0557	0596	0636	0675	0714	0753
0.2	0793	0832	0871	0910	0948	0987	1026	1064	1103	1141
0.3	1179	1217	1255	1293	1331	1368	1406	1443	1480	1517
0.4	1554	1591	1628	1664	1700	1736	1772	1808	1844	1879
0.5	1915	1950	1985	2019	2054	2088	2123	2157	2190	2224
0.6	2257	2291	2324	2357	2389	2422	2454	2486	2518	2549
0.7	2580	2612	2642	2673	2704	2734	2764	2794	2823	2852
0.8	2881	2910	2939	2967	2995	3023	3051	3078	3106	3133
0.9	3159	3186	3212	3238	3264	3289	3315	3340	3365	3389
1.0	3413	3438	3461	3485	3508	3531	3554	3577	3599	3621
1.1	3643	3665	3686	3718	3729	3749	3770	3790	3810	3830
1.2	3849	3869	3888	3907	3925	3944	3962	3980	3997	4015
1.3	4032	4049	4066	4083	4099	4115	4131	4147	4162	4177
1.4	4192	4207	4222	4236	4251	4265	4279	4292	4306	4319
1.5	4332	4345	4357	4370	4382	4394	4406	4418	4430	4441
1.6	4452	4463	4474	4485	4495	4505	4515	4525	4535	4545
1.7	4554	4564	4573	4582	4591	4599	4608	4616	4625	4633
1.8	4641	4649	4656	4664	4671	4678	4686	4693	4699	4706
1.9	4713	4719	4726	4732	4738	4744	4750	4758	4762	4767
2.0	4773	4778	4783	4788	4793	4798	4803	4808	4812	4817
2.1	4821	4826	4830	4834	4838	4842	4846	4850	4854	4857
2.2	4861	4865	4868	4871	4875	4878	4881	4884	4887	4890
2.3	4893	4896	4898	4901	4904	4906	4909	4911	4913	4916
2.4	4918	4920	4922	4925	4927	4929	4931	4932	4934	4936
2.5	4938	4940	4941	4943	4945	4946	4948	4949	4951	4952
2.6	4953	4955	4956	4957	4959	4960	4961	4962	4963	4964
2.7	4965	4966	4967	4968	4969	4970	4971	4972	4973	4974
2.8	4974	4975	4976	4977	4977	4978	4979	4980	4980	4981
2.9	4981	4982	4983	4984	4984	4984	4985	4985	4986	4986
3.0	4986.5	4987	4987	4988	4988	4988	4989	4989	4989	4990
3.1	4990.0	4991	4991	4991	4992	4992	4992	4992	4993	4993
3.2	4993.129									
3.3	4995.166									
3.4	4996.631									
3.5	4997.674									
3.6	4998.409									
3.7	4998.922									
3.8	4999.277									
3.9	4999.519									
4.0	4999.683									
4.5	4999.966									
5.0	4999.997133									

SOURCE: Harold O. Rugg, *Statistical Methods Applied to Education*, Houghton Mifflin Company, Boston, 1917, appendix table III, pp. 389–390, with the kind permission of the publisher.

Table B. Distribution of t

df	Level of significance for one-tailed test					
	.10	.05	.025	.01	.005	.0005
	Level of significance for two-tailed test					
	.20	.10	.05	.02	.01	.001
1	3.078	6.314	12.706	31.821	63.657	636.619
2	1.886	2.920	4.303	6.965	9.925	31.598
3	1.638	2.353	3.182	4.541	5.841	12.941
4	1.533	2.132	2.776	3.747	4.604	8.610
5	1.476	2.015	2.571	3.365	4.032	6.859
6	1.440	1.943	2.447	3.143	3.707	5.959
7	1.415	1.895	2.365	2.998	3.499	5.405
8	1.397	1.860	2.306	2.896	3.355	5.041
9	1.383	1.833	2.262	2.821	3.250	4.781
10	1.372	1.812	2.228	2.764	3.169	4.587
11	1.363	1.796	2.201	2.718	3.106	4.437
12	1.356	1.782	2.179	2.681	3.055	4.318
13	1.350	1.771	2.160	2.650	3.012	4.221
14	1.345	1.761	2.145	2.624	2.977	4.140
15	1.341	1.753	2.131	2.602	2.947	4.073
16	1.337	1.746	2.120	2.583	2.921	4.015
17	1.333	1.740	2.110	2.567	2.898	3.965
18	1.330	1.734	2.101	2.552	2.878	3.922
19	1.328	1.729	2.093	2.539	2.861	3.883
20	1.325	1.725	2.086	2.528	2.845	3.850
21	1.323	1.721	2.080	2.518	2.831	3.819
22	1.321	1.717	2.074	2.508	2.819	3.792
23	1.319	1.714	2.069	2.500	2.807	3.767
24	1.318	1.711	2.064	2.492	2.797	3.745
25	1.316	1.708	2.060	2.485	2.787	3.725
26	1.315	1.706	2.056	2.479	2.779	3.707
27	1.314	1.703	2.052	2.473	2.771	3.690
28	1.313	1.701	2.048	2.467	2.763	3.674
29	1.311	1.699	2.045	2.462	2.756	3.659
30	1.310	1.697	2.042	2.457	2.750	3.646
40	1.303	1.684	2.021	2.423	2.704	3.551
60	1.296	1.671	2.000	2.390	2.660	3.460
120	1.289	1.658	1.980	2.358	2.617	3.373
∞	1.282	1.645	1.960	2.326	2.576	3.291

SOURCE: Table B is abridged from Table III of R. A. Fisher and F. Yates, *Statistical Tables for Biological, Agricultural and Medical Research* (1948 ed.), published by Oliver & Boyd, Ltd., Edinburgh and London, by permission of the authors and publishers.

Table C. Distribution of χ^2

Probability

df	.99	.98	.95	.90	.80	.70	.50	.30	.20	.10	.05	.02	.01	.001
1	.0³157	.0³628	.00393	.0158	.0642	.148	.455	1.074	1.642	2.706	3.841	5.412	6.635	10.82
2	.0201	.0404	.103	.211	.446	.713	1.386	2.408	3.219	4.605	5.991	7.824	9.210	13.81⁵
3	.115	.185	.352	.584	1.005	1.424	2.366	3.665	4.642	6.251	7.815	9.837	11.341	16.26⁵
4	.297	.429	.711	1.064	1.649	2.195	3.357	4.878	5.989	7.779	9.488	11.668	13.277	18.465
5	.554	.752	1.145	1.610	2.343	3.000	4.351	6.064	7.289	9.236	11.070	13.388	15.086	20.517
6	.872	1.134	1.635	2.204	3.070	3.828	5.348	7.231	8.558	10.645	12.592	15.033	16.812	22.457
7	1.239	1.564	2.167	2.833	3.822	4.671	6.346	8.383	9.803	12.017	14.067	16.622	18.475	24.322
8	1.646	2.032	2.733	3.490	4.594	5.527	7.344	9.524	11.030	13.362	15.507	18.168	20.090	26.125
9	2.088	2.532	3.325	4.168	5.380	6.393	8.343	10.656	12.242	14.684	16.919	19.679	21.666	27.877
10	2.558	3.059	3.940	4.865	6.179	7.267	9.342	11.781	13.442	15.987	18.307	21.161	23.209	29.588
11	3.053	3.609	4.575	5.578	6.989	8.148	10.341	12.899	14.631	17.275	19.675	22.618	24.725	31.264
12	3.571	4.178	5.226	6.304	7.807	9.034	11.340	14.011	15.812	18.549	21.026	24.054	26.217	32.909
13	4.107	4.765	5.892	7.042	8.634	9.926	12.340	15.119	16.985	19.812	22.362	25.472	27.688	34.528
14	4.660	5.368	6.571	7.790	9.467	10.821	13.339	16.222	18.151	21.064	23.685	26.873	29.141	36.123
15	5.229	5.985	7.261	8.547	10.307	11.721	14.339	17.322	19.311	22.307	24.996	28.259	30.578	37.697
16	5.812	6.614	7.962	9.312	11.152	12.624	15.338	18.418	20.465	23.542	26.296	29.633	32.000	39.252
17	6.408	7.255	8.672	10.085	12.002	13.531	16.338	19.511	21.615	24.769	27.587	30.995	33.409	40.790
18	7.015	7.906	9.390	10.865	12.857	14.440	17.338	20.601	22.760	25.989	28.869	32.346	34.805	42.312
19	7.633	8.567	10.117	11.651	13.716	15.352	18.338	21.689	23.900	27.204	30.144	33.687	36.191	43.820
20	8.260	9.237	10.851	12.443	14.578	16.266	19.337	22.775	25.038	28.412	31.410	35.020	37.566	45.315
21	8.897	9.915	11.591	13.240	15.445	17.182	20.337	23.858	26.171	29.615	32.671	36.343	38.932	46.797
22	9.542	10.600	12.338	14.041	16.314	18.101	21.337	24.939	27.301	30.813	33.924	37.659	40.289	48.268
23	10.196	11.293	13.091	14.848	17.187	19.021	22.337	26.018	28.429	32.007	35.172	38.968	41.638	49.728
24	10.856	11.992	13.848	15.659	18.062	19.943	23.337	27.096	29.553	33.196	36.415	40.270	42.980	51.179
25	11.524	12.697	14.611	16.473	18.940	20.867	24.337	28.172	30.675	34.382	37.652	41.566	44.314	52.620
26	12.198	13.409	15.379	17.292	19.820	21.792	25.336	29.246	31.795	35.563	38.885	42.856	45.642	54.052
27	12.879	14.125	16.151	18.114	20.703	22.719	26.336	30.319	32.912	36.741	40.113	44.140	46.963	55.476
28	13.565	14.847	16.928	18.939	21.588	23.647	27.336	31.391	34.027	37.916	41.337	45.419	48.278	56.893
29	14.256	15.574	17.708	19.768	22.475	24.577	28.336	32.461	35.139	39.087	42.557	46.693	49.588	58.302
30	14.953	16.306	18.493	20.599	23.364	25.508	29.336	33.530	36.250	40.256	43.773	47.962	50.892	59.703

For larger values of df, the expression $\sqrt{2\chi^2} - \sqrt{2df - 1}$ may be used as a normal deviate with unit variance, remembering that the probability for χ^2 corresponds with that of a single tail of the normal curve.

SOURCE: Table C is reprinted from Table IV of R. A. Fisher and F. Yates, *Statistical Tables for Biological, Agricultural and Medical Research* (1948 ed.), published by Oliver & Boyd Ltd.,, Edinburgh and London, by permission of the authors and publishers.

Table D. Distribution of F

$$p = .05$$

n_2 \ n_1	1	2	3	4	5	6	8	12	24	∞
1	161.4	199.5	215.7	224.6	230.2	234.0	238.9	243.9	249.0	254.3
2	18.51	19.00	19.16	19.25	19.30	19.33	19.37	19.41	19.45	19.50
3	10.13	9.55	9.28	9.12	9.01	8.94	8.84	8.74	8.64	8.53
4	7.71	6.94	6.59	6.39	6.26	6.16	6.04	5.91	5.77	5.63
5	6.61	5.79	5.41	5.19	5.05	4.95	4.82	4.68	4.53	4.36
6	5.99	5.14	4.76	4.53	4.39	4.28	4.15	4.00	3.84	3.67
7	5.59	4.74	4.35	4.12	3.97	3.87	3.73	3.57	3.41	3.23
8	5.32	4.46	4.07	3.84	3.69	3.58	3.44	3.28	3.12	2.93
9	5.12	4.26	3.86	3.63	3.48	3.37	3.23	3.07	2.90	2.71
10	4.96	4.10	3.71	3.48	3.33	3.22	3.07	2.91	2.74	2.54
11	4.84	3.98	3.59	3.36	3.20	3.09	2.95	2.79	2.61	2.40
12	4.75	3.88	3.49	3.26	3.11	3.00	2.85	2.69	2.50	2.30
13	4.67	3.80	3.41	3.18	3.02	2.92	2.77	2.60	2.42	2.21
14	4.60	3.74	3.34	3.11	2.96	2.85	2.70	2.53	2.35	2.13
15	4.54	3.68	3.29	3.06	2.90	2.79	2.64	2.48	2.29	2.07
16	4.49	3.63	3.24	3.01	2.85	2.74	2.59	2.42	2.24	2.01
17	4.45	3.59	3.20	2.96	2.81	2.70	2.55	2.38	2.19	1.96
18	4.41	3.55	3.16	2.93	2.77	2.66	2.51	2.34	2.15	1.92
19	4.38	3.52	3.13	2.90	2.74	2.63	2.48	2.31	2.11	1.88
20	4.35	3.49	3.10	2.87	2.71	2.60	2.45	2.28	2.08	1.84
21	4.32	3.47	3.07	2.84	2.68	2.57	2.42	2.25	2.05	1.81
22	4.30	3.44	3.05	2.82	2.66	2.55	2.40	2.23	2.03	1.78
23	4.28	3.42	3.03	2.80	2.64	2.53	2.38	2.20	2.00	1.76
24	4.26	3.40	3.01	2.78	2.62	2.51	2.36	2.18	1.98	1.73
25	4.24	3.38	2.99	2.76	2.60	2.49	2.34	2.16	1.96	1.71
26	4.22	3.37	2.98	2.74	2.59	2.47	2.32	2.15	1.95	1.69
27	4.21	3.35	2.96	2.73	2.57	2.46	2.30	2.13	1.93	1.67
28	4.20	3.34	2.95	2.71	2.56	2.44	2.29	2.12	1.91	1.65
29	4.18	3.33	2.93	2.70	2.54	2.43	2.28	2.10	1.90	1.64
30	4.17	3.32	2.92	2.69	2.53	2.42	2.27	2.09	1.89	1.62
40	4.08	3.23	2.84	2.61	2.45	2.34	2.18	2.00	1.79	1.51
60	4.00	3.15	2.76	2.52	2.37	2.25	2.10	1.92	1.70	1.39
120	3.92	3.07	2.68	2.45	2.29	2.17	2.02	1.83	1.61	1.25
∞	3.84	2.99	2.60	2.37	2.21	2.09	1.94	1.75	1.52	1.00

Values of n_1 and n_2 represent the degrees of freedom associated with the larger and smaller estimates of variance respectively.

SOURCE: Table D is abridged from Table V of R. A. Fisher and F. Yates, *Statistical Tables for Biological, Agricultural and Medical Research* (1948 ed.), published by Oliver & Boyd, Ltd., Edinburgh and London, by permission of the authors and publishers.

$$p = .01$$

n_1 / n_2	1	2	3	4	5	6	8	12	24	∞
1	4052	4999	5403	5625	5764	5859	5981	6106	6234	6366
2	98.49	99.01	99.17	99.25	99.30	99.33	99.36	99.42	99.46	99.50
3	34.12	30.81	29.46	28.71	28.24	27.91	27.49	27.05	26.60	26.12
4	21.20	18.00	16.69	15.98	15.52	15.21	14.80	14.37	13.93	13.46
5	16.26	13.27	12.06	11.39	10.97	10.67	10.27	9.89	9.47	9.02
6	13.74	10.92	9.78	9.15	8.75	8.47	8.10	7.72	7.31	6.88
7	12.25	9.55	8.45	7.85	7.46	7.19	6.84	6.47	6.07	5.65
8	11.26	8.65	7.59	7.01	6.63	6.37	6.03	5.67	5.28	4.86
9	10.56	8.02	6.99	6.42	6.06	5.80	5.47	5.11	4.73	4.31
10	10.04	7.56	6.55	5.99	5.64	5.39	5.06	4.71	4.33	3.91
11	9.65	7.20	6.22	5.67	5.32	5.07	4.74	4.40	4.02	3.60
12	9.33	6.93	5.95	5.41	5.06	4.82	4.50	4.16	3.78	3.36
13	9.07	6.70	5.74	5.20	4.86	4.62	4.30	3.96	3.59	3.16
14	8.86	6.51	5.56	5.03	4.69	4.46	4.14	3.80	3.43	3.00
15	8.68	6.36	5.42	4.89	4.56	4.32	4.00	3.67	3.29	2.87
16	8.53	6.23	5.29	4.77	4.44	4.20	3.89	3.55	3.18	2.75
17	8.40	6.11	5.18	4.67	4.34	4.10	3.79	3.45	3.08	2.65
18	8.28	6.01	5.09	4.58	4.25	4.01	3.71	3.37	3.00	2.57
19	8.18	5.93	5.01	4.50	4.17	3.94	3.63	3.30	2.92	2.49
20	8.10	5.85	4.94	4.43	4.10	3.87	3.56	3.23	2.86	2.42
21	8.02	5.78	4.87	4.37	4.04	3.81	3.51	3.17	2.80	2.36
22	7.94	5.72	4.82	4.31	3.99	3.76	3.45	3.12	2.75	2.31
23	7.88	5.66	4.76	4.26	3.94	3.71	3.41	3.07	2.70	2.26
24	7.82	5.61	4.72	4.22	3.90	3.67	3.36	3.03	2.66	2.21
25	7.77	5.57	4.68	4.18	3.86	3.63	3.32	2.99	2.62	2.17
26	7.72	5.53	4.64	4.14	3.82	3.59	3.29	2.96	2.58	2.13
27	7.68	5.49	4.60	4.11	3.78	3.56	3.26	2.93	2.55	2.10
28	7.64	5.45	4.57	4.07	3.75	3.53	3.23	2.90	2.52	2.06
29	7.60	5.42	4.54	4.04	3.73	3.50	3.20	2.87	2.49	2.03
30	7.56	5.39	4.51	4.02	3.70	3.47	3.17	2.84	2.47	2.01
40	7.31	5.18	4.31	3.83	3.51	3.29	2.99	2.66	2.29	1.80
60	7.08	4.98	4.13	3.65	3.34	3.12	2.82	2.50	2.12	1.60
120	6.85	4.79	3.95	3.48	3.17	2.96	2.66	2.34	1.95	1.38
∞	6.64	4.60	3.78	3.32	3.02	2.80	2.51	2.18	1.79	1.00

Values of n_1 and n_2 represent the degrees of freedom associated with the larger and smaller estimates of variance respectively.

Table D. Distribution of F *(Continued)*

$$p = .001$$

n_1 / n_2	1	2	3	4	5	6	8	12	24	∞
1	405284	500000	540379	562500	576405	585937	598144	610667	623497	636619
2	998.5	999.0	999.2	999.2	999 3	999.3	999.4	999.4	999.5	999.5
3	167.5	148.5	141.1	137.1	134.6	132.8	130.6	128.3	125.9	123.5
4	74.14	61.25	56.18	53.44	51.71	50.53	49.00	47.41	45.77	44.05
5	47.04	36.61	33.20	31.09	29.75	28.84	27.64	26.42	25.14	23.78
6	35.51	27.00	23.70	21.90	20.81	20.03	19.03	17.99	16.89	15.75
7	29.22	21.69	18.77	17.19	16.21	15.52	14.63	13.71	12.73	11.69
8	25.42	18.49	15.83	14.39	13.49	12.86	12.04	11.19	10.30	9.34
9	22.86	16.39	13.90	12.56	11.71	11.13	10.37	9.57	8.72	7.81
10	21.04	14.91	12.55	11.28	10.48	9.92	9.20	8.45	7.64	6.76
11	19.69	13.81	11.56	10.35	9.58	9.05	8.35	7.63	6.85	6.00
12	18.64	12.97	10.80	9.63	8.89	8.38	7 71	7.00	6.25	5.42
13	17.81	12.31	10.21	9.07	8.35	7.86	7.21	6.52	5.78	4.97
14	17.14	11.78	9.73	8.62	7.92	7.43	6.80	6.13	5.41	4.60
15	16.59	11.34	9.34	8.25	7.57	7.09	6.47	5.81	5.10	4.31
16	16.12	10.97	9.00	7.94	7.27	6.81	6.19	5.55	4.85	4.06
17	15.72	10.66	8.73	7.68	7.02	6.56	5.96	5.32	4.63	3.85
18	15.38	10.39	8.49	7.46	6.81	6.35	5.76	5.13	4.45	3.67
19	15.08	10.16	8.28	7.26	6.61	6.18	5.59	4.97	4.29	3.52
20	14.82	9.95	8.10	7.10	6.46	6.02	5.44	4.82	4.15	3.38
21	14.59	9.77	7.94	6.95	6.32	5.88	5.31	4.70	4.03	3.26
22	14.38	9.61	7.80	6.81	6.19	5.76	5.19	4.58	3.92	3.15
23	14.19	9.47	7.67	6.69	6.08	5.65	5.09	4.48	3.82	3.05
24	14.03	9.34	7.55	6.59	5 98	5.55	4.99	4.39	3.74	2.97
25	13.88	9.22	7.45	6.49	5.88	5.46	4.91	4.31	3.66	2.89
26	13.74	9.12	7.36	6.41	5.80	5.38	4.83	4.24	3.59	2.82
27	13.61	9.02	7.27	6.33	5.73	5.31	4.76	4.17	3.52	2.75
28	13.50	8.93	7.19	6.25	5.66	5.24	4.69	4.11	3.46	2.70
29	13.39	8.85	7.12	6.19	5.59	5.18	4.64	4.05	3.41	2.64
30	13.29	8.77	7.05	6.12	5.53	5.12	4.58	4.00	3.36	2.59
40	12.61	8.25	6.60	5.70	5.13	4.73	4.21	3.64	3.01	2.23
60	11.97	7.76	6.17	5.31	4.76	4.37	3.87	3.31	2.69	1.90
120	11.38	7.31	5.79	4.95	4.42	4.04	3.55	3.02	2.40	1.56
∞	10.83	6.91	5.42	4.62	4.10	3.74	3.27	2.74	2.13	1.00

Values of n_1 and n_2 represent the degrees of freedom associated with the larger and smaller estimates of variance respectively.

Author Index

Subject Index

273